A GUIDE TO

THE GUIDE TO THE PERPLEXED

A Guide to *The Guide to the Perplexed*

A READER'S COMPANION TO MAIMONIDES' MASTERWORK

Lenn E. Goodman

STANFORD UNIVERSITY PRESS
Stanford, California

Stanford University Press
Stanford, California

Printed in the United States of America on acid-free, archival-quality paper

Library of Congress Cataloging-in-Publication Data
Names: Goodman, Lenn Evan, 1944- author.
Title: A guide to the Guide to the perplexed : a reader's companion to Maimonides' masterwork / Lenn E. Goodman.
Description: Stanford, California : Stanford University Press, 2024. | Includes bibliographical references.
Identifiers: LCCN 2023020619 (print) | LCCN 2023020620 (ebook) | ISBN 9781503629530 (cloth) | ISBN 9781503637474 (paperback) | ISBN 9781503637481 (epub)
Subjects: LCSH: Maimonides, Moses, 1135-1204. Dalālat al-ḥā'irīn. | Judaism—Early works to 1800. | Jewish philosophy—Early works to 1800. | Philosophy, Medieval—Early works to 1800.
Classification: LCC BM545.D35 G659 2024 (print) | LCC BM545.D35 (ebook) | DDC 181.06—dc23/eng/20230504
LC record available at https://lccn.loc.gov/2023020619
LC ebook record available at https://lccn.loc.gov/2023020620

Cover art: © Bodleian Libraries, University of Oxford

Contents

Abbreviations

B.	The Babylonian Talmud
b.	ben or ibn, son of
BYU	Brigham Young University
CM	Maimonides' Commentary on the Mishnah
CUP	Cambridge University Press
DK	Hermann Alexander Diels and Walther Kranz, *Fragmente der Vorsokratiker* (6th ed., 1952)
ED	Saadiah, *K. al-Mukhtār fī 'l-Amānāt wa 'l-Iʿtiqādāt* (familiarly known as *Sefer Emunot ve-Deʿot*)
HUCA	*Hebrew Union College Annual*
HUP	Harvard University Press
J.	The Jerusalem Talmud
JHP	*Journal of the History of Philosophy*
JLA	*Jewish Law Annual*
JNES	*Journal of Near Eastern Studies*
JPS	Jewish Publication Society
JQR	*Jewish Quarterly Review*
JRAS	*Journal of the Royal Asiatic Society*
JSQ	*Jewish Studies Quarterly*
JSS	*Journal of Semitic Studies*

JTS	Jewish Theological Seminary of America
K.	*Kitāb* (Book)
LCL	Loeb Classical Library
LL	Littman Library of Jewish Civilization
M.	The Mishnah
MT	Maimonides, *Mishneh Torah*
NE	Aristotle, *Nicomachean Ethics*
OUP	Oxford University Press
PAAJR	*Proceedings of the American Academy for Jewish Research*
SGA	*Studia Graeco-Arabica*
SM	*Sefer ha-Mitzvot* (Maimonides' Book of the Commandments)
SUNY	State University of New York
UC	University of California

Two Notes to the Reader

Biblical passages quoted here follow the versions used in the Goodman-Lieberman translation and commentary of the *Guide*. They are set in italics rather than set off by quotation marks. The modified King James–y diction used helps disambiguate pronoun reference and the like. It also helps remind readers that the biblical text is already ancient to the Rambam and his contemporaries. Maimonides' creative and insightful readings and paraphrases stand out by the typically more informal, conversational tone he favors in the *Guide*. The slight contrast in the rendering of his biblical landmarks and prooftexts allows his insightful glosses and paraphrases to show up as neither arbitrary nor trivial as he lays out his understanding of the biblical texts he seeks to open up to his reader.

References to the works of Plato and Aristotle here are to the Stephanus and Bekker texts, respectively. The *Guide* itself is cited by part and chapter, and/or by the pages of Munk's classic edition, by part and page number, recto or verso. Thus III 51 refers to Part III, chapter 51 of the *Guide*; and 2.67b refers to Part 2, page 67 verso in Munk's edition. Munk page numbers are shown throughout the Goodman-Lieberman translation for those who wish to consult the Judaeo-Arabic text.

A GUIDE TO
THE GUIDE TO THE PERPLEXED

Introduction

Moses Maimonides, called the Rambam in traditional Jewish circles—using a scribe's convenient acronym of his Hebrew name, Rabbi Moshe ben Maimon—is known in English language texts as Maimonides, the Greek patronymic reflecting the impact of his writings in Latin translation. His name in Arabic, Mūsā bin Maimūn, signals his fame among Muslim scholars. He was born in Cordoba in 1138[1] and died in Cairo in 1204. Tradition has it that he is buried in Tiberias. Even in Cordoba, which he and his family had to leave when he was a child, a handsome, if fanciful, statue of a seated man honors his youthful presence. Indeed, he continued decades after the family's exile to call himself ha-Sefardi, "the Spaniard" in Hebrew, never losing his links to Andalusia and its heritage in philosophy, the sciences, and Jewish law. But more on that later.

His own contributions link those fields: Maimonides was a master in the sciences pursued by the learned in his day, especially geometry, astronomy, and logic. His writings reveal skill and clarity in argument—and, what often matters more, insight in choosing premises, analyzing assumptions, and synthesizing seemingly disparate positions. A practicing physician, he wrote ten Arabic medical works, some in multiple volumes, and all in the Galenic tradition of scientific medicine. His medical works are exemplary of the most up-to-date standards of medical theory and practice, notable for their care with terminology and for eschewing the astrological assumptions and excursions that sometimes attach themselves to Galenic works and even to those of Galen himself.

As for Halakhah, Maimonides would become the most formidable exponent of Jewish law to arise since the completion of the Talmud, guided by his conviction that *all* of God's laws must make sense and directly or indirectly serve human needs. For God, of course, has no needs but gave the Torah, as its name implies, for the guidance of His people. Beyond his role as a foremost Jewish jurist, today universally acknowledged and acclaimed, readers of the Rambam's *Guide to the Perplexed* will readily observe that he was a penetrating reader of biblical and rabbinic poetics, whether he found it in the form of metaphor, allegory, or homiletic symbolism.

Maimonides' *Sefer ha-Mitzvot* (Book of the Commandments, *SM*), written in Arabic, catalogs the 613 mitzvot that rabbinic tradition held the Torah to contain. His listing (not the only one to be attempted) opens with *I am the* L*ORD thy God* (Exodus 20:2), placed first among the positive mitzvot, and *Thou shalt have no other God before me* (20:3), first among the negative. These two precepts, as the Rambam saw it, bear prescriptive force, as they must if they are to ground every other biblical norm. They are not mere affirmations of fact, as though God's existence made no demands on us. For Maimonides, recognition of God's unique ultimacy anchors His moral and legislative authority. But the recognition that these two mitzvot call for is no arbitrary fiat. Rather, as Maimonides sees it, these two items in the Decalogue speak directly to reason, articulating, as he will argue, a pair of core truths, an axiom and its corollary, that Moses voiced for Israel at Sinai and that all those present grasped for themselves in the measure of their understanding (II 33, 75a).

The *K. al-Sirāj*, or Book of the Lamp, Maimonides' Arabic commentary on the Mishnah, tracks the six Orders of that ancient halakhic code. It includes the celebrated Eight Chapters, his introduction to Pirkei Avot, the well-known gathering of the rabbinic sages' teachings, which typically express ethical and edifying maxims. Often studied on its own, given the ethical focus of the remarks from the Sages collected in Mishnah Avot, the Eight Chapters elicits from the Torah a scheme of virtue ethics designed to help us better our character. By so doing it lays the foundation needed if we are to reach our highest goal and attain the deepest and purest form of worship: active and passionate knowledge of God.

Moshe Halbertal highlights Maimonides' originality when he explains how innovative the *K. al-Sirāj* is in treating the Mishnah independently, as no mere springboard to talmudic study but the backbone of Halakhah.[2] Maimonides' seven years' labor in preparing his commentary—much of it undertaken in conditions of hardship, exile, and persecution—aimed to bring the Talmud's "chaos," as Halbertal puts it, into systematic order, finding reason and principle in the Mishnah's ritual, penal, civic, and public laws. Maimonides apologizes for any errors his commentary might contain, since parts of it were composed on shipboard or on the road. He continued throughout his life to revise and emend his findings based on his maturing judgment and deeper study. In a letter, he explains how he'd needed to correct passages where he'd followed too closely the lead of the Geonim, as the spiritual leaders of "Babylonian" Jewry were called.[3] Remarkably, the Rambam's own fair copy of this work has survived, and almost all of it has been published, showing the hundreds of revisions that reflect his growing mastery and authority in Halakhah as a body of law kept alive by organic but not radical change (II 49, 84b; III 25, 57ab).

In one revision that sheds light on what Menachem Kellner and David Gillis call his universalism, Maimonides sets aside the mishnaic dictum (M. Bikkurim 1.4) that in bringing first fruits to the Temple, a proselyte does not recite the ritual declaration thanking God for the land *the Lord promised our fathers* (Deuteronomy 26:3). God had promised Abraham that he would be *the father of many nations* (Genesis 17:5). So *pace* many of the early Sages, and rejecting his own prior view (but following the Jerusalem Talmud), Maimonides holds—as he ruled in his responsum regarding the status of Obadiah the Proselyte—that a convert, as an adopted child of Abraham, makes the same blessings as any other Jew. As Isaiah said, *One shall say, "I am the Lord's and another call himself by Jacob's name"* (44:5).[4]

The Mishnah commentary paved the way for the fourteen-volume code of Jewish law that Maimonides boldly called *Mishneh Torah* (hereafter *MT*), using the traditional title of Deuteronomy, where the Torah's laws are restated. The work, unprecedented in scope and unequaled in conceptual penetration, codifies the full range of Halakhah, tracing rabbinic prescriptions to their biblical roots, setting the entire halakhic edifice on its intellectual foundations,[5] spelling out its moral and spiritual aims, and purging the Talmud's frequent repetitions, digressions, obiter dicta, and asides. Even citations are omitted, along with the byplay of debate and dissent across the centuries that sets the Sages in conversation with one another.

The backgrounds of debate and deliberation can clarify the intentions of a law. But they may also leave key issues unresolved. The Talmud and the literature spilling from it can appear a seething cauldron. But where another code might draw sharp crystals from such a supersaturated solution, Maimonides finds a living organism, integrated by the clear purpose of the whole: to better the lives of all Israel by enhancing the people's material well-being, improving their relations, refining their character, and opening up doorways to the realization of the affinity to God that all human beings share, the affinity attested when Genesis affirms that mankind, male and female, are created in God's image (1:27). To Maimonides, that means that all human beings are blessed with reason and the power to perfect it and so come to know God and emulate His goodness.[6]

Although it tracks the major sections of the Mishnah, the Talmud is not tightly thematic. But the very act of codifying a body of law is pregnant with a key premise of legal rationalism, that laws serve purposes. For it is by their purposes that legal prescriptions are most usefully marshaled for practical and intellectual use. In the Yale Judaica Series translation, the *MT* is called simply *The Code of Maimonides*. But in Jewish traditional circles, where it remains a key halakhic reference and a focus of extended, even devotional, study, it is often called the *Yad Ḥazakah*, or the *Yad* for short, echoing Deuteronomy 26:8: *With a strong hand and an outstretched arm did the Lord bring us forth from Egypt*. For the numerical value of the letters of the word *yad* (hand) is fourteen, recalling the work's fourteen volumes. The epithet sidesteps calling the work by the same name as Deuteronomy.[7] But *strong hand*, a phrase well known from its appearance in the Passover Hagaddah, also reflects the confidence readers gained from the work's reliability—and its power in rendering halakhic rules intelligible. A law whose purposes are understood can be intelligently observed, interpreted, elaborated, refined, explained, justified, even cherished. In the same spirit, Maimonides ends his *Guide to the Perplexed* by laying out the warrants he sees for every class of biblical mitzvot, first in general terms and then, when he feels able, in more specific detail. The guiding principles he finds—grouped under the three headings of material, moral, and spiritual/intellectual well-being—are the distillate of his extended and sensitive studies of Halakhah.[8]

Maimonides' aim in his great code was to marshal the rules, norms, and principles of Halakhah as "a transparent, accessible system." That system had grown, and its written corpus had become, as Halbertal puts it, "an uncontrollable organism, laden with disputes and fragmented give and take recorded in Aramaic, a language not used in daily life." History had made its structuring principles somehow remote. One who labored to master it "could not be assured of the ability to extract practical legal rulings from the Talmudic morass. He would always remain justifiably concerned that he had failed to understand the complex debate, that he had chosen wrongly among the wealth of opinions . . . that he had missed a reference to his subject elsewhere in the Talmud, in some remote, unrelated context—a distinct possibility, given the Talmud's freewheeling structure—and that the overlooked reference might have fundamentally changed the picture."[9]

Maimonides' goal was to introduce order that would allow the body of Halakhah to function as a living and perspicuous system, giving students, scholars, and those in need of practical rulings clear and dispositive guidance. "I have been zealous on behalf of the LORD God of Israel," he wrote, "seeing a nation lacking a true and comprehensive book of its own laws and lacking true and clear beliefs. I acted for God's sake alone."[10] Ideas were crucial from the outset. For Halakhah lays out a way of life, but its norms reduce to an empty game unless anchored in understanding—practical and moral, intellectual and spiritual.

Halakhah, for Maimonides, would not remain a morass. Looming before him at the outset, its magnificent disorder may have resembled more a mountain than a swamp. But with the *Commentary on the Mishnah* and *SM* under his belt, he faced the Law with a sense that he could be the man equipped to master it—and so help others, mapping its every foothold of practical or theological relevance. This task he saw as critically necessary:

> For the purpose intended in the collation of the Talmud has been aborted and lost. The object of today's scholars is only to kill time in talmudic disputing, as if the point were just to hone their skills in debate. That was not the original intention. Debates and disputes arose only incidentally, when words seemed to allow one person to read them one way and another to read them differently, and each mounted arguments to show that his reading should

> prevail. But the prime intent was just to make known what must be done or avoided in this case and others like it. My object was to go back to the original intent, to make the demands of Halakhah easy to remember and, indeed, understand. For its norms had gotten lost in the welter of debate. I left all the rest for those more disposed to such an exercise.[11]

There had been prior essays toward a halakhic code, but none was complete or systematic. Among those earlier codes, Maimonides especially admired the pioneering work of Isaac al-Fāsī (1013–1103), who had come to Andalusia after forty years of halakhic work while living near Fez, as the surname by which he is known announces. Al-Fāsī became head of the yeshiva at Lucena, near Cordoba, in 1089, soon after completing his code, sometimes called the "Little Talmud." His students included the poet/philosopher Judah Halevi (ca. 1075–1141) and Halevi's lifelong friend Joseph Ibn Migash (1077–ca. 1141), who succeeded al-Fāsī at Lucena and was the teacher of Maimonides' learned father. But not since Judah the Patriarch and his colleagues compiled the Mishnah, Maimonides wrote, had anyone set out the full range of Halakhah.[12] And the body of law registered in the Mishnah had grown immensely in the Babylonian and Jerusalem Talmuds and in the forests of discussion that spread within and beyond them.

The need Maimonides addressed lay not in the realm of praxis alone. The intellectual need was in some ways even greater, given the varying sophistication of the Sages (and their audience) and the oblique and elliptical modes of rabbinic discourse, heavily reliant on allegory, parable, and dialogue, often allusive and presumptive of immediate and intimate familiarity with Scripture and with the full range of rabbinic dicta and homilies, and chary of overt confrontation with the issues of theology. Yet despite the rabbinic habits of obliquity and indirection, values and ideas are prominent anchors and aims in Halakhah, not least in its claim to divine authority. Nor, as Baḥyā Ibn Pāqūdah explained, can one adequately observe the Torah's prescriptions if one does not understand their aims and observe them with appropriate intent.[13]

Heralding the clarity of mind that Maimonides brought to all his work, from his efforts to rationalize the nomenclature of *materia medica* to his very early work defining key terms and stating basic rules of logic, *MT* flies proudly on its masthead a line from the Psalms, quoted, with characteristic verve, in the medieval manner to elicit a facet of meaning not salient on the surface: *Then shall I be unabashed to scrutinize all Thy commandments* (119:6). The challenge Maimonides took up is to see and set before his readers the good sense in the Mosaic laws, which God Himself had promised would be plain to the nations of the world:[14] *Follow and keep them. For this is your wisdom and discernment in the eyes of the nations, who will hear all these laws and say, "What a wise and discerning people is this great nation!" For what nation is so great as to have the divine so near as the* LORD *our God is to us whenever we call upon Him, and what nation is so great as to have laws and rules as just as this entire Torah that I give you this day!* (Deuteronomy 4:6–8).

Maimonides' goal in the *Mishneh Torah* was to render Halakhah accessible to all who might need it. That, he says, is why he wrote the work in mishnaic Hebrew, not biblical Hebrew or Aramaic—nor in Arabic, opaque to most European Jews.[15] He treasured Torah study and devoted much of his waking and working life to it. But he did not consider such study life's purpose or highest goal. The Torah was given as a guide to life for Israel in every generation (1.13b), but life itself is for living actively and thoughtfully. The Torah aims to show us how best this can be done (2.84b). A lifetime spent conning over halakhic debates without seeing a resolution to them was not a life well spent. Our moral goal, as Maimonides stresses, is to perfect our character in acts of kindness. Our intellectual goal, to know God,[16] is best attained by seeing the expressions of God's grace and wisdom in nature. The two goals join hands in a virtuous circle, good character pointing implicitly toward God and kindness and generosity inspired, in turn, by ever clearer and sharper awareness (even in the midst of an active life) of God's constant presence (I Introduction, 4a; III 51, 125a–126b).[17]

Some of the Rambam's contemporaries worried that the *Mishneh Torah*, as the title he gave it allowed them to suspect, was meant to *be* the Halakhah (rather than represent it). Pinḥas ben Meshullam, chief Jewish judge of Alexandria, a man of Provençe, voiced the fear that Maimonides aimed to replace the Talmud—hence his failure to name his sources.[18] "God forbid!" Maimonides replied in a lengthy letter. He did teach al-Fāsī's code and other rabbinic works. He wrote the *MT*, in the first instance, he declared, as his own aide-mémoire but then to help others navigate the Talmud's depths—and learn the sentence of the Law.

Halbertal gives Pinḥas's question a full hearing and ultimately confirms the Rabbi's fears.[19] Those fears, we can say, partly with the aid of hindsight and partly with an appreciation of Maimonides' own history and practice, seem a bit overwrought. But Maimonides clearly did aim to displace talmudic study as a way of life. If that is what Rabbi Pinḥas feared, his fears were not groundless: Maimonides did not celebrate the aim of spending one's life wandering in the woods of talmudic speculation and disputation. The *Mishneh Torah* was and remains a practical reference, giving every Jew access to the halakhic rulings needed to guide decision-making. It also enabled every committed reader to see and appreciate the conceptual and moral roots and implications of Jewish law as an integrated system. But Halakhah was itself a guide, not a world to live in. Obscurantism and the life bred by it were not precious to the Rambam.

Among those who, ever since the destruction of the Temple in Jerusalem in the year 70, thought of halakhic study as a way of life—and indeed the ideal way of life—Rabbi Pinḥas's worries have persisted to this day, marked by concerns about the omission of citations from the *MT* and its elision of ancient debates. Nothing said here will stanch the wound still throbbing at the site of the Roman conquest, when rabbinic study and the liturgy it bred displaced the spiritual life once centered on the Temple in Jerusalem. But in matters of Halakhah, Maimonides, we can say, seems never to fly naked: He never substitutes mere personal opinion for well-precedented, well-grounded halakhic judgment. Rabbinic scholars who probe the internal consistency and external groundings of the rulings recorded in the *MT*, long topoi of halakhic scholarship, consistently find halakhic foundations for them, often anchored in rather deeper and more faithful understanding of the ancient texts than lesser readers have reached. Given Maimonides' vast learning and his access to some texts no longer extant, Jacob Dienstag writes, it would be "an endless task" to trace all his sources. But despite eight-and-a-half centuries of critiques invited and intensified by its prominence, the *Yad Ḥazakah* retains a commanding place as a halakhic work.[20]

The *Guide*, like Maimonides' Code, shows his deep respect for tradition. But in the *Guide*, the focus shifts from practice and precept to theory and theology. The division of the house, tellingly, intensifies between those in love with philosophy as the love of wisdom and those insensitive to it or allergic to it. Where the *Yad* seeks order, intelligibility, and principle in Halakhah, the *Guide* turns to Aggadah, the vehicle that bears the themes of Jewish theology lightly rather than dogmatically, in midrashic, homiletic fancy, its narratives, providing a setting for the doxological precepts of the Torah in much the way that Jewish praxis and the Jewish ethos find their roots in the biblical mitzvot.

Not least among the miracles made possible by the Judaic reliance on narrative and midrash is that the Torah, in its broadest sense (which, for traditionalists, includes the rabbinic literature), can teach without dogmatism. It does so, as Maimonides is at pains to make clear, partly by its poetry and partly by the symbolism embedded in its ceremonial practices—although here, in the ritual laws that the Torah uses to make institutions of ideas, there are sanctions. Just as he wrote the *Mishneh Torah* to make Halakhah accessible to human understanding, it was to discover to his reader the rationality of the Torah's ideas that Maimonides, making a new start in 1185 after setting aside two earlier exploratory and explanatory projects,[21] wrote the *Guide to the Perplexed*.

PART I

Building Blocks

ONE

Setting the Scene

Jews had lived in Iberia since antiquity. Indeed, some locate Tarshish, where Jonah hoped to flee (1:3), in southern Spain, as far as possible across the Mediterranean from the port of Jaffa, where the reluctant prophet put to sea. After defeating Carthage (in the third century BCE), Rome ruled Spain. Jews seem to have lived in Iberia at least by the first century of the Common Era, their numbers swelling after Bar Kokhva's defeat in 135. In time they prospered, but as Rome Christianized, serious efforts were made to obliterate Iberian Judaism. Persecution continued under the Visigoths and intensified when their rulers abandoned Arianism and turned Catholic (in 589). Onerous taxes, invidious laws, expulsions, forced conversions, pogroms, expropriations, and seizure of children for baptism persisted down to 711, when an army of Muslim Arabs and Berbers invaded and made Andalusia their own. Many Jews saw the invaders as liberators and aided the Islamic forces, who left Cordoba in Jewish hands and collaborated with Jews in Granada, Malaga, Seville, and Toledo. Jews were now *dhimmīs*, subject to special taxes and discriminatory laws, enforced with varying degrees of severity. But the contrast with Christian oppression made Muslim Spain a magnet to Jews.

The rise of Islam in the seventh century had brought ethnic Arabs and, in time, their non-Arab clients and vassals to military and political prominence and dominance. The once mighty Persian Empire fell to Muslim Arab armies, as did some of the richest Byzantine provinces. Egypt, Syria, North Africa, and southern Spain were Islamized. In the Muslim East, the first four "Rightly Guided" caliphs, lieutenants to Muḥammad, the prophet of Islam (ca. 570–632), were succeeded by Arab dynasts, the Umayyads, with their capital in Damascus. Then came the ʿAbbāsid Revolution, fanned by nascent Shīʿite legitimism and ethnic resentments, when the denizens of Persian provinces and newly conquered lands in Central Asia found that accepting Islam did not always put them on equal footing with the Arab conquerors. The Umayyads were overthrown in 750.

Not far from ancient Babylon and Ctesiphon, once the glory of the defeated Persian Empire, the ʿAbbāsids built their capital on the Tigris, calling it the City of Peace. The ancient name, however, stuck: Baghdad became a metropolis. Umayyad stragglers were ruthlessly hunted down. But Umayyad claimants in North Africa managed to establish a regime of their own in Spain. Its greatest ruler, ʿAbd al-Raḥmān III (r. 912–961), united the fractious country, declared himself caliph, and pushed back Christian and Shīʿite threats to his rule.

Classics

The early ʿAbbāsids saw the cultural heritage of the fallen Iranian Empire and the Byzantine provinces as priceless spoils of war. Muslim monarchs and notables sponsored the extensive translation of Greek classics into Arabic, preserving ancient works and creating, on the fallen nurse log, a new literature unlike anything known in Europe before the Renaissance.[1] The sciences and practical arts of ancient Greece and the lands to the east were eagerly assimilated and their disciplines cultivated and enlarged. To the learned, the industrious, and the entrepreneurial, the wealth of foreign sciences, arts, and lore was too valuable a resource to ignore. Muslims learned the art of papermaking from Chinese war prisoners in 752, and as early as the third century, Central Asians had been making high-grade stock from cotton rags rather than use the mulberry fiber favored in China.[2] From India, the newly Islamicate peoples gleaned worldly wisdom from the fables of the *Panchatantra*. They mastered advanced techniques of sericulture and ceramics in the great cities of the Silk Road. And there, too, at Balkh (the former Bactria, conquered by Muslim armies in the mid-seventh century), the debates of Muslim missionaries with local erudites of Sarāstivādin Buddhism first conceived the dimensionless atoms distinctive of the early schools of Islamic theology,[3] whose views Maimonides will challenge in his robust defense of natural causality (I 51, 58b; I 73).

Greek medicine, architecture, engineering, and astrology were among the arts prized by the conquerors. Hundreds of works were translated into Arabic under Islamic patronage, often by Christian scholars whose knowledge of Greek gave them entrée to the newly accessed treasure house of truth. The earliest interest was in practical arts like medicine and mechanics, but the appetite for learning broadened swiftly, and understanding of what counts as practical varied widely and expanded rapidly. Knowledge of mathematics and astronomy was clearly critical for merchants, builders, architects, and engineers, just as anatomy, physiology, and botany were for physicians. But command of logic was critical for anyone locking horns with Greek-trained Christian clerics in Alexandria or Damascus. And logic verged into metaphysics when debate was joined with Christian theologians who had long sparred with one another in turning Aristotle's *Categories* to account in debates about the Trinity. Formal study of grammar and lexicography proved vital in interpreting the Qur'ān, not least for converts new to Arabic. But equally vital were new methods of history-writing advancing beyond the anecdotal entertainments and genealogical lore of Arabia. Chronicles, annals, and biographical dictionaries were written. Before long, there were thematic universal histories seeking cultural wisdom as well as practical and diplomatic lessons from the past.[4]

Works of practical value were soon seen to be inseparable from their framework and foundations in theory: Astrology, in demand for calculating horoscopes and siting new cities, needed astronomy. A monumental achievement was the ninth-century translation of the *Syntaxis Mathematica* of Ptolemy (ca. 100–ca. 170), known well to Maimonides and still named today by its Arabic title, *Almagest*. One group of Christian translators made over into Arabic (often via an intermediate Syriac draft) some 129 Greek works of Galen (129–216/7), the great medical writer and sometime physician to Marcus Aurelius. Maimonides tracks Galen's medical contributions and cites him regularly in the *Guide* on philosophical as well as anatomical issues, welcoming his wisdom but disagreeing when he finds him wanting or unfriendly to the Torah (I 73, 106b,

117b, II 10, 21b; II 15, 33b, III 12, 18ab). Galen knew that medicine operates on philosophical footings, ethical, epistemological, cosmological, and metaphysical. One of his works is titled *That the Best Physician Is Also a Philosopher*.[5]

Of vital importance to philosophically inclined readers of Arabic were Galen's summaries of Plato's dialogues. The works available included the *Cratylus, Sophist, Statesman, Parmenides, Euthydemus, Republic,* and *Laws*.[6] For the *Timaeus*, a key work for any scriptural monotheist, given Plato's poetic myth of the world's creation, there was, besides Galen's summary, a commentary by Plutarch, which prompted a supercommentary by the formidable physician al-Rāzī, whose *Theology* Maimonides openly loathes but whose medical writings he respects. Galen's précis of the *Timaeus* drops the contextual byplay and cuts to the bone of Plato's argument, opening with Plato's contention that a temporal reality must have had a beginning. Writings by Neoplatonists, including Plotinus, Porphyry, and Proclus, were readily available in Arabic, although some were disguised as works of Aristotle, furthering the Neoplatonic effort toward the synthesis of the Platonic and Aristotelian philosophical heritage.

Most of the great Muslim and Jewish philosophers of the Middle Ages were themselves physicians in the Galenic tradition, their clinical work linked with their intellectual explorations and creative speculations. In mathematics, as in medicine, theory and practice reinforced each other. The Hindu number system, with its revolutionary idea of zero;[7] the arithmetic of Nicomachus of Gerasa; and the geometry of Euclid and his successor, Apollonius (whose work on Conic Sections is quoted in the *Guide*), meant far more than the ability to write a bill of lading or survey a field after the Nile flood. It meant the ability (accurately) to calculate the earth's radius, predict eclipses (II 24, 53b), and speculate on the dimensions of the cosmos (III 14, 28a) and even on the meaning of infinity (I 73, 115ab, II Introduction 5ab). In the same way, philosophical theology and metaphysics linked with Aristotelian virtue ethics and Platonic virtue politics through the ideas of human nature, agency, and destiny—all prominent themes in Maimonides' reflections.

There was resistance, to be sure, to the flood of new ideas in the rising culture of imperial Islam. Greek logic was welcomed by some but pilloried by others as the mere grammar of the Greeks, unneeded by articulate speakers of Arabic.[8] Arabic letters did, in truth, have sciences of grammar and lexicography—although the critics little knew that these studies, too, had deep Greek roots.

Al-Kindī, the first major physician/philosopher of Islam, known for his Arab ethnicity as the "Philosopher of the Arabs," was a sponsor and user of translations from the Greek. Echoing Aristotle, he urged in his *Metaphysics* that one should welcome truth from any source where it can be found. But although favored by the ʿAbbāsids in the early days of the translation movement, Kindī fell out of favor and was imprisoned late in life, when a new caliph arose who knew not the worth of philosophy and courted clerics of a narrower, avowedly traditionalist cast.

The translation movement did not end with the ʿAbbāsids. ʿAbd al-Raḥmān III was the proud possessor of an illustrated Greek manuscript of Dioscorides' *Materia Medica*, a treasury of pharmaceutical knowledge presented to him by the Byzantine emperor and soon made over into Arabic by a monk sent to do that work. Aiding the monk, especially with the names of the herbs cataloged in the precious work, was the monarch's Jewish physician Ḥasdai b. Shaprūṭ (905–75), the caliph's right-hand man, repeatedly entrusted with delicate diplomatic missions to Christian rulers in Spain and negotiations with the Byzantines. Leader of his fellow Jews and spokesman in their behalf at court, Ḥasdai was the patron, among others, of the poet and lexicographer Menaḥem ben Sarūq and of Dūnash ben Labrāṭ, who first introduced in Hebrew the Arabic prosody that would come to dominate Andalusian Hebrew poetry.

In time, thinkers and scholars writing in Arabic would claim the intellectual heritage of antiquity as the legacy of an ancient Near Eastern patrimony.[9] There were affinities, of course, treasured and cultivated by synthetic thinkers like Maimonides. But the tale was just a tale, perhaps lending cover to the learned and creative efforts that were irrepressible among Arabic literati. Maimonides himself harbored thoughts of an ancient Hebraic *prisca scientia* (I 71). Yet notions of a *philosophia perennialis* to be recovered or reconstructed from Hebrew texts did little to protect his own work from the critics who found its themes and theses alien. The *Guide to the Perplexed*, his philosophical masterpiece, would be denounced to Church authorities and burnt along with the *MT* not long after his death.[10] In some quarters, its teachings and arguments are still held suspect, heretical, inauthentic, or insincere, often on grounds of a perceived inevitable clash between Athens and Jerusalem.

Exile

The sense of loss still visible in Maimonides' habit of signing himself a man of the West poignantly echoes in personal terms his abiding sense of the ancient loss of Israel's life in her own land. Explaining the lapse of prophetic inspiration as a result of exile and defeat, he argued, following the Talmud, that joy and confidence are critical to inspiration: Prophets cannot fulfill their mission when weighed down by the lassitude and grief suffered by Israel in exile (II 36, 80a).

In 1148, when young Moses was just ten years of age, Cordoba fell to the Almohads, a militant Islamic movement whose forces invaded Spain from North Africa. The conquerors called themselves *al-Muwaḥḥidūn*, "the Monotheists." The definite article is a bitter testament to the zealots' claims: If the Almohads were the monotheists, just what were Jews and Christians, or even fellow Muslims in the fallen lands? The implicit charge: The now failing regime of the Almoravids had not held true to the path and precepts of Islam, and communities of other faiths and practices had failed by the only standard that mattered.

Apocalyptic moments and movements are not rare in Islamic history. As Ibn Khaldūn (1332–1406), the great North African social theorist, explains, tribal energies and loyalties can expand beyond appeals to a shared pedigree and build something of a juggernaut if fired by religious zeal, empowering those who ride under the same banner. They can overwhelm an urban-centered power that has grown soft enjoying the amenities of city life and increasingly reliant on others—most dangerously on fighting forces other than its own.[11]

The Almoravids, *al-murābiṭūn*, were that decaying movement now. They, too, had united Berber tribes in the name of Islamic renewal. Their name, too, had been a battle cry, proclaiming their origins in a fortified Sufi conventicle (*ribāṭ*) at the mouth of the Senegal River. They had conquered the Maghreb early in the eleventh century and overwhelmed Andalusia soon after. At their peak, they and their tributaries held much of Iberia and North Africa. But the dynasts had softened, much as Ibn Khaldūn would find all too natural. Beset by Christians to the north and by Muslim rivals in Iberia and the Maghreb, they could not withstand the Almohad onslaught.

Berber mercenaries had come to Iberia even before the Almoravids, at the behest of Hishām, the Umayyad ruler who abandoned the relative tolerance of ʿAbd al-Raḥmān III and his philosophically inclined son al-Ḥakam (r. 961–976).

Al-Ḥakam had amassed an impressive library of scientific and philosophical books, among which ʿAbd al-Raḥmān's Jewish minister Ḥasdai b. Shaprūṭ had been sure to include many Jewish works, laying a foundation for Jewish learning in the West and rendering Andalusian Jewish scholars far less dependent on the academies of Baghdad.[12] Hishām, seeking favor from the clerics (*ʿulemāʾ*) and arms to prop up his tottering regime, had purged al-Ḥakam's library, and now he was overwhelmed by the outside forces he had called upon.

Gnawed away in the early decades of the eleventh century, the Umayyad state fell in 1031, its dominions split up into small principalities under local leaders known as *Mulūk al-Ṭawāʾif* (*reyes de taifas* in Spanish). These "Party Kings" had sought political and military expertise and cultural éclat by drawing to their courts a diverse array of learned and tough-minded ministers and aides, including such Jews as the self-made polymath Shmuel Ibn Naghrela (993–1056), wazīr to the Berber Zirid dynasts of Granada. Shmuel, known as the Nagīd, led Granada's forces in the field but studied Talmud by night and wrote religious and secular Hebrew poetry modeled on Arabic genres and motifs but redolent of the Psalms, Ecclesiastes, and Proverbs. A patron of other poets and scholars, he wrote an Arabic work on Hebrew grammar and founded the yeshiva at Lucena.

But lest we absorb too rosy an image of the *convivencia* of Jews and Muslims in the Iberian Golden Age, we must add that the Nagīd's son and successor was murdered by a mob in 1066, his body crucified in the city gate.[13] After the ensuing massacre of Granada's Jews, the community struggled back to life, only to be destroyed by the Almoravids in 1090.

It was the weakness of the factional kings that brought the Almoravids to Spain. Despised by the *ʿulemāʾ* for their cultural openness, the Party Kings had struggled against the forces of the Reconquista, and when Toledo fell to the Christians in 1085, it was to Berber forces that the surviving Muslim powers turned. The Almoravid leader Yūsuf b. Tāshufīn (1061–1106) advanced into Spain the next year. He defeated the armies of Alfonso VI of León and Castile, but he could not yet retake Toledo. Knowing well that the *Reyes de Taifas* were weakened by their rivalries and had lost much popular support through resentment of their prodigal spending, heavy taxes, religious openness, and laxity, he returned in 1090, defeating all but one of them by 1094. When he died in 1106, reportedly at the age of one hundred, Almoravids ruled northwest Africa and much of southern Spain. But their sway was not to last. Alfonso I of Aragon defeated them at Saragossa in 1118. By 1147, the Almohads had conquered Marrakesh, the capital the Almoravids had founded in North Africa; slain their last ruler; and were ready to sweep into Spain. Their conquest of Cordoba in 1148 was a fateful change for the Maimon family and for all Jews in the Islamic West.

The Almoravids took pride in an admiring letter supposedly sent to Ibn Tāshufīn by the great Muslim theologian al-Ghazālī (1058–1111). As a young jurist teaching in Baghdad, Ghazālī had issued a fetwa in support of Ibn Tāshufīn as the legitimate Sunnī ruler in the West, seeing him as loyal to the caliph in Baghdad.[14] The Baghdad caliphs had long been mere figureheads by now, but Ghazālī still saw the caliphate as the anchor of Islamic unity, even as the caliph accepted the armed power of local sultans—Seljuqs in the East or Almoravids in the West. Such powers were needed, as he saw it, to champion Islam against its enemies, external (be they Byzantine or Catholic) or internal, like the Party Kings, too ready to align with Christian princes or with the Ismāʿīlī Shīʿites. Celebrated as the "Proof of Islam," Ghazālī was revered for his sober Sufism; his forty-book pietist classic, *Reviving the Religious Sciences* (*Iḥyāʾ ʿUlūm al-Dīn*); and his biting critique of the Islamic philosophical school, *The Incoherence of the Philosophers* (*Tahāfut al-Falāsifa*). Core arguments of the *Tahāfut* defended belief in the world's creation against the Philosophers' thesis of its eternity. Eternalism, Ghazālī charged, was tantamount to atheism. For an eternal world seemed to have no need of God.

There is a certain irony in the Almoravids' clutching for Ghazālī's mantle. For the Almoravid dynasts had little taste for theological inquiry,[15] and their authorities had burnt Ghazālī's books in all their dominions.[16] It was the Almohads who made him their culture hero. Ibn Tūmart (d. 1130), the Almohad founder, was said to have been inspired by the purity of Ghazālī's monotheism. Fancifully, it was claimed he had met him and witnessed his fury on hearing that the *Iḥyāʾ* had been burnt.[17] Ghazālī, we are told, had called on God to destroy the Almoravid regime, and Ibn Tūmart had prayed it would be by his hand. Like other Ashʿarite theologians, Ghazālī called claims to personal agency *shirk*, or polytheism: God is the true author of all events and actions. A human being is but the pen in the hand of the scribe. The story of the encounter was palpably Almohad propaganda. Ghazālī was far off to the east in Ṭūs when his book was burnt. But the tale cunningly frames Ibn Tūmart's response as no mere personal threat but a prayerful vow of devotion to the use he hoped God would make of him.

The Almohad conquest was founded on terror. Ibn Tūmart had cemented his power in a bloody forty-day purge (*tamyīz*) of tribes and tribesmen deemed spiritually lax, disloyal, or corrupt.[18] With massacres and forced conversions, his disciple and successor ʿAbd al-Muʾmin expanded Almohad domains to an empire. Hundreds of thousands were slain in North Africa.[19] Part of the movement's mission, as the Jewish philosopher and historian Abraham Ibn Daʾud (ca. 1110–ca. 1180) wrote, was to wipe out the nation and erase the name of Israel. No yeshiva remained in Almohad domains, and no Jew survived who openly rejected Islam.[20]

Ibn Tūmart had proclaimed himself the Mahdī, precursor of the Messiah, and ʿAbd al-Muʾmin pressed claims of his master's infallibility. Calling himself the Mahdī's caliph, he abandoned even nominal allegiance to the ʿAbbāsids. The Almohads' square coins, their austere salafist architecture, and their archaizing calligraphy signaled the radical and totalizing intent of their regime. There was a new call to prayer, sometimes using Berber language. The Qur'ān and *Ḥadīth* swamped the familiar jurisprudence of the Mālikite school, and a new class of religious authorities was installed, schooled in Ibn Tūmart's writings, trained in special Almohad seminars, and paid by the regime.[21]

The movement clearly had intellectual pretensions. Ibn al-Qalānisī (d. 1160), a non-Almohad source, calls it a *madhhab fikr*, a school of thought. But the aim was not to free but to control its subjects' thinking. Yet Abū Yaʿqūb Yūsuf (r. 1163–84), who succeeded his father, ʿAbd al-Muʾmin, had a soft spot for philosophy. He was the best of friends with Ibn Ṭufayl, the philosopher/physician whose fictional fantasy, *Ḥayy Ibn Yaqẓān*, sought to reconcile Avicenna's philosophy with the theology of Ghazālī. The two men enjoyed each other's company and conversation and spoke freely about the question of the world's eternity, even in the presence of the young Averroes (1126–1198) when Ibn Ṭufayl introduced him at court. Ibn Ṭufayl once laughingly suggested, as he lined up for his pay, that if the puritanical regime wanted music theory, he could teach that too.[22] It was at his suggestion, in 1168, that the Commander of the Faithful, as the Almohad monarch was styled in his caliphal title, commissioned Averroes, scion of a long line of *qāḍī*s, to write his massive three-tiered commentaries on Aristotle's works. For Abū Yaʿqūb felt a need for fuller exposition of their Arabic translation.[23] Later, in Latin translation, Averroes' commentaries guided generations of European readers.

But free intellectual inquiry, as Averroes saw it, was not for the masses. One path was open to the rare philosophical seeker. Quite another was laid out for the commonfolk. Ibn Ṭufayl's philosophical bildungsroman would be welcomed among the early movers of Europe's Enlightenment as a challenging invitation to independent thinking when it was translated into Latin, first in 1493 at the instance of the Renaissance humanist Pico Della Mirandola and then in 1671 by the English Arabist and Hebraist Edward Pococke. Later, from Pococke's Latin and still later from the original Arabic, it was translated into other European languages. But although *Ḥayy Ibn Yaqẓān* was often read, in its European translations, as an invitation to engage independently in natural science or spiritual exploration,[24] Ibn Ṭufayl himself sharply distinguished from the masses those rare souls whose talents and virtues made them capable of safe and responsible thinking. For the hoi polloi, a more parochial repertoire of symbols, rituals, and creeds seemed both fitting and necessary, given the moral and intellectual limitations of ordinary minds.

Not without reason are notions of "double truth" fathered upon Averroes, who carefully discriminates truths to be shared widely from those reserved for the wise. He boldly rebutted Ghazālī's critique of the Islamic philosophers, line for line, in his tartly titled *Incoherence of the Incoherence*. But in his *K. Faṣl al-Maqāl wa Taqrīr mā bayna al-Sharīʿa wa-'l-Ḥikma min al-Ittisāl* (On Drawing a Line between Religion and Philosophy and Determining Their Relations), he labored to find a place for philosophy and the sciences alongside religion—in his milieu, more readily called law than faith. In his paraphrase of Plato's *Republic*, he named the Almoravids as masters of tyranny, but not the Almohads. We'll find Maimonides twitting Averroes, albeit not by name, for trying to accommodate Almohad dogma by painting the eternalism that his Muslim contemporary espoused as somehow compatible with an anthropocentric teleology (III 13).

For the Almohads, as a movement, the very idea of independent thinking was anathema. They cherished memories of Ibn Tūmart's browbeating a distinguished Mālikī jurist for imagining that a question of Sharīʿa law might have more than one sound answer. And they prized a book ascribed to Ibn Tūmart as a hallmark of jurisprudence for dismissing the old ideal of *kull mujtahid muṣīb*, that any juridical authority's ruling is sound.[25] Mālikī jurists and theologians were, in fact, in mortal danger under the Almohads as presumed Almoravid diehards. It was now a capital offense not to hail Ibn Tūmart as Mahdī. And the once protected status of *dhimmī* was abolished: Jews and Christians were mere infidels; as the historian al-Marrākushī (fl. 1185–1224) reports, they were now deemed *mushrikūn* (polytheists), polar opposites of *muwaḥḥidūn*, and targeted for death should they fail to embrace Islam.[26]

While still in North Africa ʿAbd al-Muʾmin had massacred the Jews of Tlemcen, Sijilmasa, Marrakesh, Fez, and other cities as each fortress fell. More bloodshed followed in Spain. In a bitter elegy, Abraham Ibn Ezra (ca. 1092–1167) mourns the Almohad destruction of a dozen Jewish communities in Spain and North Africa. No Jew or Christian, the Muslim historian al-Nuwayrī reports, remained in ʿAbd al-Muʾmin's lands, nor did any church or synagogue. Forced conversion was state policy. The bitter choice, once the heat of battle cooled and the plundering turned to confiscation, was Islam, exile, or death.

Christians could go north, encouraged by Alfonso VII of León-Castile. But no such welcome awaited Iberian Jews in Catholic Spain. Exile, for them, meant a life as outcasts, and few could foresee just how urgent it would prove to be to leave al-Andalus. Given its scale, the caliph's decree could not be fully and immediately enforced. So despite the public executions, the slippage inevitable in any would-be totalitarian regime prompted delays and fed hopes that the rigors of this latest persecution would pass—and pass they did, but not until the Almohad dynasty itself had crumbled in the mid-thirteenth century. Meanwhile, false comforts, as Maimonides ruefully reflects in his early *Iggeret ha-Shemad* (Letter on the Persecution), were fraught with tragic outcomes.

Andalusian Jews who were able and had some recourse or some sense of the future fled into exile. Thousands were martyred. But many did recite the *Shahādah*: "There is no god but God, and Muḥammad is His prophet." For those hoping to remain Jewish at heart or in secret practice, the barb was in the tail. Affirming one God might seem harmless enough. Muslim scorn for thoughts of the Trinity made Christians a ready target of Almohad zeal. But for Jews, the sore point lay in accepting Muḥammad as a prophet. God, surely, could speak to anyone He pleased (yet see 2.73b–74a). But to the conquerors, accepting Muḥammad as "seal of the prophets" (Qurʾān 33:40) meant embracing every particular of Islam as understood by the authoritative exegetes of the revealed book and the vast canon of beliefs and practices deemed authentically

Muḥammadan. And apostasy, once the *Shahādah* was pronounced, meant death in this world and damnation in the next.

Joel Kraemer suspects that ʿAbd al-Muʾmin, the true founder of the Almohad state, may have relaxed his oppressive policy somewhat toward the end of his reign, needing Christians and Jews to help manage his new won empire. He made a treaty with Genoa and, in 1153, allowed Moroccan Christians to import high-value goods. But a clampdown followed: In 1162, many of the forced Jewish converts of Granada, along with Mozarab Christians, supported a revolt. The Almohad heir, Abū Yaʿqūb Yūsuf, sent by his father, retook Granada and slew the rebels. Almohad policy hardened, and Jewish conversions increased. Abū Yaʿqūb succeeded his father the following year.

Recalling the ninth-century persecution of his fellow Ashʿarites by the then dominant Muʿtazilite sect, Ghazālī had stressed in the *Iḥyāʾ* that lip service alone, the mere "husk of the husk" of monotheism, suffices to save one's neck, as he put it. One cannot, he wrote, open men's hearts to prove them sincere. But the Almohads cared little for such niceties, even from Ghazālī. Inquisitions into the faith and practice of nominal converts scarred their rule. Yet many of the Jews who professed Islam retained Jewish allegiance and the clandestine Jewish practices still possible for them.

For a time, perhaps, lip service seemed to suffice. Nominal converts, as Maimonides wrote, went through the motions, and Almohad officials played their part. But then came calls for sincerity and the imposition of strict rules and disabilities on "new Muslims." Ibn ʿAqnīn, Maimonides' compatriot in exile, reports that even after their conversion, new Muslims could not own slaves, marry "old" Muslims, or consort with them. Marrākushī describes the coarse, awkward, and humiliating dress mandated in a decree by Abū Yūsuf (al-Manṣūr, r. 1184–1199), Abū Yaʿqūb's son and successor. Holding the converts' sincerity suspect, he declared, "They pray in the mosques, teach their children to recite the Qurʾān, and comport themselves according to our custom and religion, but God alone knows what their hearts conceal, or their homes contain."[27]

The plain words of the Qurʾān, "No force in faith" (2:256), seem firmly to exclude coerced conversions. But the same verse continues: "True guidance is clearly sundered from error." That sharp division of faith from falsehood opened a door to persecution of those who stubbornly spurned Islamic truth. The Qurʾān exhorted Muslims: "Do battle in the path of God, and know that God hears and knows" (2:244). Muḥammad's self-image as the embattled leader of embattled followers bred a sharp duality: The sense of persecution and exclusion shared by early Muslims fused with triumphalist hopes. So in a telling verse, the Qur'ān urges, "Battle them until resistance ends and all religion turns to God" (8:39; cf. 61:4). Other verses (15:94, 16:125, 29:46) enjoin tolerance and dialogue. But such openness is qualified variously, and in keeping with the Qur'ānic doctrine of *naskh*, or abrogation (2:106), conciliatory passages were seen as canceled by later warlike verses.

The Almohad persecutions made many a Muslim thinker run with the fox and hunt with the hounds. Often it seemed unclear, even to the thinkers themselves, just which role they were cast in. So crypto-Jews were not alone in pursuing a modus vivendi. Even the caliph played a different role in his bloody reprisals at Granada from his pleasant welcome of Averroes when Ibn Ṭufayl presented him at court. In 1195, around the time of Abū Yūsuf's severe sumptuary decree, Averroes was exiled, perhaps as a sop to the clerics, and sent to once heavily Jewish Lucena, charged with pagan beliefs related to his supposed Jewish ancestry. The instigators seem to have been rival jurists.[28] After much effort, in time, he was restored. But by then the Maimon family was long gone.

They seem to have fled Cordoba soon after the conquest. They may have remained in Spain for another five years, but for obvious reasons, little is known of their whereabouts. From the biographical dictionary of Ibn al-Qifṭī (d. 1248), we learn that young Moses took instruction in philosophy and the allied sciences of mathematics, astronomy, and logic while still in Spain. Evidently, he studied medicine too at this time with both Jewish and Muslim physicians. At this early stage, we learn from Ibn al-Qifṭī, the young Rambam, not yet clinically experienced, tended to be cautious and was careful to consult with other physicians about difficult diagnoses.[29] But even in his mature medical work, he favored clinical consultation—as able physicians still do today.

In his mature medical writings, after cautions against ill-informed doctor-shopping and arbitrary switching from one therapy to another, and agreeing with Rāzī that splicing disparate medical plans may well compound their errors, Maimonides writes, "But if physicians consult with one another, as kings and statesmen do, and they debate and dispute to reach a decision about what should be done, that approach is best and is the one to be preferred."[30] Maimonides candidly admits the weaknesses of medicine and his own therapeutic limitations.[31] "In this art of medicine," he writes, "as al-Fārābī states, as in seamanship and agriculture, outcomes may not depend on what we do. A physician may do all that he should in the best way possible, with no error on his part or that of the patient, and still not achieve the cure he sought. The reason is clear. For what is at work here is not medicine alone but nature."[32] We hear a mature and calm voice here, but the conditions that allowed Maimonides to speak with such calm authority still lay in the future.

Exiled from Cordoba, the Maimon family may have made their way to Christian Spain for a time. If so, the little that the Rambam says of Christian lands suggests a rather negative impression. He remarks on the filth of European cities, where swine might roam the marketplace (III 47, 111a)—hardly a common sight in a Muslim-ruled city. In 1159/60, when he was twenty-one, the family—mother, father, his brother David (then in his teens), and three sisters—left Spain for Fez. Maimon, the paterfamilias, was about sixty.

Fez, a venerable city in today's Morocco, was founded by the Shīʿite Idrisid dynasty in 808. Like other Maghrebi cities, it had been a center of Jewish learning, home to many Iberian Jews who had come to North Africa when, as Halevi wrote, the Jews of al-Andalus found themselves caught between the hammer of the Reconquista and the Almoravid anvil. Yet six thousand Jews were massacred in Fez in 1033 by militant Berber tribesmen, and many women were simply carried off. Fez fell to the Almohads two years before Cordoba and was a power base for the movement. Isaac Husik called it the very lion's den. What, then, drew the family to this city in the Almohad heartland? Language may have influenced their choice. So might ties of friendship, or of trade, on which the family's livelihood depended. But Fez, clearly, was the eye of the storm.

It is not known with certainty if the family were among the crypto-Jews displaced spiritually as well as geographically by the Almohad conquest. The question is controversial, but there is good evidence from multiple sources that they were.[33] Maimonides himself seems to confess it in his *Iggeret*. His father had circulated a Letter of Consolation the year they reached Fez, comforting his fellow Jews and urging them not to despair but to keep the faith and such Jewish practices as they could: They were still Jews and should not torment themselves over their forced dissimulation.[34] A critic, now unknown, had urged martyrdom rather than utter the *Shahādah*, branding it a wicked denial of God.

To renounce Judaism but retain secret Jewish practices, he wrote, only compounded the sin. That stung. Maimonides wrote a vehement response, refuting the critique with a barrage of halakhic learning and scarcely bridled contempt for its unnamed author, whom he calls "a would-be scholar, who did not suffer what befell most Israelite communities in this time of oppression—God end it!" Islam, he argued, is not idolatry, and the nominal converts should not be condemned but welcomed by their fellow Jews once able to return. "In no way do I defend myself," he wrote. "No. I say, *We lie in disgrace, covered with shame. We have sinned before the* L*ORD our God, we and our fathers!* (Jeremiah 3:25). . . . We know where we stand and do not try to hide it—*We know our guilt,* L*ORD, and our fathers' wrong. We have sinned against Thee* (Jeremiah 14:20)."[35]

Herbert Davidson, zealous to defend Maimonides from any thought of even nominal conversion, impugns the sources that attest it. He rejects Maimonides' authorship of the *Iggeret* and speculates that the responsum it rebuts was fictitious; its brief, a strawman. He even denies that Almohad policy confronted Jews with choices of Islam or death.[36] But clearly the Almohad reign of terror had made dissimulation seem prudent, and any perceived laxity in its enforcement ill prepared Iberian Jews for what was to come.

For a time, Maimonides writes, the hidden loyalties of many a nominal convert had been an open secret:

> In every persecution in the Sages' time the transgressions imposed involved overt actions. They were ordered, as they relate in the Talmud, not to study Torah or circumcise their sons, but to sleep with their menstruous wives and profane the Sabbath.[37] But in this persecution no act at all is demanded, just uttering some words about believing in that man. If one wants to keep all 613 commandments covertly, one can. There's no one to stop him. If he decides, on his own, to profane the Sabbath or some such thing, no one forced him. These conquerors make one do nothing but say those words, and they know very well that we don't mean what we say but speak only to evade the king's edict by paying lip service to his faith.
>
> So anyone slain rather than accept that man as a prophet can only be said to have performed a *mitzvah*. A great reward awaits him with God since he laid down his life to hallow God's name. But if anyone asked me whether to die or so confess, I would say, "Do it, and do not be slain—but do not stay in

> that ruler's domain." One should stay at home until able to leave that realm; and, if one must go out to work, he should practice his Judaism in private.[38]

Davidson's strongest argument against the letter lies in its treating as martyrs those who died rather than embrace Islam. For in earlier persecutions, the Sages forbade martyrdom unless what was demanded was murder, a sexual crime, idolatry, or public and exemplary breach of any item of the Law. Citing the *MT* (Laws of the Foundations of the Torah 5.4), Davidson finds it hard to believe that Maimonides would comfort penitent Israelites by condoning their sin and not condemn those who accepted death when they should not have done so. But here Davidson's strongest argument proves his weakest, partly because it is a priori. Few of us know what we might have done when faced with threats of death, or how we might judge others who chose death before dishonor. It's hard to imagine anyone so priggish or callous as to condemn as sinners those who died refusing to renounce their faith. Maimonides' stance, even as he confesses his own sin, is not evidence against his authorship of the letter but an enduring emblem of his character.[39]

Among the evidence for the family's years as nominal Muslims is Ibn ʿAqnīn's testimony. In his voluminous commentary on the Song of Songs, he recalls quiet hours of Torah study with Maimonides when both were crypto-Jews in Fez. Proud of his ties to the now celebrated luminary, he adds the verses he wrote on his friend's departure, calling him the insignia of the age; his arguments, a sword brought to the Torah's aid:

> My heart, too, set sail when my friend put out to sea.
> It forgot its homeward way and has not returned to me.
> I would restir the fires of friendship, if only I knew how.
> But how can I relight them, when my soul is with him even now?[40]

Ibn al-Qifṭī was a close friend of Ibn ʿAqnīn's, and his father was deputy at Jerusalem to al-Qāḍī al-Fāḍil, Maimonides' later patron in Cairo. When the Almohad decree was first promulgated, Ibn al-Qifṭī writes, Jews who had little in the way of possessions went into exile. But those who felt well rooted or had much to lose remained in Andalusia. Maimon's family, hoping to ride out the storm, had gone through the motions: studying the Qurʾān and praying in Muslim fashion. Only later did they leave. Ibn Abī ʿUṣaybiʿa's biographical dictionary confirms the story: Maimonides had accepted Islam. Indeed, he had memorized the Qur'ān and had studied Islamic law—labors hardly out of character.[41] Ibn Abī ʿUṣaybiʿa may have gleaned these details from Maimonides' son Abraham, his colleague at the Nasiri hospital in Egypt. Perhaps in deference to Abraham, Kraemer suspects, he adds the qualifying phrase "It is said."[42]

Faced with new rounds of persecution, the family could see that their refuge in Fez had become a trap. The *Iggeret* telescopes into a single sentence, couched as advice, the outcome of their agonized deliberations and the bitter lessons of the experience they shared with so many other Jews: "My counsel to all those I love and to any who ask my advice is to leave this place and go where one can practice his religion and follow the Torah, uncoerced and unafraid."

The family left Morocco and, after a stormy voyage in which their vessel was nearly swamped by a great wave, landed safe in Acre in the spring of 1165, the Land of Israel now under Crusader rule. Maimonides thanked God he had been saved from the sea—and the persecution.[43] He vowed to mark the storm's date each year with a fast of two days, including a day of perfect solitude in worship and study—alone with God, he wrote, as he had been at sea. Only pressing necessity might interrupt his seclusion. As his fast closed each year, he and his family would celebrate with gifts for the poor. He was not yet married, but he vowed to charge all his descendants to keep the same anniversary.

In the fall, the family traveled to Jerusalem and Hebron. At the site of the ruined Temple, they prayed, as many Jews still seek to do today. The journey from Acre to Jerusalem was dangerous and difficult, given the ongoing strife of Muslims with the Crusaders, the depredations of brigands, and the fees extracted for traversing tribal territories. The Jews and Muslims of Jerusalem had been massacred by the Crusaders in 1099 or sold as slaves if taken alive. Jews seeking refuge in the synagogues had been burnt alive. Jews now were banned from living in Jerusalem, as they had been by Hadrian and again by Constantine. But Maimonides, his father, and his brother David, with their friend Japhet ben Eli, were able to reach the city and walk there in reverence and awe.[44] They traveled on to Hebron, where Jews and Muslims had been expelled in 1099. There, Maimonides writes, he kissed his ancestors' graves. The tomb at Machpelah, purchased by Abraham (Genesis 23), held special meaning for the Rambam. For he saw Abraham as the founder of rational monotheism.[45] He would name his son Abraham, and the epigram he set at the head of each of the three parts of the *Guide* was the verse he understood as the Patriarch's proclamation of the universal God (Genesis 21:33).

The family did not remain long under Crusader rule. In a year, they left for Egypt and, after a time in Alexandria, settled in Fusṭāṭ or old Cairo. Built as a garrison city by the conquering general ʿAmr b. ʿĀṣ in 641 soon after the Muslim conquest, it had become the first great city of Muslim Egypt and by Maimonides' time had grown to some two hundred thousand souls, about four thousand of them Jewish. But by now it was a suburb of Cairo, the capital of the Fāṭimid dynasts, Ismāʿīlī Shīʿites whose caliph claimed descent from Fāṭima, Muḥammad's daughter and wife of his cousin ʿAlī. The Fāṭimids had conquered Egypt in 969 and built Cairo under the sign of Mars (al-Qāhira) in triumph after centuries as rebels and persecuted subversives in Sunnī-led lands.

By the eleventh century, Cairo rivaled or even outstripped Baghdad among the great cities under Islamic hegemony. It was a cosmopolitan center of letters as well as commerce. Its House of Learning (*Dār al-ʿIlm*), founded by the Fāṭimid caliph al-Ḥākim (r. 996–1021), had housed secular texts in logic, mathematics, astronomy, medicine, grammar, and Arabic philology, as well as works in the Islamic sacred sciences. Here scholars had read and copied manuscripts from the royal library. The institute had been destroyed in riots in 1068, but its collection was rebuilt in the Fāṭimid palace.[46] Also in Fusṭāṭ, its importance to later historians as yet unknown, was the Geniza, or repository, of the Ben Ezra Synagogue, where many thousands of Jewish manuscript documents were preserved (although in considerable disarray) lest any occurrence of the name of God in their sacred texts, letters, contracts, or legal writs be desecrated. Among these treasures, as we now know, are letters to and from the Rambam and manuscripts in his own hand.[47]

TWO

Learning

In 1167/68, soon after settling in Fusṭāṭ, Maimonides completed his commentary on the Mishnah. Begun when he was twenty-three, much of the work had been researched and written during the family's unsettled years. Still a classic today, the commentary brought him fame as a halakhist. He had gained impressive mastery of rabbinic texts but also of the sciences long cultivated in the Greek philosophical tradition and now part of the patrimony of learned readers of Arabic. The astronomical calculations embedded in the *MT* show that Maimonides began work on it almost immediately on completing the Mishnah commentary, barely pausing to collate the 613 mitzvot in the Book of the Commandments, his catalog *raisonné* of the biblical precepts, the work that frames the trellis on which he trained what would become the sturdy branches of the *MT*. He completed the *Yad* after ten years of devoted labor, in 1178.[1]

Maimonides' Jewish learning began in childhood with his father's teaching. Maimon was descended from a long line of rabbis. He had studied under Ibn Migash in the now lost yeshiva of Lucena, a center of Jewish life from the ninth century, when Muslims were restricting the growth of the Jewish community in nearby Cordoba. Maimonides treasured his father's records of Ibn Migash's teachings, citing the master's halakhic analyses with admiration in the introduction to his Mishnah commentary.[2] Maimon had written biblical and talmudic commentaries and works on the laws of prayer and ritual purity. A handful of his responsa are known to survive, attesting to his work as a sensible and credible halakhic authority. A commentary of his on an Arabic astronomical work reveals his pursuit of the scientific inquiries his son, too, would follow.

From Ibn ʿAqnīn and others, we know the curriculum of Jewish learning familiar in Spain: A boy was expected to know the Tanakh and to be at home in the Talmud by bar mitzvah age. Serious students would move on to poetry and formal grammar and delve into the talmudic commentaries and halakhic codes like al-Fāsī's. Biblical study was not subordinated to talmudic learning as was common in Europe. Memory was critical. One could memorize without understanding, the maxim went, but one could not understand without memorizing.[3] Scriptural words gain enriched meaning and resonance as one learns and grows, and the alchemy of memory and experience bred rich results in Maimonides' case as he probed biblical and rabbinic texts to elicit their themes, moral, legal, and spiritual/intellectual. Beyond the artful erudition prized by scholars and poets of the day, his exegeses and excursions reveal his deep absorption of biblical and rabbinic ideals and themes, elaborated with faithful creativity.

Mastery of Halakhah is evident in the Mishnah commentary, the *MT*, and the Book of the Commandments. The same works reveal Maimonides' pathway toward that mastery, through careful study of the Babylonian and Jerusalem Talmuds and their many satellites, down to the work of Andalusians like al-Fāsī and Ibn Migash. Constitutions and statutes may be foundational, but jurists know that the cutting edge in legal practice lies in the most recent decisions. With all his sensitivity to the biblical roots and rabbinic branches of Halakhah, Maimonides was keenly aware of that fact of legal life, reflected in Ibn Migash's ruling that recent responsa take precedence over vexed talmudic dicta and debates. The same outlook is reflected visibly in Maimonides' preference for Andalusian practice over Baghdad precedent and Geonic authority.[4]

Unlike many traditionalists who spoke self-effacingly of "the decline of the generations," Maimonides saw periods of efflorescence as well as decline in the past. He recalled with a mixture of regret and lost pride the former glory days of Jewish and general learning in Andalusia and worried about the loss of broader learning in his own day.[5] Well aware of progress in mathematics and the sciences (II 4, 13b; 9, 19b), Maimonides did not fail to notice stagnant pools as well as fresh springs in rabbinic thinking (I 71, 1.94ab; 74, 121b).[6] Biblical law itself, he argues, advances: Ancient Israelites needed animal sacrifices. For that was the mode of worship familiar in ancient times. But the Torah regulates and restricts such offerings in time, place, and modality, paving the way for higher modes of worship in prayer and the quiet meditation of the heart (III 32). Beyond the halakhic cabinet of rabbinic learning, Maimonides was a master of aggadah, the homiletical narratives and parables that weave the tissue of rabbinic theology, bound into distinctive thematic patterns by often unseen subtexts. Unfazed by the aggadic idiom, he treats the Sages' anthropomorphisms as clear evidence that the ancient Rabbis were not misled by biblical imagery but freely joined in the prophets' poesy (I 46, 52ab). In the *Guide*, he, too, draws on the midrash creatively, seeking (and sparking) insights and pursuing conceptual coherence but cutting clear of what he finds fanciful or superstitious—for the Sages were not above quarreling with Scripture, sometimes to halakhic advantage but also, at times, to homiletical perversion. Citing a famous rabbinic remark upholding God's transcendence, he writes, "I wish all their words were like it" (I 59, 1.73b).

Confronting the Sages' endorsement of remedies suggestive of sympathetic magic, Maimonides picks his way gingerly through the ancient texts: Some of the old nostrums, he suggests, may have had an empiric basis, if only psychosomatically, and so were permitted—as long as they stayed clear of overt pagan exuviae (III 37, 80b). But he balks at a midrashic statement ascribed to R. Eliezer that God made the heavens "of the light of His garment." For beyond its anthropomorphism, the image suggests discomfort with ex nihilo creation (II 26, 56a; 13, 2.27a).[7]

At home in the targumim, the interpretive Aramaic translations of the Tanakh ascribed to Onkelos the Proselyte and Jonathan ben Uzziel, Maimonides admires Jonathan's handling of biblical imagery (I 7, 17b; 30, 33ab, II 29, 60b, 47, 100a; III 2, 4b, 6a) and both men's resolving of biblical anthropomorphisms (I 27, 30ab; 36–37, 44a–45a, II 26, 56b; 35, 75b–76a; 41, 88b).[8] He pores over the Onkelos manuscripts he can put his hands on, seeking a nuance to help explain a subtle shift in the anticorporealist paraphrases he admires (I 48). But an Onkelos or Jonathan, he grants, cannot interrupt the flow of his translation to spell out his intent (I 28, 31ab). Clearly, the Targums, long familiar to readers of the Torah, sensitize hearers to such imagery and help them see in the boldest biblical anthropomorphisms deeper hints of God's transcendence. In that sense, the targumim underscore the Rambam's own explications of the thrust of the references to God that he reads as poetic tropes.

In the same colophon that marks his completion of *K. al-Sirāj*, Maimonides mentions that while at work on that commentary, he was actively studying the sciences given currency and new life in Arabic by the translation movement. The Galenic medicine and Ptolemaic astronomy vividly present in the work[9] allowed him to frame a critical grasp of what a science is, how a scientific art is practiced, and how sound arguments are shaped.

Maimonides had explored astronomy while still in Andalusia. In his *Treatise on the Calendar*, published when he was just twenty, he suggests that he might have dug deeper into the mathematical and theoretical facets of the subject had his reader not needed just a simple, practical handbook.[10] But practicality remains a leitmotif all through his oeuvre. The abiding concern in his medical works but also in the *MT* and the *Guide* is with what the reader needs to know, and his eye holds steadily practical even as his gaze rises to metaphysics. For the *Guide*, too, is a therapeutic work, addressing the doubts and anxieties expected to beset a critical mind confronting the narratives and prescriptions, theological and cosmological premises and problematics, of the Torah (I Introduction, 3ab, 6a, 9a, 11b).

The practical tenor of Maimonides' works is underscored by his following the Arabic custom of answering the stated or perceived needs of the person notionally addressed in a work, to whom, in effect, it was dedicated. That second-person perspective is sharpened by Maimonides' sustaining a rapport with the reader as his argument unfolds in the *Guide*. The reader's anticipated needs vividly demarcate the gulf the work seeks to bridge. Those needs are topical but also universal, for the Torah, Maimonides affirms as his argument takes flight, is a timeless guide (I 2, 1.13b). So his own guidebook, meant to make critical sense of revelation, should have lasting relevance as long as critical minds take the Torah seriously.

Maimonides' lifelong study and thinking in sacred and secular domains make it hard to put a date on any one phase of his intellectual growth. But the matter and manner of the disciplines he probed show up clearly in his writings. So does his commitment to those disciplines: Their theses and norms—adopted, qualified, bracketed, or rejected—are living themes in his work. Pressing the distinction of real sciences from sham and bluff (1.6a; 3.66a), he scoffs at blowhards "innocent of science" who invoke the authority of the sciences to buttress a dogmatic eternalism (2.33b). Equally unimpressive to him are the would-be champions of tradition "who know no science worthy of the name" (1.9b). In facing questions about creation, he writes, "Best to avoid what wretched homilists and exegetes do, who think knowing how to gloss a phrase is all the science they need and that the windier and wordier their treatments run the better. Reason is what we need to probe this subject, a mind honed by the rigorous sciences and at home with the secrets of the prophets" (2.65b). Polemic, jargon, "high-flown style," and pleonastic verbiage only diminish a work (1.118a).

Perhaps even before his short work on the calendar, Maimonides wrote *On the Art of Logic*—possibly for a Muslim jurist, for he praises the man's lucid and eloquent Arabic prose and peppers the little handbook with Qur'ānic phrases.[11] Reflecting close study of al-Fārābī,[12] the work focuses on logical terms, as requested. But it deals, perforce, with the boundaries of sound reasoning and the grounds of argument. So it also touches on key issues of epistemology. Demonstrations, Maimonides writes—that is, rigorous or apodeictic arguments—do not rest on mere analogy; they generally avoid induction (except for complete induction, as Avicenna explained). Dialectical arguments do use induction.[13] That will matter in the *Guide*. For Maimonides sees no apodeictic proof for (or against) creation and deems such proofs impossible. So the *Guide* will turn to dialectical arguments in support of creation (2.35ab, 43b–44b, 49b).

Having defined dialectical and rhetorical arguments as resting, respectively, on conventions and traditions, the Rambam's little handbook on logic caps its typology of arguments with a line about poetry, which Arabic logicians included in the Organon, as a persuasive art. Poetry, Maimonides writes, echoing Fārābī and Avicenna, uses comparisons to praise or dispraise.[14] This thought will prove critical in the *Guide*. For it helps explain the vital role of imagination in prophecy: Imagination likens one thing to another—as scriptural imagery likens God to things we admire—even as the biblical text teaches one that nothing is like God (1.51a, 61a; 3.20, 43a). We'll see Maimonides' keen sensitivity to biblical poetics and rabbinic homiletics at work all through the *Guide*.

The opening lines of the work, reviewing its first reader's skills and prior studies in astronomy and its mathematical roots and recalling the decision to work with him on logic before testing out his evident poetic skills on biblical puzzles (1.2a), are pretty clearly prescriptive, too, meant to prequalify prospective readers of the *Guide*. The little curriculum sketched on its first page might aid any serious reader. It is hardly idiosyncratic. But in its subtext of prescriptions, Maimonides also gives us a glint of personal history, tracing his own path of learning in the sciences, a path traveled by striving cognoscenti in Islamic domains from al-Fārābī's time to his own and earlier, harking back to Hellenistic Alexandria.[15]

Fārābī, whose thoughts Maimonides prized, called mathematics foundational pedagogically, since it mirrors reality: One starts with abstractions—numbers and magnitudes—and then seeks to see where one's learning applies, in optics, astronomy, music, statics, and mechanics. By working in this way, one can learn not just what is so but why.[16] Logic and mathematics together lay foundations for mastering the natural sciences and moving on to cosmology, constructing a universe, with metaphysics in or beyond its upper stories. Maimonides' love of logic and the value he found in logic, in mathematics, and in the natural sciences resonate with the perennial love of learning precedented a millennium before his time in the work of Philo, who, in a kindred spirit, prescribed a like structuring of one's studies, for which the floorplan had been laid out by the Stoics:

> The ancients, they say, likened philosophical discourse, with its three parts, to a field, comparing the part that deals with nature to the trees and plants; the ethical part, to the fruits and crops, for which the plants exist; and the logical, to the surrounding fence. For, just as a wall around a field protects the fruits and plants that grow there from those who wish to steal in, bent on mischief, to plunder what grows there, the logical part of philosophy is a metaphoric barrier safeguarding the other two parts, ethics and physics: It unravels ambiguities and equivocations and bares fallacies and sophistries with clear and unambiguous language and proofs that leave no room for doubt. It destroys seductive guile, the soul's worst snare and deadliest foe, and smooths the mind like wax, to receive the flawless, reliable imprint of the sciences, natural and moral. (*De Agricultura* 14–16, LCL 3.114–17)

In a traditional cultural milieu, ethics might not seem to belong to the same edifice as other sciences, perhaps because religious tradition is expected to provide the necessary and sufficient moral guidance. But teachers like Yaḥyā b. ʿAdī, Miskawayh, and Ghazālī naturalized an Aristotelian virtue ethics in their religious traditions, as Maimonides would do in his own, revealing the roots of the Torah's mitzvot in its comprehensive project to improve human life and character among its recipients.

History might be neglected among students of philosophy, if only because Aristotle had not considered it a science, given its focus on particular events rather than their general patterns. Even so, Maimonides was heavily reliant on history in building his own science of politics. And Miskawayh did write history as well as ethics, deeming both inquiries critical in public as well as private life. Maimonides, in a similar humanistic spirit, will show particular sensitivity to history (2.39, 84b; 3.121ab), not least in his evolutionary (and contextual) treatment of the history of religions. Inquiry, Maimonides knows, demands work and patience. Anyone, he writes, might love to know the shape of the cosmos, what can or should be meant by angels, and how the soul transcends the body. But how many would drop everything, even for a week, to pursue such questions? The inspired poetry of Scripture can help turn one in the right direction (1.38a–39a). But surefooted advance depends on the sciences. That makes patience more than a moral virtue. To Maimonides in the *Guide*, patience means prerequisites.

If theology is the regal science, addressing deep longings felt by "thinkers of every stripe and in every era" (1.34a), the sciences gathered by Aristotelians under the name of physics, and covering all studies of the natural world, are the high road to cosmology. But logic and mathematics are the gateways; and cosmology, for its part, leads on to theology. For if we hope to grasp how God rules the world (by emanation—that is, by the gift of the forms that exercise sway over matter—as the *Guide* will teach, and not by magic, as imagination might propose), we can see a path from physics in its broad sense to cosmology and on to metaphysics, often named by Aristotle as theology, its salient branch.

Theology, Maimonides writes, is riven with partisanship and perplexity. There's much less contention in the natural sciences, and none in mathematics (1.34ab). Logic and mathematics "train the mind in reasoning, enabling one to reach the truth, to understand things as they really are and purge the confusions (and resultant distortions) that befuddle most inquirers' minds—taking the incidental for essential, say" (1.38b). These formal disciplines teach us what certainty is, how it is won (1.57a), and how to tell proof from mere persuasion (2.32a, 33a). A mind trained in logic and mathematics is not stocked but honed. So it is here that disciplined inquiry must begin.[17]

Stepwise advance is the key. Each science builds on what went before. So taking things out of order, as Maimonides sees it, creates only instability. The patience he counsels, therefore, is a lively motif all through the *Guide*, counterpoised against the impatience he labels with the Arabic term *tahāfut*, echoing the title of Ghazālī's twenty-round takedown of the Islamic philosophical school. That title, *Tahāfut al-Falāsifa*, is conventionally translated as *The Incoherence of the Philosophers*. But Maimonides, relying on the word's semantic base, uses the term consistently to warn of a collapse, a downfall resulting from headlong, ruinous haste (1.9a; 5, 16b, 103a; 3.31a, 40ab, 135a), typified for him biblically by the overeagerness that fatally marred the vision of Israel's ancient elders (Exodus 24:11), rendering their epiphany all too corporeal. The contrast, biblically (1.16ab), is with the humble Moses (Numbers 12:3), who did not rush to see what was not his to behold but modestly *hid his face* (Exodus 3:6). The rabbinic contrast is between Akiva's learned diligence and the restive Elisha ben Avuya, whose impatience as to the problem of evil cost him his spiritual footing.

Elisha was no Job. Job had called on God to explain his sufferings and those of other innocents; but his character had readied him for a higher understanding, grounded in the recognition that vulnerability is an inevitable concomitant of the gift of being (Job 1:21)—and opening the mind to the insight that suffering as well as joy may bring (2.69b; 3.45a–46b). Elisha knew how to question God's justice. But he lacked the resource to answer his own questions, and he sorely lacked the patience to await a better answer than presented itself at first blush. No Akiva he. Akiva discovered profundities in the Torah's every word and found meaning, as admiring successors put it, even in the crown serifs adorning certain of its letters. Pointedly resistant to any facile reduction of the cosmos to its presumptive element (2.68b), Akiva was ready, when the time came, to see even his own martyrdom as a lesson and a way of loving God with his all.

Honey, eaten to excess, is the biblical motif Maimonides finds to represent intellectual impatience: A bit is good, but excess, even of knowledge, can be destructive if it leads one to take on more than one can handle (1.26a; II 30–32). Patience, as Maimonides sees it, nurtures an open mind. But minds, like eyes, can be strained (1.16ab, 31, 35a). Falling into a quandary, one may rush toward global rejection—or willfully embrace ill-founded views, talk oneself into believing what one cannot know, and pretend (to oneself or others) that things are proven that cannot be proved. In thought, as in action, Maimonides reasons, finding a middle ground is precious. So moral maturity is as critical as logic on venturing into metaphysics. Haste breeds frustration, fostering credulity and wishful thinking at one extreme, disgust and blanket denial at the other. Akiva, a paragon of intellectual patience as Job is of its moral counterpart, entered the Pardes, or pleasure park, of inquiry. But unlike Elisha and the rest, he emerged unscathed, neither overreaching nor hasty to discredit anything not proved impossible (1.35ab).

It's all too easy to confuse critical thinking with skepticism and take negativity for skepticism's yield rather than suspension of judgment and a call for deeper inquiry. Too often overlooked is the home truth that the highest criticism is self-criticism. One might deny *either* side of a disjunction. So doubt has an affirmative as well as a negative face. Maimonides' stance, reflecting how he forged his own thinking, was not to try to suspend all beliefs that can be doubted, as Descartes would one day propose in his effort give inquiry a fresh start, but to weigh the problems clinging to all sides of a seeming dilemma—of creation, say, or the suffering of innocents—and then choose the view least burdened with difficulties (2.12a, 32a, 50a; cf. Plato, *Phaedo* 85cd). It's at such a point that the tradition of Moses and Abraham is rightly heeded (2.50a–51a; cf. 2.29b), not to clinch the case—for conviction still needs argument—but to urge one to keep listening and searching.

One domain that Maimonides explored was what we might now be tempted to call anthropology. That field did not yet exist as a formal discipline in his time. Saadiah, Fārābī, the Ikhwān al-Ṣafā', Ibn Ṭufayl, and others had considered religious and social institutions in broad, generic terms. Drawing on experience and wide reading, they registered observations as to the general principles at work in human communities and domains of practice and belief. Travelers and historians did write about the peoples encountered within and beyond the expansive Islamic empire. But far ranging as it was, their work was often almost anecdotal. Not until Ibn Khaldūn did a systematic learned work address the material, social, technological, intellectual, and spiritual conditions of human life. His *Muqaddimah*, or Prologue to the study of history, compared the lives and ways of nomads with those of city folk in ecological, economic, sociopolitical, moral, and religious terms. Nomads, as Ibn Khaldūn saw it, were the predecessors of city people—and often their successors when tribal forces united under a religious banner, as the Almoravids and the Almohads had done.

An appetite for understanding led Maimonides to probe cultures beyond the one he knew best, and Ibn Khaldūn himself may have drawn on some of Maimonides' reflections on the moral impact of desert life (2.80a; 3.52b–53a). But where Ibn Khaldūn relied on experience gained in his dealings with Arab and Berber tribes, Maimonides' study of other cultures relied on books. In the texts of Greek philosophy and science, he saw religious presumptions remote from those of the Hebrew prophets, and modes of argument and exposition sharply contrasting with those of the rabbis (2.33b). The reflections of ancient philosophers on method, their own and those of their rivals, invited comparison and critical scrutiny, and Aristotle's masterful marshaling of the rules of reasoning in the Organon court admiration and emulation. But much remained foreign. Translators had tactfully turned Greek gods into angels, but Arabic readers had trouble with, say, Aristotle's thoughts about tragedy in a culture where theaters were unknown.

Star worship was familiar enough to the rabbinic sages that they made star worship a standard name for polytheism, and Maimonides was catholic enough in his sensibilities to view pagan piety with some intellectual sympathy. Paganism still must be effaced, as the Torah demands, since it accords worship where it is not due (3.70a, 79a). But idols, Maimonides writes, echoing Iamblichus's apologetic response to Porphyry's ancient critique, are not deities. For pagans were not fools: "No pagan, you see," Maimonides wrote, "ever worshipped on the assumption that his idol was the one god. No one ever imagined, or ever will, that the form he cast in metal, or worked in wood or stone, created and rules heaven and earth. Idols are served only as symbols of something that mediates between us and God" (1.43b).

A hearty appetite for understanding led Maimonides to probe pagan piety well beyond its philosophical rationales. The sources available to him were not extensive. Nor were they all that they pretended to be. But although he found the beliefs they bruited often grotesque and many of the practices they prescribed bizarre, he urged their study if one hoped to understand the religious culture against which Abrahamic monotheism had rebelled and the context in which the Mosaic law was framed.[18] Just as he urged the study of logic and mathematics as training grounds in critical thinking, not preludes to mere skepticism, and just as he prized astronomical and biological studies not as alternatives to religion but as portals to an ever-growing discovery of God's wisdom and grace, he urged the study of alien cultures not as a warrant for relativism but as a chrestomathy of moral, social, and spiritual alternatives embodying much that was sound alongside much that was ignorant or degenerate.

Foremost among the sources available to the Rambam here was the *Nabatean Agriculture* of Ibn Waḥshiyya. The book purported to be the Arabic translation of an ancient text. It was hardly that, but it did contain rich veins of pagan lore and legend, recipes and rites meant to ensure, say, that one's fruit trees not drop their fruit prematurely. To Maimonides, the text was a gold mine of data as to the sorts of practice and belief from which the Torah had freed ancient Israel (2.84b; 3.64b). Pagan beliefs localized and particularized the powers presumed to be divine and set the gods into unseemly rivalries and conflicts with one another. Pagan practices were onerous and undignified, if not downright inhuman (3.64a, 67b, 78b–79a). But the pagan world was a formative backdrop to the emergence of the Mosaic law, especially in its ritual dimensions. One cannot understand the symbolic freighting borne by any ritual norm if one is ignorant of the alternatives it rejects.

Diligent study of all the pagan texts he could get his hands on made Maimonides' work in this dimension of the *Guide*, as Sarah Stroumsa puts it, "the first systematic Jewish attempt to carry out a comparative study of the history of religion." The "painstaking cultural study of which he was so proud" was motivated by the Rambam's effort "to understand the laws of the Torah within their cultural context."[19] The big theme he drew from such explorations belongs, if named in his own theocentric terms, fell under the rubric of grace (*talaṭṭuf*) and was typified in his thinking by the retention of a (strictly regulated) cult of sacrifice and of other modes of (pagan) worship, including a temple, rituals of prostration, and the like. The provision of mother's milk to the young of mammals when they are unready for solid food and God's leading Israel through a hostile desert when the newly freed slaves were hardly ready to do battle for the promised land are, for Maimonides, paradigm cases of such accommodations (3.69b–70b).[20]

Polytheism was in clear conflict with the demonstrated absoluteness and unity of God. And pagan notions of propitiation clashed with the biblical and philosophical ideas of God's perfection, universal grace, and justice. Pagan notions of venal, even needy gods (1.79a; 3.79ab), preserved in astrology and in theurgic uses of "names" and talismans, degrade divinity as well as morality, where the ideas of freedom and responsibility are vested. And they sap the foundations of the sciences, behind which (in the case of astrology) they hide. The residua of pagan notions pollute the scientific arts like medicine (let alone agriculture and animal husbandry), peopling nature with unseen capricious powers. Since pagan thought and practice are inimical to science and to coherent thoughts about divinity, it's easy to see why Maimonides adds to the Torah's anathema (rooted in abhorrence for ancient pagan cults of child sacrifice and temple prostitution; cf. 3.64a) his own hostility toward paganism and paganizing superstitions. But study of the context from which the religion of Abraham and Moses emerged and diverged shows him what the Torah adopted or adapted and where it freed Israel from the pagan matrix. Generically, the idea of worship is preserved. So are practices like the building of temples and expressions of reverence and awe in rituals like prostration and prayers of praise and petition. Most challenging among the survivals was the institution of animal sacrifice. Maimonides saw its preservation as a concession—mother's milk, as he put it—accommodating the spiritual infancy of ancient Israel, a people not yet ready for solid spiritual food (3.69b–71a).[21]

Often, where reason has trouble discerning the grounds for a biblical law (since the specific modalities of any legal norm are underdetermined by its broad purposes), Maimonides sees ripostes to the practices of neighboring ancient peoples, reversing their symbolism, as if semiotically to refute the theses implicit in pagan ceremonial. So Israelites, in worship, face not the sun but the site where God first revealed His true nature to Abraham (3.98ab). Otherwise mystifying biblical prohibitions preserve, like fossils, the imprint of a forgotten pagan practice—seething a kid in its dam's milk, say (3.111b), or interweaving linen and wool in a garment, as if to link in cosmic symbolism the animal and vegetative worlds (3.80b). We better understand the prominence of sheep and goats in the Torah's sacrifices if we know something of the fauns and satyrs that haunted pagan wildlands (3.101b, 104b–105b).

Maimonides' probing of the *Nabatean Agriculture* and the other pagan sources that he cites attests to the breadth of his pursuit of understanding, ranging well beyond traditional Judaic texts. We do not know how early these explorations began in his case. But clearly, they continued long into his life. For the *Guide*, written in his late years, actively engages with these pagan texts as it seeks to fathom religious phenomena, beliefs, and rituals, generically and to see the wisdom of the Mosaic Torah in context by candling it against the pagan backdrop out of which it emerged and from which it liberated Israel.

Formation

The formal disciplines of logic and mathematics are foundational for Maimonides because they teach us rigor and pave the way to thoughts that rise beyond the sensory world. Such thoughts hark back to Plato's vision of a cosmos built to a rational plan (2.16b–17a) and to the wry comment that Plato fathers upon Socrates, lampooning the notion that astronomy leads the mind to "higher things" because it raises our eyes to the heavens (or the ceiling!). Astronomy is of vital import to Plato, since its mathematical foundations wean the mind of physicality and introduce us to the ideal realm.[22] To Maimonides, as to Fārābī, mathematics anchors a serious education in the sciences because it traces the deep structure of reality. To all three men—Plato, Fārābī, and Maimonides, as to Einstein centuries later—mathematics is the poetry of the cosmos, opening to the keen inquirer glimpses of the mind and plan of God. The natural sciences, for Maimonides, like nature itself, reflect the gift of form, internal in the mind and perceived externally in the cosmos.

Beyond the lessons of rigor and the elevation of our intelligence, seeing reason implicit in nature and explicit in sound thinking, Maimonides' study of geometry and logic honed a powerful skill in analysis and enhanced the insights of a mind adept at synthesis. Consider the achievement of Euclid. Much of the matter of geometry was familiar before Euclid wrote. But geometrical facts were unintegrated, unsystematic. Euclid widened the scope of geometry but also teased out its roots and gave it rigor of the kind that mathematicians most value and admire by seeking the minimal set of definitions, axioms, postulates, and undefined terms that together allow deduction of a system. It was for this reason that Euclid titled his book *The Elements*. The order of exposition was synthetic, but the order of discovery was analytic: The elements anchored geometry as a system. Maimonides applied the same technique in his jurisprudence, seeking the general principles that structure God's Law and eliciting from individual mitzvot the moral foundations in virtue ethics that their themes subtend. He used the same analytic and synthetic skills in appraising the two chief systems of cosmology and metaphysics that vied for credence in his day: the schools of kalām, or Islamic dialectical theology, typified for him in the doctrines of the occasionalist *mutakallimūn*, and those of the *Falāsifa*, the Philosophers, as the Muslim exponents of Neoplatonic Aristotelianism called themselves, the school best represented in Arabic by Fārābī and Avicenna and their ilk, thinkers who appropriated to themselves the very name of philosophy, transliterated from the Greek as *falsafa*.[23]

Maimonides ordered the elements of the doctrine developed by the Islamic philosophical school in twenty-five premises that yield the core theses of a philosophical theology: the existence, unity, and incorporeality of God.[24] Supplemental premises are needed, he allows, to shore up the structure he traces, but all twenty-five, he grants, are well sustained by argument in Aristotle's *Physics* and *Metaphysics* and their commentaries (2.4b). Indispensable to *Falsafa*, however, as Maimonides sees it, was one further premise: the world's eternity, unproven and unprovable, but critical to the Philosophers' case. He treats it as a postulate, which he grants to its exponents for the sake of the argument.

Foreshadowing a tension between philosophy and kalām that lends a quiet sense of drama to his work, Maimonides promises at the outset of the *Guide* to explain the aims and arguments of the kalām schools and assay their rigor (1.2b). He had studied all the works of kalām he could find, he says.[25] His verdict, in the end, had proved negative (1.95b–96a, 98a). To bring his reader to a like conclusion, if by a less arduous route, he will rehearse the core arguments of kalām cosmology and metaphysics and their underlying assumptions. Here, as in his treatment of the Philosophers' system that follows, the exposition is synthetic, but its groundwork is analytic, bearing the fruits of his own extensive study.

Maimonides' theological goals, as he would lay them out in the *Guide*, chimed with those of the Mutakallimūn and, for that matter, with the theists (*muḥaqiqūn*, exponents of the Truth) among philosophers: to show the existence, unity, and incorporeality of God. But he aims to do so without resort to the less than rigorous methods he had seen in the kalām—and, if possible, without leaning on the Philosopher's posit, of the world's eternity. The Mutakallimūn, resting on the radical contingency of all finite or determinate being, had treated creation as the linchpin of their system and suspended their world from that skyhook. Maimonides had reached the conclusion, by the time he wrote the *Guide*, that creation could not be demonstrated. But neither, he found, could the world's eternity.

Despite the drawbacks he saw in the Philosophers' worldview, it did seem best to Maimonides not to give creation the lead in theology but to support it dialectically once the more rigorous arguments of the Philosophers for God's existence, unity, and incorporeality had done their work. He saw room in nature for God's will. For clearly not every fact could be reduced to necessity or deduced a priori, as the Aristotelian eternalist project seemed to promise. The determinism latent in the Philosophers' intellectualism did seem to rob God (and humanity as well) of volition and to close the door on the idea of an open future. But as long as the Philosophers held the high ground of rigor, there was no need to condemn them as unwitting atheists as Ghazālī had done. Far better to adopt the irenic stance of Ibn Ṭufayl and recognize that eternalists, like scriptural monotheists, could make a case for God's existence. Theism could survive on their account, too, although the God of Moses and the Patriarchs was preferable ultimately to the God of the Falāsifa.

The biblical God, as Maimonides saw things, was the Creator of a world that need not have existed. For there was no contradiction in its failure to exist. Here lay the spark of inspiration that Avicenna had seen in the theology of the kalām. And like his creationist predecessors, Maimonides could affirm clearly that the world would never have existed had God not given it being. Nor, he could argue, would it continue to exist but for its sustenance by God's grace—the same grace that first gave it being. The point is salient in the opening words of the *MT*, which recognize God as the ultimate and sustaining Cause of all else that is. But now, in the *Guide*, that affirmation is voiced in the language of the Philosophers when Maimonides affirms (I 69) that God is the world's formal and final cause as well as its Maker. Biblically, in Genesis, we encounter God as the Creator. On the Aristotelian account, as Maimonides read it, God was the Prime Mover responsible ultimately for the eternal rotations of the spheres and the resulting cycles of nature. Beyond that, in Neoplatonic terms, God was the Source of the forms that structure all things and that, by so doing, give nature its abiding reality. So as the Creator and Sustainer of the cosmos, God remained the ultimate cause: Here the Philosophers' view was not at odds with the teaching of Abraham and Moses.

The Philosophers' brief, as Maimonides read it, was far more coherent and perspicuously developed than the views to be found among the fissiparous schools of kalām. We can follow the variety of kalām views in the doxography painstakingly (but fairly) assembled by al-Ashʿarī (873–935), which lists dozens of issues over which Muslim theologians differed from one another and catalogs the positions taken by each school or figure on each question.[26] Kalām diversity makes Maimonides' analysis especially impressive, as he reduces to system the protean debates of the kalām.[27] With typical terse modesty, he caps his analytic work in a phrase, alluding to the disparate views and many schools of mutakallimūn (1.104b). But his account, homing in on what he found most telling and most problematic in the method and matter of kalām, reflects extensive study, begun, perhaps, in high hopes but ending in disappointment.

Kalām, as an enterprise, reflects the interactions of early Muslim missionaries and apologists with non-Muslims in the course of the expansion of the Islamic Empire and its successor states. Exponents of Islam found themselves called on to explain and defend the precepts of their faith among non-Muslims, who did not share their faith or their outlook and who often had the advantage of extensive training in interfaith (and intrafaith) apologetics and polemics. But kalām matured among professional theologians even as its schools and sects split and splintered. The name assigned generically to its practitioners, *mutakallimūn*, might be translated, rather too literally, as "talkers," and that was how these men were labeled when Arabic texts citing them were made over into Latin: Scholastics knew them as *loquentes*. But the force of the Arabic term is best understood in terms not of talk but of argument. Traditionalists in Islam, including the Mālikī jurists prominent among the Almoravids, faulted the mutakallimūn for relying on theological argument where tradition (*Ḥadīth*), harking back to the sayings and doings of Muḥammad and his companions, supplied the necessary and sufficient canons of normative practice and belief.

Mutakallimūn, by contrast with doctrinaire traditionists, were trained to debate the fine points deemed critical in theology, aiming to win over listeners and silence adversaries. So a typical kalām handbook was built around talking points, listing gambits and ripostes for use in disputation. Readers of Aquinas know the pattern well from his wrapping his thesis-and-argument format in a frame that opens each question by stating objections to the intended doctrine and ends by answering those objections. Kalām theology is called "dialectical" because Fārābī, who prided himself on his mastery of logic, branded it as such. Kalām arguments typically used hypothetical-propositional reasoning rather than Aristotelian syllogistic. That preference may reflect the ancient Stoic bias against class logic, grounded, perhaps, in fears that the categorical judgments required in sound Aristotelian syllogisms may lie beyond our reach. The studied neglect of class logic by the mutakallimūn reflects their suspicion of the sciences of nature to which the *Falāsifa* were committed. The hypothetico-deductive mode of reasoning gave color to Fārābī's judgment that kalām arguments were dialectical not just for their roots in disputation but because they fell short of rigorous proof and indeed relied on premises plainly open to dispute.

A dialectical argument, in Aristotelian terms, relies on premises shared with an interlocutor, premises that may or may not be true. In kalām, the shared premises might be scriptural if the disputants held shared scriptural commitments. But Muslim mutakallimūn were as likely to differ in their readings of the Qur'ān as in their theology. What crippled their arguments in Maimonides' eyes was that their premises were suppositious (1.95a; 2.40a); their inferences, tendentious if not outright fallacious. Had he, even in youth, lacked good reason to prize the power and clarity of the Aristotelian logic that he saw in Fārābī and Avicenna, he had ample cause to do so by its contrast with kalām hypotheticals, which seemed to press ahead in willful innocence of the problems posed by elementary sophisms like the fallacy of division (1.108ab).

The two kalām schools most prominent on Maimonides' horizon were Muʿtazilite and Ashʿarite. The Muʿtazilites, in the ascendant in the early days of the ʿAbbāsid caliphate, were moral realists. They defended free will and called themselves the exponents of monotheism and theodicy. Maimonides, like the Philosophers, agrees with the Muʿtazilites about God's absolute unity (1.57a, 77a)[28] and justice (1.92b; 3.35a). He welcomes their affirmation of free will—although he doubts their capacity to sustain that commitment, given their inflated ideas of divine agency (1.110b; 3.33b). Muʿtazilites held that God owes it to us to inform us of His expectations—and that He has done so through prophecy. So we are both responsible to obey and capable of obedience, earning reward or punishment accordingly. Maimonides is sympathetic but skeptical of the Muʿtazilites' notions of divine accountancy, especially when they seemed Pollyanna-ish as to the suffering of innocents—let alone when they went so far as to expect innocent beasts to be requited in the hereafter for their sufferings, an extreme view that even Saadiah had embraced (3.34a, 36ab).

The Ashʿarite school, founded by its namesake, Abū 'l-Ḥasan al-Ashʿarī, in reaction to Muʿtazilism, which he had championed for years before framing what he saw as a more authentically traditional (submissive and resigned) theology of sheer grace, denied that we humans can author or "create" our own acts. Ashʿarites resolutely denied our moral competence to judge God's justice: Right and wrong were coextensive with obedience or disobedience. But if God chose to punish obedience and reward disobedience, ours not to reason why (3.35a).

Both of these schools, and others, had difficulties with human agency—and typically with natural causation more broadly. Here lay Maimonides' core material issue with the kalām. Some mutakallimūn did struggle to defend human freedom, as the Muʿtazilites did in affirming human moral responsibility. Even the Ashʿarites did so in a way, when they professed that while we do not "create" our acts, we do "acquire" or appropriate them. Maimonides brands that view as double talk (1.58b). But despite such labored efforts, the mutakallimūn, as Maimonides saw it, put real human agency out of reach. And they sank natural causality. Their piety presumed a rivalry between divine and natural powers, making causal efficacy, as it were, a zero-sum game, neglecting the possibility that causation, in reality, might operate on more than one level, natural and divine, with God delegating natural efficacy to His creations. For the elements and compounds found in nature exercise their own effects by way of the natures God gave them; animals can act by their volitions, and human beings can exercise free choice as well.

Maimonides distills the arguments of the Mutakallimūn to twelve premises meant to vindicate the thesis that the world began. From here it seemed to them easy to prove the existence of God and then God's unity and incorporeality. Maimonides shares the desiderata. But he finds the kalām arguments flawed. Some he found laughable. At the root of the problem was the distortion of the idea of creation by the stress kalām arguments put on it. Seeking to prove that the world began (and thus needed a creator), the Mutakallimūn made every event a miniature act of creation. Aiming to magnify God's might, they negated every delegated power assigned to a creature. Every atom in the universe depended wholly and solely on God. Special postulates were introduced meant to elevate God's creative action and eliminate more than the most minimal presence to be found in the objects of God's creation: The kalām atom had no size, no duration or nature of its own; it had no essential properties but only the "accidents" God gave it for the instant it was vouchsafed. For each atom was created anew at every instant with the accidents that God pleased to give it.

The heart of the kalām, as Maimonides saw it, was occasionalism: God was not just the ultimate but the only cause, the only real actor. Natural or "horizontal" causality was an illusion. What we familiarly call the cause of an event was only its "occasion." That account, as Maimonides complains, erases nature itself (2.40a; 3.55b). It obviates the work of the senses and precludes the very possibility of natural science. As a result, it vitiates such arts as medicine, architecture, and mechanics. The goal Maimonides would embrace and make central to the project of the *Guide* was to reconcile divinity with natural science and the practical or technical arts rather than set them at odds. If food, or water, or even air does not sustain us, he asks, and if God's pleasure is all that keeps us alive, why did God create all these things that were not needed, on the kalām account, to attain His purpose (2.69b; 3.24a)?

The Mutakallimūn stood poles apart from the Philosophers, who championed the sciences and believed that Aristotle and his Neoplatonic successors had proved creation impossible and the world eternal, the laws of nature unchanged throughout the infinite revolutions of the heavens. Maimonides believed neither creation nor eternity to be demonstrable. Indeed, he found it ill advised to mount an argument meant to be conclusive for or against creation. For all such arguments backfire in the end by rendering creation not a fact but a necessity. The rigor sought in apodeictic proofs rubbed off onto God, transforming the free and wise Creator into a mere mechanism—or, on the kalām account, a madcap busybody with nothing better to do than oversee the fall of every leaf and dictate the fate of every nymph on the surface of a pond (3.33a, 36a).

If an eternal world depends on God, creation must be continuous, and God's act becomes automatic—or, more strictly, an algorithm timelessly spewing forth temporal "implications" (3.42a). But creation, as pictured by kalām occasionalists, demands constant re-creation of every atom (or another, like or unlike it) at every instant that God wills a given body to exist. Binding God to produce all that occurs, occasionalism negates the divine wisdom discovered by the sciences, visible in the processes of nature, and relied on in the arts. Ironically, the dependence of every event on God's immediate act vitiates the very idea of creation that it was meant to vindicate. For creation is empty if creatures are given no powers of their own—living beings seeking their needs and humans making the choices that God-given reason empowers us to make.

Occasionalism left God no room for delegation of powers. So God no longer governed by way of nature, and the imperatives that animate any scriptural revelation hung by a raveled thread. For human will and choice, now ineffectual, became irrelevant. The very ideas of loyalty, faith, trust, and obedience—all notions of virtue and vice, and every divine command—were emptied of content. The Mutakallimūn had sold logic as well as science and morals to buy the theology they coveted. But that theology was unsustainable. For sound views demand sound premises. But kalām arguments began where good arguments should end: The Mutakallimūn had posited premises designed to yield the conclusion they wished for: that only God can act. But honest minds, Maimonides urged, do not try to build a world around their wishes:

> I say, as Themistius did, that reality does not conform to our beliefs; true beliefs must conform to reality. Studying the works of these mutakallimūn that I could access, just as I studied those of the Philosophers that I could, I found that, with all their diversity, the mutakallimūn all use the same method: They pay no mind to facts. . . .
>
> When I reflected on this approach, my soul recoiled violently, and rightly so. Their supposed proofs that the world began were deeply flawed, seeming cogent only to those who cannot tell proof from persuasion or sophistry. To one who knows the arts of logic, it is obvious that all these suasions are riddled with flaws and rest on unproved premises. (1.95b–96a)

Maimonides marks a turning point in his history here. Kalām occasionalism had sacrificed human agency, the sciences, the practical arts, and nature itself (1.97b) on the altar of a presumed theological expedient. That was a sacrifice that Maimonides was not prepared to make. Reason demanded that he reject kalām occasionalism. He must look to the more rigorous methods of *Falsafa* and forge his own synthesis of scriptural monotheism with naturalism and the sciences, human agency and responsibility. Declaring his allegiance to the methods and values of philosophy, he writes, "In intellectual matters, one must follow where the argument leads and believe what is soundly proven" (2.19a; cf. 2.49b–50a, 3.63a). He marks his commitment by reference to his Andalusian roots: "The Andalusians among our people all hold to the Philosophers' tenets and favor their views, so long as they do not contradict biblical principles. You will not find any who follow the Mutakallimūn on any point" (1.94a).

Focus

Further insight into Maimonides' intellectual and spiritual growth can be gleaned from the exercises he prescribes for those hoping to win the constancy in God's presence that he sees as our highest human goal, the key to providence, and gateway to immortality. If the mind is our link to God (I 1),[29] we strengthen that bond through thoughts of God, our highest way of worship: "All our devotional practices—reading the Torah, praying, and performing the other mitzvot—aim only to train us to focus on His precepts and free us from worldly distractions, engrossed, as it were, in Him and lost to all else" (3.125b).

The lives of Abraham and Moses show us, Maimonides argues, how it is possible to engage actively in the world yet preserve that higher focus (3.120b, 126b–27a). The secret is to act for God's sake in all that we do (cf. M. Avot 2.12). Once one is firmly resolved and sincerely committed to such a life, even worldly actions are no longer distractions, and the false dichotomy between an active and a contemplative life dissolves. Here, as in steering a course between doubt and credulity, moral preparedness is critical, lest we confuse actions performed for God's sake or thoughts directed toward Him in love with those directed toward some imagined surrogate, pragmatic paymaster, or projective fantasy (1.77ab).

Maimonides outlines a stepwise regimen for advancing toward what he sees as our singular spiritual goal: In reciting the *Shemaʿ* or praying the *ʿAmidah*, one must clear the mind of distractions. After some years, one will be ready, in reading the Torah or hearing it read, to give undivided attention to its words and their meaning. Likewise with the prophets. Secure on this plateau,

> You will be able to see to all your needs and wants in life, any worldly concerns—eating, drinking, bathing, talking with your wife or youngsters or ordinary people. I have left you plenty of time, all that you will need, to think about your property, your household affairs, and your bodily welfare. But in the time for religious observances, fill your mind with what you are about, as I explained. And when you are by yourself or lying awake in bed, guard those precious moments and turn your thoughts solely to intellectual

> worship of this kind, which brings you close to God, standing in His presence, in the genuine way I taught you, using reason, not the passions of fancy. This, as I see it, is the goal that can be reached by one who knows, if he brings his soul to merit it by the discipline I have described. (3.126ab)

Maimonides has not prescribed what he has not tried; he writes from experience here. So beyond a spiritual vademecum, his outline retraces his own spiritual path.

THREE

Cairo

Just months after the family reached Egypt, Maimon died. Maimonides himself suffered from the illnesses he found endemic in his new surroundings. But if he had lost a world in Cordoba, he found another in his new home. Settling in Fusṭāṭ in 1167, he lived among its largely Christian population and its Karaite and Rabbanite Jews. Here he completed his Mishnah commentary, having already written a conspectus of the laws of the Jerusalem Talmud.[1] He avoided publishing his youthful talmudic studies, but it was in Fusṭāṭ that he wrote his great halakhic code. Here he could teach science and philosophy, practice medicine and write medical works, invest in trade ventures in gems and pharmaceuticals, and play a leading role in Jewish communal life. The Fāṭimid rulers, Ibn al-Qifṭī reports, proposed him as a physician to the Frankish king at Ashkelon.[2] He declined that honor. But clearly, he was far from invisible in Egypt—quite a contrast to his days under Almohad dominion in the Maghreb.

Learning remained at the core of his life, but from the start, there was no ivory tower. Early on he took a leading role in raising funds to ransom Jewish captives. The prisoners, as Joel Kraemer explains, were civilians held by pirates or by Crusaders, who, like pirates, lived on booty. Jews had no forces to free hostages and no prisoners to trade. That made ransom critical. The usual price was one hundred dinars for a group of three, but it could run higher for distinguished captives. So the sums needed far exceeded private means. The Cairo

Geniza preserves four of Maimonides' appeals for such funds. Collaborating with a community council, he pressed the urgency of the appeal, seeking its broad circulation, assuring close control of the monies raised, and looking after the details of negotiation, the terms of release, and the housing, clothing, and other needs of the rescued victims, Karaite or Rabbanite. In cases of piracy, those liberated were often far from home when brought to Alexandria for ransom, sometimes after a lengthy captivity.[3]

Maimonides married after settling in Fusṭāṭ, by around 1173. If his age was thirty-five, that was rather late in life for his day but understandable given the family's unsettled years and not atypical among his male descendants. His bride came from a prominent and well-to-do family, and his own growing prominence in learning would have pleased them, even as his standing was enhanced by theirs. The family bond redoubled when his sister married his bride's brother. She bore several children. Maimonides himself may have had a daughter who died young, but the one offspring we know of was his son Abraham, born in 1186, when Moses was forty-eight.

His writings had begun to bring him numerous halakhic questions. His letters and the hundreds of his responsa preserved through the years show him acting, in effect, as a jurisconsult and court of appeal for far-flung communities and for rabbis seeking his rulings and advice. Among his public letters, one, in 1172, offered good counsel and good heart to the Jews of Yemen, who were facing persecution, aggravated and exacerbated by the pretensions of a false messiah who preyed upon the people's insecurity. The appeal to him from the Jews of Yemen clearly marks his stature while still in his midthirties. His reply shows the confidence of a respected halakhic authority, a striking contrast to the *Iggeret ha-Shemad*, in which he first tested his halakhic wings in the face of earlier challenges. It was hardly passive obedience that he counseled. Kraemer describes what he advised as a form of "passive resistance."[4] But what was possible—and what he prescribed—was much like what Isaiah Berlin, appraising Stoic strategies in an earlier era, called a retreat to the inner citadel, of conscience and consciousness. The citadel in this case, however, was not the moral and spiritual inner sanctum of personal isolation. Much of its strength and structure came from communal solidarity.[5]

In 1171, the Fāṭimids were overthrown, and Maimonides was taken under the wing of the Muslim statesman aptly titled al-Qāḍī al-Fāḍil, or the Virtuous

Judge (1135–1200), the right hand of the new ruler, the celebrated Saladin. Al-Qāḍī al-Fāḍil, one of history's great talent spotters, could count both Maimonides and Saladin among his finds. He had seen the military prowess, dedication, and honesty of the Kurdish general (Salāḥ al-Dīn, 1138–1193) and became the éminence grise of his rule in Cairo, a metropolis in the original Greek sense of the term, a mother city dominating the surrounding region, its sway vested in the energy and sagacity of its rulers.

The Shīʿism of the Fāṭimids had never commanded wide support in Egypt, and Saladin was no Shīʿite. He had served as a commander under the counter-crusading Zangid dynast Nūr al-Dīn, who had widened his father's conquests in Syria and forced the last of the Fāṭimid caliphs to make him his wazīr in Fusṭāṭ, displacing the predecessor, Shāwar, who had evacuated the city and burnt it in 1168, using some twenty thousand naphtha pots, for fear it would fall to the depredations of Amalric's Crusaders. Nūr al-Dīn had repulsed the Christian armies, and Shāwar was executed. By 1169, Nūr al-Dīn was succeeded as wazīr by Saladin, a native of Takrīt on the Tigris. He had campaigned with Zangid forces in Egypt and his letter of investiture as wazīr was penned by al-Qāḍī al-Fāḍil.

At that king-maker's advice, in the fall of 1171, Saladin dropped the Fāṭimid caliph's name from the salutatory address of the Friday prayers in favor of the ʿAbbāsid caliph in Baghdad, renouncing his Fāṭimid masters. When Nūr al-Dīn died in 1174, Saladin married his former suzerain's widow and founded his own, Ayyūbid dynasty, with al-Qāḍī al-Fāḍil as his wazīr. He soon wrested Syria from the Zangids and had himself recognized by Baghdad as the rightful ruler of Egypt, North Africa, Nubia, western Arabia, and central Syria, including the Land of Israel. In the course of Saladin's many campaigns, the wise wazīr twice saved his life, in one case hiring Bedouins to rescue him on finding him stranded in the desert when his troops had been routed unexpectedly in a desperate attack by Baldwin, the Crusader prince.[6]

He had earlier saved Saladin's life by exposing an 1174 plot by Fāṭimid loyalists. The coconspirators were the Nizārīs, a breakaway Ismāʿīlī sect whose tactics inspired the word assassin. The Nizārīs made two attempts on Saladin's life, just as they had slain a Fāṭimid ruler, as well as Ghazālī's patron Niẓām al-Mulk and many others.[7] In 1176, Saladin besieged the seemingly impregnable fortress of the Nizārī leader Sinān, known as the Old Man of the Mountain (d. 1192), and the two men reached a kind of détente.[8] Free to battle the Crusaders, Saladin routed them at Hattin near Tiberias in 1187. He took Tiberias and then Jerusalem. His men tore down the golden cross atop the Mosque of Omar on the Temple Mount, the site of Solomon's and Herod's Temples. The church bells were replaced with the muezzin's call still heard there today.

The fall of the Holy City ignited the Third Crusade (1189–92), led by Frederick Barbarossa of Germany, Richard the Lionheart of England, and Philip Augustus of Spain. Well remembered for his courage and his accustomed (but not invariant) nobility toward defeated foes, Saladin did battle with all three. His victories sparked a Sunnī revival in the lands he ruled. Much of his success on and off the field reflected the skills of his wazīr. Saladin was generous and patient, but he could also be ruthless. Disloyal allies and refractory foes were slain. Churches were destroyed, as mosques would have been had the tides of battle shifted.[9] Admirers of Islamic theosophical strains even today rue and resent the fate of the mystic Suhrawardī at his hands. Saladin had set a teenaged son, al-Ẓāhir al-Ghāzī, in command of Aleppo, nominally under the authority of an older son at Damascus. But Suhrawardī's syncretic illuminism had a political side to it, and al-Ẓāhir had not proved immune to the mystic's tempting him to dynastic pretensions of his own. On his father's orders, the reluctant Ẓāhir had the mystic crucified for heresy in 1191. Suhrawardī was thirty-six.[10]

A lover of poetry as well as polo, Saladin was a patron of the sciences and enjoyed the conversation of learned men of an evening.[11] His court even boasted an organ builder, reflecting the arts of the Byzantines.[12] Al-Qāḍī al-Fāḍil—poet, statesman, and learned clerk, ascetic in his habits, a merchant and a landowner—had a library of some hundred thousand volumes, doubtless open to Maimonides. He endowed a madrasa and a school for orphans. His *majlis*, or salon, hosted the luminaries of the day. He lowered taxes,[13] reorganized the military and intelligence services, and advised Saladin logistically and strategically. The sultan himself was not a skilled administrator and credited his brilliant military successes no less to the pen of his wazīr than to his own sword.[14] Where an astute powerbroker like al-Qāḍī al-Fāḍil sought out talent, Saladin, like Marcus Aurelius, was a poor judge of men, his personal honesty undercut by his "intense loyalty" to family members:

> He gave them his complete confidence and expected of them an equal confidence and loyalty in return. Himself completely indifferent to the material

> rewards of power, he seems to have had no conception of the corrupting influence of power and wealth on others, and it was, apparently, not until his serious illness in 1185 that he became fully aware of the jealousies amongst them. . . . The vast fortunes left by governors and officers . . . allow us to deduce a state of affairs of which we can sometimes find precise evidence. That Saladin was aware of abuses is evident from the frequent prohibitions of "illegal" taxes and other oppressive practices. . . . But he had little patience with the perpetual and petty, but necessary, details of daily administration, and his lack of personal supervision made itself felt.[15]

Even so, his dynasty would last until the devastating Mongol conquest in 1260.[16] Maimonides would serve at the Ayyūbid court for the rest of his life as a respected physician and a leader of Egyptian Jewry, revered for his learning and widely consulted for rulings on matters of Jewish law. His brother David, such was the plan, was to travel as a merchant while Moses continued in productive pursuit of the life of the mind.

Loss

A merchant's life, however, was fraught with peril. Merchants, pilgrims, and scholars had good reason to travel in caravans. Brigands, pirates, and hostile tribes beset travelers, robbing them and holding for ransom or selling into slavery those who survived an attack. Sandstorms and lack of good roads and good maps compounded the risks. Even in port, the customs collectors compounded the tolls of robbery. In a ruling based on the rabbinic principle that the law of the land is law, Maimonides forbids merchants from hiding gems in a hollowed-out cane, at least where the customs agents held due authority—but not if they were wont simply to take all they could get.[17]

Marco Polo (1254–1324) describes the port city of Hormuz as a hot, "sickly" place—"and if a merchant dies there, the King takes all his property."[18] Yet ships did return from India laden with silks and celadon, cinnamon, cloves, ginger, pepper, perfumes, drugs, dyestuffs, chemicals, copper, tin, and lead. Given the high cost and high risks of transport, the multiple hands goods passed through, and the taxes, duties, and expenses of tribal "protection" en route, only high-value goods were worth transporting far. Yet half the goods traded in Mediterranean markets came from India and the Far East, and the India trade was the mainstay of Egypt's wealth.[19] Saladin's control of the Red Sea and his trade treaties with Pisa, Genoa, and Venice fed the European markets and returned valuable goods, including war matériel.[20]

Soon after the family settled in Fusṭāṭ, David ben Maimon, now in his early twenties, undertook a merchant voyage for India. He and a companion sailed up the Nile to Qus, where the prosperous Jewish community warmly welcomed such wayfarers. Naively separating from the main caravan group, the two crossed three hundred miles of rugged desert for the Red Sea port of ʿAydhāb. Their three weeks' agony proved fortuitous. The main group, from whom they had parted, was robbed and wounded; some died of thirst, as David wrote home to his brother. His letter, miraculously preserved in the Cairo Geniza, described the journey and looked forward to what now seemed the easy part, passage by sea to India. Yet as he had to report, recent ships had foundered, carrying travelers known to both men, with losses of property, although not of lives.[21] David had made the journey for his brother's sake, he wrote but assured him it was not from any sense of pressure from him. "What was was," he wrote. His wife must be told not to worry: "He who saved me from the desert and its terrors will save me from the sea."[22]

There was good cause for worry. There were storms, reefs, and shallows in the shark-infested waters. The ships in the India trade hugged the shore. They were light and maneuverable but highly dependent on maintenance. Marco Polo wrote of what he saw:

> Their ships are wretched affairs and many of them get lost; for they have no iron fastenings, and are only stitched together with twine made from the husk of the Indian nut. They beat this husk until it becomes like horse-hair, and from that they spin twine, and with this stitch the planks of the ships together. It keeps well and is not corroded by the sea-water, but it will not stand well in a storm. The ships are not pitched, but are rubbed with fish-oil. They have one mast, one sail, and one rudder, and have no deck but only a cover spread over the cargo when loaded. This cover consists of hides, and on the top of these hides they put the horses, which they take to India for sale. They have no iron to make nails of, and for this reason they use only wooden trenails in their shipbuilding. . . . Hence 'tis a perilous business to go on a

voyage in one of those ships, and many of them are lost, for in that Sea of India the storms are often terrible.[23]

The journey from Cairo to India, via ʿAydhāb and Aden (the halfway point) was over 3,600 miles. David and all he had were lost at sea. He left behind his young wife and their little girl. Much of the family wealth had been invested in the journey. There was no insurance. David's death left Maimonides prostrate for nearly a year. He took to his bed with fever, inflammation, confusion, and distress. Eight years after receiving David's letter, he recalled the news of his death as the worst day of his life. Still disconsolate, he remembered the child he had dandled on his knee, the boy he had taught, the young man who went to the marketplace to earn a livelihood, "while I remained safe."[24]

Personal grief mingled with a sense of guilt and a broader theological grief still visible when the *Guide* paints the image of a ship sunk, "drowning some or all of those on board." Was the loss of great and good men no different from the ruin of an ant hill (3.32b)? What could one say or think of David's hopeful bravado, trusting in God's care, and his brave, formulaic words, steeling himself to reassure a wife and brother? Quoting from Galen, Maimonides assays the impact of ill fortune as a consequence of our embodiment: "Do not delude yourself with the vain hope that from semen and menstrual blood an animal could come that will not die or suffer pain, that will move perpetually or shine like the sun" (3.19b).

Alongside the vulnerability that is the price of our embodiment (and thus, of our creation), Maimonides acknowledged the risks we choose, sea voyages among them—as well as royal service (3.20b). That thought brings the matter close to home. For no one served in a royal court, as Maimonides would do for decades, without knowing the risks. Even victims, as he came to see it, share responsibility for the harms they suffer. That thought helps him make some sense of the Sages' words "No death without sin" and their calling the least pain that one suffers a punishment—and the least joy a reward (3.34b–36a).

'Punishment,' taken so broadly, cannot regard only moral, legal, or ritual infractions. The Sages' thesis, as Maimonides reads it, falls closer to the thought that every action has an equal and opposite reaction: The very act of claiming space or breathing air makes one, in a sense, an aggressor. The elements bite back; insensate nature (3.95b) is indifferent. God is good. That anchor point is held fast. Creation is a blessing, an act of grace (3.131a). But creation means finitude, and finitude brings vulnerability. The prospect of knowing God is the light worth the candle. Only so is there personal providence, when the mind that links us with God rises above matter's reach and the body's vulnerability (3.45a–46a).

To state the case so tightly frames as a mere inference the bitter fruit of the painful grief Maimonides struggled through in his year of mourning. Elisha ben Avuya had lost his spiritual moorings, so the Sages said, on merely witnessing the loss of a good son to his sense of filial duty. But in David's loss, that parable turned concrete. To free himself from survivor's guilt, Moses had to accept his brother's gentle, liberating words: David had chosen the journey for his sake, but not out of pressure to do so. Accepting that gracious release, Moses steps into David's shoes: He, too, has made a pact with danger by entering into royal service.

Parnassah

Jewish tradition expects the bereaved to stay closeted in mourning—but also, as the days of mourning end, to "rise" and resume their lives. No less than the Patriarchs (3.126b), Maimonides had responsibilities to shoulder. Clearly, he would be a scholar like his father. David was to have been the breadwinner. But things were different now. There was a practical problem to face beyond the theological quandary and the personal pain. Much had been lost at sea, and there was a family to support. Maimonides had never been idle. He had written and published from an early age, and he had practiced medicine and taught. But now the family needed a livelihood.

Any prospect of earning a living as a rabbi was anathema to him. He had published his dismay at the thought of rabbis' taking pay for their teaching or halakhic rulings (*CM* Vows 4.3). Such work was heaven's mandate (1.22b; 2.23b–24a), demeaned if made into paid labor. In *MT* he calls it blasphemous to exploit Torah study to shirk earning a living. To make a trade of Torah learning or teaching, he wrote, dishonors the Torah and damps its light. It harms the practitioners and loosens their grip on immortality. It was in that strong sense that he read the mishnaic rebuke, "Do not make Torah a spade to dig with" (M. Avot 4.7; see *MT* Laws of the Study of Torah 3.10).

Rabban Gamliel, son of Judah the Patriarch, had said, "Fair it is to combine Torah study with a life in the world (*derekh eretz*). The twofold labor puts sin out of mind. All Torah study not coupled with a trade is empty in the end and leads to sin" (M. Avot 2.2). *Derekh eretz* here, Maimonides explained, means "a worldly occupation"; the sin warned against amounts to theft. To the Sages, as Joseph Hertz wrote, "no honest toil, no matter how hard or repugnant, was deemed beneath the dignity of a scholar, so long as it safeguarded his independence, and saved him from being a burden on others. Like the Prophets of old, the Rabbis would take no pay for their teaching or official activities. They were either manual laborers or they followed some calling or craft. Hillel was a woodcutter, Shammai, a builder; R. Joshua, a blacksmith; R. Chanina, a shoemaker; R. Huna, a water-carrier; R. Abba, a tailor; others were carpenters, tent-makers, farmers, and merchants."[25] To the Sages, Rabbi Hertz notes (ad M. Avot 1.10), idleness did not mean nobility, nor did nobility mean idleness. "Better to do without," Maimonides wrote, quoting the Talmud, "than to be dependent on others or cast oneself on public charity. 'Better to strip hides in the market than say, "I am a great sage, I am a priest, support me."' So did the Sages command. Among the great sages were hewers of wood, bearers of beams, drawers of water for gardens, ironworkers, and blacksmiths. They did not seek public assistance or accept it when offered."[26]

From his first published work, his Letter on the Persecution, Maimonides showed a deep loathing for the pretensions of the half-learned. The concision and rabbinic erudition he strove for in that *Iggeret*, alongside its realism and humanism, reveal what he prized in the learned and hoped for from himself. His contempt for the judgmental, half-baked learning of the adversary he declined to name persists in his attitude toward all too many of "the self-professed sages of Israel" (2.17a). Ignorance, prolixity,[27] and superstition were their obvious faults. But their overblown claims to authority were capped by what he saw as willful dependence on the charity of the community.[28] Summing up the themes of Maimonides' halakhic magnum opus, Isadore Twersky writes,

> Some of the most impassioned and protreptic prose of the *MT*, for example, expresses his opposition to the existence of an institutionalized and salaried rabbinate, dependent on the largess of patrons or charitable contributions. . . . The religious indignation, moral pathos, and de facto inflexibility

of his position become even more poignant and meaningful in the light of his own turbulent biography and its remarkable consistency in this area, in defiance of all challenges, pressures, and temptations.[29]

Spiritual leadership, as Maimonides saw it, was a mandate, compelled by the flow of understanding that those graced with it must share, even to their cost—even at the risk of death (2.81ab). To retain one's learning in hopes of a return on one's investment betrays the law of being that floods the cosmos with a light and insight that are not one's property to barter or withhold (3.2b). Inspired knowledge was the true guide of life. So the sacred dignity of sharing knowledge joins hands with the demands of probity: Halakhic rulings must serve neither elite interest nor popular whim, as the Torah warns: *Pervert not justice by preference of the poor or deference to the rich: Judge thy neighbor justly* (Leviticus 19:15).

If rabbinical work was not to be Maimonides' trade, medicine was the clear option, reflecting his study of the sciences and philosophy. He had studied medicine while still in the Maghreb. He had clinical training, experience, and repute, and he valued medicine. It was not just another craft like carpentry or weaving, he wrote, but a special way of serving God. Good health and bodily fitness are not the be-all and end-all of life (Eight Chapters 5, *MT* Ethical Laws 3.3). But to allay pain and preserve human lives are worthy ends, both of them critical to mankind's higher goal (3.45b, 60a, 131a, 133a).

Pursuing his medical practice, Maimonides continued to consult with senior physicians and colleagues, gleaning insight into diagnostics, therapeutics, materia medica, and dosages from their clinical experience and their writings. Always eager to share what he knew, he taught medicine as well as practicing it. His students included his sister's son, who bore the sobriquet al-Talmidh al-Zakī, the Brilliant Student, and became a physician in Anatolia.

Maimonides served as a physician to al-Qāḍī al-Fāḍil, to Saladin,[30] and to the sultan's son and successor, al-Malik al-Afḍal. His letter to Ibn Tibbon, written in his late years, describes how he rode each day from Fusṭāṭ to the palace, about a mile and a half away, attending to the ruler, his family, and court, returning home in the afternoon for a meal, then seeing private patients, often into the evening. On Shabbat, after congregational prayers, he gave public lectures[31] until breaking for afternoon prayers. Little time remained for casual banter, but Maimonides was a good correspondent, his letters lovingly preserved by his successors, along with his responses to rabbinical queries and pleas for help and advice from far-flung communities.

Of his ten medical works, half were written for members of the Ayyūbid court. The rest were essentially textbooks and reference guides based in part on his own clinical experience alongside the medical knowledge gathered in the Galenic tradition. The ten included the multivolume *Medical Aphorisms*; a supercommentary on the Galenic *Aphorisms of Hippocrates*; *On Hemorrhoids*, based in part on Avicenna and (in the judgment of Gerrit Bos, our leading scholar of Maimonides' medical work) probably in part on a lost work of Rāzī's; *On Asthma*, written for a Muslim patient; a collection of medical responsa; and a work on the nomenclature of drugs, herbs, and their variants and substitutes, vividly illustrative of Maimonides' abiding commitment to the resolution of ambiguity so critical in the *Guide*.

Reliance on memory is prominent in Maimonides' study and practice of medicine and in his medical writing and teaching—as it was in his juridical and philosophical work. The occasional verbal slip in his biblical quotations in the *Guide* shows that he did not balk at quoting even sacred texts from memory. But his prodigious memory fed the syntheses and analogies that underwrote his creativity. He knew the medical literature, as Bos details, well enough to disentangle complex terminological issues as to the fine anatomy and diseases of the eye, and he knew Galen's many texts well enough (sometimes by heart) to catch him in contradictions from one work to another and to discredit his authorship of a work falsely ascribed to him in Arabic, seeing that its terms were not Galen's—a finding confirmed by today's scholarship.[32]

There's a glimpse of the court milieu in the topics of some of his medical works: One, on protection from poisons,[33] is dedicated to al-Qāḍī al-Fāḍil—tellingly, for among the luminaries of the wazīr's *majlis* was a poet whose enduring loyalties to the fallen Fāṭimids made him a principal in the 1174 plot against Saladin.[34] For al-Malik al-Afḍal, who suffered from digestive problems and depression, Maimonides wrote *The Regimen of Health* and *On the Elucidation of Some Symptoms and the Response to Them*. The latter, Bos explains, was written when Maimonides "was old and weak and thus unable to attend al-Afḍal personally." The sultan had failed, perhaps, to trim his lifestyle and diet as the earlier work had prescribed. *On Coitus* was written for a nephew of Saladin's who wanted a regimen to enhance his stamina, since he had many slave girls.[35]

Maimonides shows what he thinks of court values when he pictures a decadent who risks "grave dangers like sea travel or royal service to win such superfluities" as jewels and other luxuries but "blames fate, and rails at fickle fortune for denying him the wealth to buy wine enough to keep him ever drunk and girls decked out in gold and jewels to excite him beyond his capacities" (3.20b).

Scientific medicine in Maimonides' day was respectful of texts centuries old, like those of Hippocrates and Galen, but expected the old texts to be continually updated by the clinical experience of philosopher/physicians like Rāzī, Avicenna, and Maimonides himself. Maimonides may scorn Rāzī's theology, but he values his medical work—and agrees with him in seeing progress in science and in his Galenic distaste for passions like anger.[36] Among the medical "moderns" besides Rāzī and Avicenna, he highly respects Westerners like Ibn Wāfid and Ibn Zuhr (Avenzoar, 1090/1–1161/2). And although he admires Galen, he calls him out when he finds the "Imām" of physicians overstepping his expertise[37]—making a mystery of time (1.106b) or calling apes merely grotesque (3.55b).

Maimonides cherishes Hebrew for its chaste usages (3.14b). But he sees language as conventional, not natural, let alone divinely fashioned. He reads the delicacy he finds in Hebrew diction as reflecting and projecting an ethos of piety, but not inborn ethnic purity.[38] So he does not wax chauvinistic, as Galen does, calling Greek "the sweetest" of languages and comparing foreign tongues to "the squealing of pigs and croaking of frogs."[39] Nor will he turn to astrology, as Galen does in charting the course of fevers (3.80a). He prizes Galen's counsel on the value of exercise (3.55a) and welcomes his explaining mortality and morbidity as natural results of our embodiment (3.19b). But he stands up for tradition when he finds Galen lampooning the Mosaic account of God's powers.[40]

The Torah calls God a healer (Exodus 15:26), but Maimonides rejects the notion that healing, any more than agriculture or industry, should be left to God alone. Medicines and other therapies are as relevant to our well-being as food: Natural causes are efficacious, and human activity is right to enlist them (III 13, 17). The future is not sealed, or it would make no sense for human beings to be given commandments—including safeguards like setting a railing on the roof to prevent tragic falls (Deuteronomy 22:8). Medical treatments, he argues, must be anchored in natural science, not talismans, incantations, or magical "names" (I 61; 3.80ab).[41] Even the authority of science, often pled in behalf of astrology, cannot exempt it from dismissal (2.26b). Using the term Isaiah uses (47:13) to condemn those who turn to astrology to divine the future, he writes that such stargazers (*ḥozim ba-kokhavim*) have only "hot air and drivel" (*hevel va-riq*) to offer.[42] Of necromancy and the like he writes, "All these things are false and fraudulent, used by ancient pagans to induce the nations of various lands to adopt them. They are wrong for Israel, who have the sophistication and good sense not to be taken in by such nonsense or even entertain the thought that there's anything to it. As it says, *There is no enchantment in Jacob, and no divination in Israel* (Numbers 23:23)."[43] Superstitious nostrums only enshrine pagan fears. Their clear mark is lack of empirical warrant (3.80ab).[44]

Life and health are core values in the Torah and rabbinic texts.[45] Following the Sages, Maimonides derives the positive (and public) duty to heal the sick from the commandment to restore lost goods (Deuteronomy 22:2).[46] He extends that obligation, as Elinor Lieber wrote, to "an extreme type of humanism in a thoroughly Judaized form."[47] For he reads Hippocrates' famous aphorism "Life is short; the art is long" to mandate providing patients with all the necessary "externals." Hippocrates' holistic approach, he said, reveals the ancient physician's "formidable moral virtues," making it a medical duty to reach beyond medicine alone. A physician should render treatment as easy and pain-free as possible, guard against error, and eliminate barriers to healing: "If the patient is poor and is in a place that aggravates his illness, but he cannot afford another, one should move him and provide the nutrition and medication he needs." Such care is obligatory, being essential to the goal sought.[48]

A community of 120 souls or more, Maimonides ruled, must have a surgeon, and no prudent person should move to a place without a physician and surgeon (*MT* Sanhedrin 1.10, Ethical Laws 4.23). To avoid health risks is a religious obligation (*MT* Ethical Laws 4.1) demanding a wholesome diet, regular bathing, and avoidance of tainted foods and dangerous substances. The Torah commands us not to disgust ourselves (Leviticus 11:43). So one must eat nothing normally deemed disgusting—and never eat with dirty hands or a dirty tablecloth or use in the kitchen or at the table utensils from the surgery or the bathroom.[49]

Health, for Maimonides, means human flourishing in a broad, dynamic sense with moral and mental dimensions. It demands open communication and collaboration between patient and physician.[50] At the communal level, building on the halakhic obligation to keep tanneries downwind of homes and on a neighbor's right to sue to eliminate hazards and nuisances like foul odors, fumes, dust, and smoke, Maimonides outlines a system of local health rules.[51] Characteristically, he generalizes the biblically prescribed roof railing (Deuteronomy 22:8) to ban any environmental hazard: Wells and pits must be covered, and negligence of such dangers must be punished.[52]

FOUR

A New Life

Leadership

Since the eleventh century, Egyptian Jewry had been led and represented at court by a *Raʾīs*, or head chosen by community leaders and confirmed by the Muslim regime. The *Raʾīs* was known as the Nagīd, but that biblical title had fallen into disuse until regained by Maimonides' son Abraham and borne by five generations of Maimonides' descendants. He himself held the title only briefly, from 1171, but he fulfilled many of its duties informally without the title. The *Raʾīs* was a Rabbanite but still responsible for Karaites and Samaritans, and Maimonides showed care and fairness toward all his constituents. He did consider Karaites sectarians (*minim*), but his responsa charge that they be treated with respect in ritual matters and with honesty and courtesy in daily relations; they, in turn, must not mock the Rabbanite Sages, past or present.

Maimonides' conscientious rejection of rabbinical remuneration was tested in his leadership role. For, as the Sages say, one may be tested by prosperity as well as hardship.[1] He passed both tests brilliantly. As Twersky writes, "[He] of course, did not receive any financial aid or official remuneration from the Jewish community, even after he emerged as its untitled leader, combining the duties of rabbi, local judge, appellate judge, administrative chief responsible for appointing and supervising community officials, and overseer of the philanthropic foundations (to which he was especially dedicated). His advice to students mirrors the same unshakeable conviction as does his criticism of past practices."[2]

Among the responsibilities Maimonides shouldered was the restoration of the synagogue known as that of Moses, a site of Jewish pilgrimage on the west bank of the Nile known for the festivities marking the traditional anniversary of Moses' birth. He carefully saw to the appointment of judges to deal with routine halakhic cases. As early as 1167, he was active in framing *takkanot*, rulings of the rabbinical council. Among the rules was a Solomonic decision clarifying the workings of majority rule in its judgments. The reforms were unimpeded by pushback from the Exilarch in Baghdad. Rabbanite (rather than Karaite) usages as to ritual baths were restored; marriage and divorce procedures were clarified, specifying the need for a proper officiant; and rules were reformed, requiring a wife's consent to her husband's taking a second wife or (if she were abroad) calling for him to deposit the *ketubah* payment due her should she sue for divorce. The Talmud had rationalized such norms as forestalling incest between unwitting half-siblings, but Maimonides read them as protecting "the well-being of the daughters of Israel."[3]

Maimonides' stature did not set him above the worldly fray. A tax farmer known to his detractors by the derogatory epithet Zuta ("Shorty") had bought the office of Nagīd in Fāṭimid days. Well hated and widely reviled for his tyrannous exactions, he regained the lucrative post as the Fāṭimids faded. Maimonides, then new in Egypt, hearing bitter complaints, evidently appealed to the wazīr and had the man deposed. When Zuta's later efforts at bribery left the Ayyūbids unmoved, he denounced key Jewish adversaries as Fāṭimid plotters. Reinstated, he abused his authority to spy on other Jews. A generation later, he would be featured as the villain in a satirical burlesque written in the allusive style of a *maqāma* (an artful and poetic prose piece) modeled on the Book of Esther and titled *The Scroll of Zuta*. He had styled himself Sar Shalom, the Prince of Peace (echoing Isaiah 9:5), but to his detractors, he was Shor Shalem, the perfect ox.

Around 1180, exploiting a communal rift in Alexandria, Zuta raised a violent rabble against Jewish leaders, pressing the messianic pretensions implicit in his boasted title. Maimonides and others intervened, again with help from the court. By 1185, the Rambam could inform Rabbi Pinḥas, newly arrived from France, that Zuta's power was spent. Maimonides' moral eminence enhanced his authority in the struggle. But it hardly hurt that al-Qāḍī al-Fāḍil was perspicacious; and Saladin, incorruptible. Courage, too, was needed, however. For Zuta was no stranger to violence. In the same candid letter that recounts the devastation of his brother's loss, Maimonides confides that soon after reaching Egypt, he survived an attempt on his life.[4]

Late in his life, the perils of the Almohad persecution resurfaced. In about 1190, one Ibn Maʿīsha, a Muslim scholar of Almoravid sympathies, arrived in Cairo. Finding there, as a prominent Jew, the man he remembered as a Muslim convert in Fez, he charged Maimonides with apostasy from Islam, a capital offense. Ibn al-Qifṭī preserves the story; *his* source may well have been Ibn ʿAqnīn. Fortunately, al-Qāḍī al-Fāḍil heard the case himself and saved Maimonides, ruling a forced conversion invalid.[5] The Qāḍī knew his Qurʾān, but he also saw little need to enforce a decree of the hated Almohads.[6]

Living

Music, Maimonides wrote, can calm the soul. So can strolling in a lovely garden or sitting by a riverbank. Wholesome foods are essential, but tasty foods can pique a flagging appetite. Gilt walls or golden threads shot through a garment are hardly necessities, but such things may raise the spirits, dispel melancholy, and revive the mind for new bouts of exploration—"as the Sages said, 'A nice house, an attractive wife, and a comfortable bed for the scholar'" (Eight Chapters 5, citing B. Shabbat 25b, Berakhot 57b).

We have no reason to say that Maimonides' own marriage was not a happy one, but it seems unlikely that his wife was his intellectual companion. Along with his warmth toward students and fellow seekers, Sarah Stroumsa finds tones of deep loneliness in his correspondence, not unlike those of contemporaries who sought the peaks of rational inquiry in the intellectual love of God.[7] A sense of isolation from less probing souls is evident in Maimonides' sometimes outspoken expressions of alienation from the vaunted authority of would-be religious leaders of lesser learning and less-penetrating mind. But so is the welcome he and others like him accorded one another, sometimes across great distances, geographical, temporal, or confessional. A less welcome expression of the same sense of intellectual isolation are Maimonides' unguarded and unmuted dismissals of the intellectual capacities of women, who were generally excluded from intellectual commerce and then judged as if they were responsible for the exclusion.[8]

Maimonides despises the priapic culture of the court and scorns recreational sex. But like Saadiah, he rejects ascetic extremes. So when the Torah requires a Nazir, on completing his vow to abstain from the fruit of the vine, to make a sin offering *for his sin against the soul* (Numbers 6:11), Maimonides echoes the Sages' judgment that the soul sinned against is the Nazir's own (Eight Chapters 4, citing B. Nazir 19a). Sukkot, when Jews celebrate the harvest and respite from agrarian labors, is observed by dwelling in shanties open to the sky, commemorating Israel's desert encampments (Leviticus 23:32–43). But then we repair to "spacious, well-built homes" in a festival that "caps our rejoicing in ways not feasible in booths" (3.96ab). For the mind and spirit, as for the body, Maimonides holds, balance is best. Justice, he adds, means balance, and the Torah's balance is clear, commanding "nothing onerous or excessive like celibacy or sacred journeys" (2.84b–85a)—or the taxing ceremonial of ancient pagan cults, let alone their child sacrifices (3.108a).

For all the self-demand of his work ethic, Maimonides knew how to relax. He hated drinking parties (3.13b), but he had seen them and remarks on how trivial he found it that pious (but chauvinistic) elders could frown on the songs sung there in Arabic, even if their themes were honorable, yet countenance Hebrew songs, even with off-color lyrics.[9] The content is what matters, not the choice of language. Maimonides disliked small talk but enjoyed intelligent conversation. A poet friend, Ibn Sana' al-Mulk (1162–1212), a Sunnī protégé of al-Qāḍī al-Fāḍil's, tells of an extended theological discussion with him along with a Shīʿite from Aleppo, all "lovers of conversation."[10] "Galen," the poet wrote, "treats only the body. Abū Imrān (Maimonides) treats body and soul—

> Were his learning applied to the ills of our age,
> Its blindness his wisdom would banish.
> He'd find a salve to heal any complexion—
> And make even the moon's blotches vanish."

Maimonides completed the *Guide to the Perplexed* in 1191, after some five years of work on its final composition. In his last thirteen years, as Moshe Halbertal notes, he wrote only medical works. By 1199, although beaten down by age and ill health, he was still at work as a physician and active in learning and teaching. His hand had begun to tremble. In the summer of 1196 or 1197, he had needed an emergency visit from a physician, as he did again in 1199, just before sending Ibn Tibbon Part III of the *Guide*. A severe famine and epidemic struck Cairo in 1200. In 1204, Maimonides died, on December 13 according to his grandson David.[11] Ibn Tibbon had completed his translation of the *Guide* on November 30.[12] Maimonides was buried initially in Fusṭāṭ, but his wish, Ibn al-Qifṭī writes, was to be buried in Tiberias, and tradition has it that he was. A dignified modern monument marks the site. His works are his true monument.[13]

FIVE

Believing

Thirteen Articles

Many moderns have heard of the physician's oath ascribed to Maimonides and used by some new-fledged physicians in lieu of the Hippocratic oath. But the oath ascribed to the Rambam, although much in his spirit, was first published in 1783 by Markus Herz and is not known earlier. It seems to have been composed by Dr. Herz himself. A better-known composition is authentic: the Thirteen Articles of Belief,[1] well known in the *Ani Ma'amin* credo and versified in the Yigdal hymn, both still widely sung in synagogue services and elsewhere.[2] The idea of a formal Jewish creed was new in Judaism, and Maimonides' making such a list is often said to reflect Islamic influence. In rabbinic Judaism, as Menachem Kellner explains, faith was classically understood in terms of trust in God and loyalty to the covenant; belief became a prominent issue when Jews interacted with Christianity and Islam, where beliefs became emblems of identity and keys to salvation. In Christianity, indeed, faith came to be seen as a source of certainty.

There is a clear interest in beliefs when the Mishnah (Sanhedrin 10.1) excludes the World to Come for those who deny the revelation of the Torah or its promises of resurrection. Also excluded was the *apikoros*—broadly, a heretic but more pointedly, given the echo of Epicurus's name, a denier of providence.[3]

We see a watershed moment, as Kellner explains, when Saadiah Gaon, living in Muslim Baghdad and contemporary with prominent Muslim doxologists and doxographers like al-Ashʿarī, structures his great philosophical summa around the project of transforming beliefs (*amānāt*) into convictions (*iʿtiqādāt*).[4] As Yosef Kafiḥ wisely stressed, that pioneering work bears the title in manuscript *K. al-Mukhtār fī 'l-Amānāt wa 'l-Iʿtiqādāt*, or *The Book of Critically Chosen Beliefs and Convictions* (Hebrew, *Sefer ha-Nivhar ba-Emunot ve-Deʿot*).

Maimonides thinks little of creeds rattled off without serious thought about the ideas they bear (1.56b). The articles of belief he assembles do not play the role that an Islamic creed or Christian catechism is often meant to play. He did not relist them in the *MT*—although the relevant precepts can, of course, be found there.[5] Nor did he make their embrace a condition of conversion to Judaism. There are half a dozen or more beliefs that he thought vital in Judaism but did not include among those he laid out in *CM*. Yet he did take seriously the thirteen he listed.[6] The reason, I believe, is that he sees these beliefs as stepping-stones to knowledge. As such, they help him resolve a serious conundrum. To see just how, we need to reflect on Plato's distinction between knowledge and belief.

Knowledge, for Plato, grasps pure ideas; beliefs occupy a lesser plane and are about physical things. Knowledge, by definition, is true; beliefs may be mistaken. For most practical purposes, Plato proposes, true belief is as good as knowledge: If I want to travel to Larissa, true beliefs can get me there (*Meno* 97). But although true belief works as well as knowledge for most practical purposes, one cannot teach well using only beliefs. A good teacher needs to explain. Beliefs alone may not reach the real causes or true natures of things. Cogent argument, as Plato's dialogues seek to show, can purge "the false conceit of knowledge" and raise one's thinking beyond the plane of belief toward knowledge, replacing subjective certitude with objective certainty. Maimonides agrees, stressing how argument, insight, and evidence can lead from belief to certainty.[7]

Here's the conundrum: The Mishnah promises all Israel (and the Tosefta adds the righteous of all nations) a portion in the World to Come.[8] Maimonides accepts the more inclusionary view: "The pious of the nations of the world (*ḥasidei umot ha-ʿolam*) have a portion in the World to Come."[9] If that means immortality, Maimonides is convinced (again following Plato) that the rational soul wins immortality by linking with pure ideas: The mind becomes what it knows. We realize our affinity to God as we assimilate the eternal ideas that are God's wisdom, expressed in nature's plan (2.16b–18a). That thought is a mainstay of the Philosophers. But most human beings, even the most righteous, are not philosophers. And most of us, most of the time, are dealing with physical things in practical ways, not rising above the plane of mere belief. The tension here is palpable between an intellectualist elitism and the Mishnah's broad promise.

Maimonides dissolves the conundrum and relieves the tension with help from al-Fārābī's theory of prophecy.[10] True prophets, as he learns from Fārābī's (still Platonizing) account, are human beings who win philosophical insights but whose powerful imaginative gift enables them to translate pure ideas into symbols (and symbolically freighted actions) that make ideas accessible to those unready to rise above the sensory world. The idea of God's goodness may thin to abstraction for many—although philosophers see it as the most concrete reality, on which all else depends. But a prophet can translate the seemingly abstract idea of God's goodness or perfection into precepts and admonitions—to love one another as we love ourselves, to return lost objects, to use fair weights and measures, to help even an enemy reload his sprawling ass (Exodus 23:5; Deuteronomy 22:4).[11] And prophetic symbols open up onto the conceptual plane (1.6b–7a). So God commands us to be holy as He is holy (Leviticus 19:2)—that is, to reach toward self-transcendence by perfecting what is most distinctively human and so most divine in ourselves. In keeping with that quest, the so-called Holiness code that accompanies God's charge to pursue holiness—that is, as Maimonides reads it, to seek self-transcendence by perfecting our humanity—details numerous moral and symbolic practices by which our higher goal can be approached.[12]

The true beliefs that prophets project stand in for knowledge. They point to the ideas they represent, giving access to the many who are unattuned to pure concepts (3.59b). Anyone sensitive to prophetic poetry or alive to the symbolically fraught usages of ritual is guided to an implicit grasp of higher ideas by the tropes spun from pure light by a prophet's poetic imagination. Even to those who live largely on a practical plane (or fancy that they do), generous moral standards and just laws convey an implicit ownership in the ideals underwriting the norms that true piety respects. The portion promised to all Israel (and to the righteous of all nations) reflects just such an understanding. It need not be voiced. Yet the invitation to grasp it conceptually and articulate it explicitly, in the measure of one's capacity, is open to all who cherish the symbols that bespeak it or enact it in ceremonial acts and moral praxis.[13]

Maimonides was still in his twenties when he wrote his treatment of *Perek Ḥelek*—the famous mishnaic Chapter on the Portion, as it's traditionally called—where he embeds his Thirteen Articles, answering to the need to mitigate the Platonizing elitism of the intellectualist case for immortality. But it was Plato himself, as mediated by al-Fārābī, who taught him how: Poetry and its moral and ceremonial counterparts bridge the gap, making way for the pure of heart.

Maimonides' Thirteen Articles of Belief can be stated as follows:

1. God is real, perfect in every way; all else depends on Him. The elements of this belief unite in the conceptual thesis behind it: There is a Necessary Being. Only a perfect being can be necessary; all else must be contingent and so dependent. As a Necessary Being, God is unique (1.42a). Because all contingent being and, indeed, temporality itself depend on God, He is called the universal Creator. Hence the element of belief: There is no apodeictic proof of *ex nihilo* creation, but Maimonides finds good reason to believe and uphold it, and he did add it to the fourth of his articles of belief in his own master copy of the Mishnah commentary.[14] God's existence stands on higher ground, as a necessary truth, seen by all Israel at Sinai in the measure of each individual's understanding and voiced in words by Moses (II 33).

   Maimonides did not, to begin with, include creation among his Thirteen Articles, perhaps because, when he first drafted *CM*, he remained unsure of the status of *creatio ex nihilo*, which he will enhance and burnish in the *Guide*. Yeshayahu Leibowitz argues that Maimonides here shunned reducing God's absoluteness to mere functionality, even in as broad a role as that of the Creator.[15] He may also have chosen not to exclude sincere theists who saw God as the universal Cause, even if they did not call Him Creator. But in the end, he came to see creation as a tenable and therefore credible view, and he upheld it, not least because it anchored a belief in miracles—and, above all, the miracle of prophecy, from which Israel has the Law.

2. God is one, not as a species or a genus or any composite is one. God is simplex, indivisible. It follows that He is immutable and impassive (1.42ab). God's unity reflects His absoluteness as a Necessary Being.[16] Any composite is contingent, dependent on the cause or causes that sustain its unity, and on the nonexistence of anything that might disrupt that unity.

3. God is incorporeal, not a body or a physical force, energy, or power of any sort. God has none of the accidents that pertain to bodies, such as motion and rest. The anthropomorphisms prominent in Scripture are metaphorical, pointing beyond themselves toward recognition of God's perfection (I 26).[17] Corporeality is inconsistent with God's unity. For not only are all bodies divisible into parts, but all are compounds of matter and form.

4. God is eternal. Popularly, this might seem to mean that God has always existed and always will. But temporality would subject God to change. For time is the measure of change. God, in truth, is timeless. Time itself is a feature of nature: It, too, began. Ex nihilo creation reflects God's absoluteness: There was no prior matter on which God's creative act depended (II 26).

5. Only God merits worship or ultimate obedience. There is no divine intermediary or intercessor and no higher standard of value. God's goodness and justice are absolute and inseparable from Him (1.19a; 3.35a, 130a). God's rule and law (*pace* the Ashʿarites) are wise and just in the same sense that human reason rightly understands justice and wisdom (2.100b; 3.22a, 35a, 36a, 64b, 75b, 115b).

6. God addresses humanity through prophets. Prophets, like philosophers, know higher truths, but their imaginative gifts enable them to convey such truths poetically to others (II 40–45).

7. Moses, the greatest of prophets, will never be surpassed. God addressed him directly, and this revelation, to Moses, did not depend on the imagination (Numbers 12:6–8) but came through the clarity of his intellect. The Mosaic Torah is the best of laws, addressing our material needs and welfare, moral betterment, and spiritual/intellectual perfection. All authentic prophets work within the framework of the Mosaic Law. Rival laws may echo its precepts. But they are, at best, imitations (I 13, 1.145a, 2.73a, 79a, 3.126b; Eight Chapters 7).[18]

8. The Torah is from Heaven—that is, despite (Christian and Muslim) claims to the contrary, it is the same law that was revealed to Moses, complete and unaltered.

9. The Torah will not be abrogated, subsumed, superseded, or replaced in whole or part—again, despite Muslim and Christian claims. The best proof of the Torah's ultimacy is not external to it. It lies in the perfectly balanced justice of its laws in meeting human needs and guiding us toward perfection of our humanity (2.84b; 3.12a, 57b, 60a; cf. 1.9a, 2.83b, 3.16b, II 40).[19]

10. God knows and judges human actions. The basis of God's knowledge and providence, as the *Guide* will argue—uncovering the truths that mere beliefs, like a tarpaulin, reveal in outline but also conceal—is God's knowledge of the substantial forms of things, including the unique form of each one of us, the mind that is one's true human identity (III 16–21).[20]

11. God rewards obedience and punishes disobedience. But our requital is typically constitutive in our acts and their consequences, including their impact on our character and relations. The highest prize is presence with God (III 27, 51); the greatest loss is of God's presence, to which Maimonides assigns the biblical name *karet*, excision (see 3.36b).

    In introducing *Perek Ḥelek*, Maimonides writes, "Gehenna is a term for the grief that overtakes the wicked." He mentions two midrashic proposals that seek to define that grief in graphic images of fire or fever, imagery meant to restrain miscreants. But the reality that such images seek to convey is the loss of God's presence, the ultimate goal of all who are wise and the special meed of human goodness, in which wisdom is implicit.

12. God's anointed king will come. We must not seek to calculate the day but await it in patience, forbearance, and hope, though it may tarry. The Messiah, for Jews, is not a divine or quasi-divine figure but a rightful Davidic king who restores Israel's autonomy in her land; rebuilds the Temple; revives, restores, and repairs the ancient law; and rules in truth and justice (*MT* Laws of Kings 1.1, 11.1). The Messianic Age is not an apocalypse like that envisioned in the Qur'ān (and by some of the Sages). As Rabbi Samuel says, "There is no difference between this world and the days of the Messiah

but the subjugation of exiles" (B. Sanhedrin 91b; cf. II 29 and *MT* Laws of Repentance 9.2, Laws of Kings 12.2).[21]

"Let no one think," Maimonides writes, "that in the days of the Messiah any of the laws of nature will be set aside. . . . The world will follow its normal course. The words of Isaiah, *The wolf shall dwell with the lamb, the leopard lie down with the kid* (11:6), are to be taken figuratively: Israel will live securely among the once predatory heathens" (*MT* Laws of Kings 12.1). Even the depredations of once vicious nations will be quelled. For peace and prosperity will strengthen one another, fostering civic virtue and displacing imperial aggression.[22] In the Messianic Age, Israel will be respected by the people of other nations for the insight that the Torah affords those who live by it into God's true nature and intent for humankind.

13. Resurrection. Textually and contextually, it is clear that Maimonides disowns bodily resurrection. Sharply distinguishing the life principle from the rational soul, he writes, "What survives death is not the soul we are born with. That is a mere capacity. What is incorporeal and immortal is the realized and fulfilled soul" (1.92b). Following where argument leads, as he says one must (2.19a), Maimonides holds that the rational soul is incorporeal: Here lay the truth that images of bodily resurrection symbolically voice (see II 27, 57b).

As in the analytic work he would later use in the *Guide* to crystallize the theology of the kalām and that of the Philosophers, Maimonides aimed here to gather the set of beliefs that would assure all Israel of their promised share in immortality. So his listing has less in common with a Muslim creed or a Christian catechism than with those sets of "common notions" that forerunners of the Enlightenment crafted or drafted in quest of a natural religion. The universalism of Maimonides' listing makes it a doxastic counterpart to the seven Noaḥidic commandments. Its inclusive scope is qualified only by its including affirmations of commitment to Israel's law: The Torah will not be superseded. Too generic a body of beliefs would dissolve Jewish peoplehood, crush the covenant, and nullify every hope of vindication for Israel's role in aiding mankind's moral and intellectual perfection in a world at peace. For Israel is the little child that shall lead the world's nations to an age of peace, justice, and understanding (Isaiah 11:6).[23]

The first two articles in the Rambam's list, as Paul Fenton rightly pointed out to me, do amount to knowledge as Maimonides understands it. They are not just beliefs to be accepted on trust. For they are, in his view, demonstrable truths and, as such, apprehended by all Israel, each according to the individual's capacity. For with truths of reason, Maimonides argues, everyone is on a par, and prophetic revelation is not needed. But even those first two precepts, God's existence and uniqueness, still needed to be voiced by Moses for the Israelites assembled at Sinai. So even here, although these were truths of reason by Maimonides' account, there was an element of trust in their acceptance (and 2.75b, 3.60a). Not every implication of these two principles, moreover, was immediately grasped by those who heard Moses pronounce them.

The mishnaic passage promising all Israel a portion in the world to come, to which Maimonides welds his Thirteen Articles, also denies such a portion to those who disbelieve that the dead will be revived.[24] There are many views, he explains, about just what that world might be like. The diversity of opinions reflects the varied intellectual capacities of their exponents. But almost all the views held on that subject are incoherent and confused:

1. Some expect a return to Eden, a life of luxury free of toil and suffering, the blessed living in gemstone dwellings, reposing on silk couches beside rivers flowing with wine and fragrant oils. Such sensualists picture Gehennah as a fiery realm where bodies are tortured and burnt in ways that Maimonides confesses it would be tedious to describe.

2. Others link the hereafter with the reign of God's anointed king. They expect the blessed to live like monarchs, growing in strength and stature and filling the world. The Messiah, they expect, will live forever; the earth will yield ready-baked loaves and ready-woven garments, and many things will occur that now seem impossible. Yet there will be no afterlife for the excluded: They will no longer exist.

3. Others imagine the dead resurrected and reunited with their loved ones. They will live forever, but the unworthy will not be revived. That picture of the world to come relies on taking literally (and wishfully) certain scriptural verses and pronouncements of the Sages.

4. Still others think of the blessed state in worldly terms: fertile land, prosperity, fecundity, longevity, bodily health, security, restored dominion for Israel, and the subduing of her foes. The punishment they envision is equally earthy: durance for others under the conditions Israel now suffers in exile.

5. Most, however, fuse or confuse all these pictures, expecting the Messiah to revive the dead and lead them back to the Garden, where they will eat and drink in perfect health "as long as heaven and earth endure."

Vivid as such images are, Maimonides finds that few have given the idea of the world to come the kind of thought it warrants and needs. Few have adequately considered what this idea could or should mean, let alone parsed out just what our highest goal should be, sought the best means to attain it, or even clearly distinguished means from ends! Scholars too often elide such questions and find themselves distracted by worries about whether the dead will rise naked or clothed, in their grave clothes or fine raiment. Caught up in what they imagine are practicalities, such divines seem unable to escape the sensory realm: Will there still be rich and poor, powerful and weak, when the Messiah comes?[25]

Seeking to raise the level of the discussion, the Rambam quotes Antigonos of Sokho (fl. ca. 200–170 BCE): "Be not like servants who serve for the sake of a reward but like those who serve not for the sake of a reward; and let the awe of Heaven be upon you" (M. Avot 1.3). Fear of God, as Maimonides sees it, matures as love, and those who act in the love of God keep God's mitzvot for their own sake.[26]

"Doing what is right because it is right," as Jonathan Jacobs explains, "need not compete with, or be in tension with, acting for God's sake. In fact, many of the relevant thinkers"—Antigonos prominent among them—"held that acting for God's sake requires doing what is right because it is right."[27] Maimonides concurs: It is when actions are motivated by their intrinsic good, the good inherent in a mitzvah as a precept of God's wisdom, that we best honor God and fulfill the command implicit in our humanity, to emulate God's perfection so far as in us lies. We act for God's sake—for the sake of Heaven, as the Sages put it—when we act not for some reward, material, hedonic, or otherworldly, but in the love of God as the Source of all real obligations and in recognition of the intrinsic value of the act itself.

Maimonides scorns the consequentialism of those who bear the yoke of heaven in hopes of an otherworldly reward. Such calculations are tolerated rabbinically for the Aristotelian (and rabbinic) reason that doing the right thing for an extrinsic reason can lead to appreciation of the good inherent in an activity (or an abstinence) and contribute to our internalizing sound motives and making them our own: Virtues are acquired when we emulate virtuous actions and make virtuous habits part of our character and identity—whereas those who shoulder duties for the sake of a reward miss the point of the Sages' warning, "Do not make the Torah a crown of self-aggrandizement or a spade to dig with" (*CM* at M. Avot 4.5). For the wise, as Aristotle makes clear, following up on Socrates' words in the *Apology*, actions are not best judged by the pleasure or pain they seem to promise; on the contrary, the virtuous are most readily judged by the actions and activities they find most pleasurable or painful (see *NE* X 5, 1176a5–25). Thus, Maimonides' caution that we miss the intrinsic worth of righteous acts if we defer our hopes to a life beyond life itself, and cheat ourselves of the intrinsic worth of wise choices, confounding means and ends:

> One must not say, "I'll perform the Torah's mitzvot and engage with its wisdom so as to receive the blessings inscribed there, or to merit eternal life" or 'I'll eschew the sins the Torah warns of, to be spared the curses inscribed there and not forfeit immortality.' It is unworthy to serve the LORD in this way. One who does so serves only out of fear, and that is not the degree of prophets or sages but only of the ignorant, or of women, or children, who are trained to serve out of fear until they know enough to serve out of love. (Laws of Repentance 10.1)

True service, Maimonides argues, in keeping with Antigonos's teaching, asks no reward and seeks no incentive. It is moved, and passionately so, by love and thus by the intrinsic worth of the good God commands. This was the standard set by Abraham, who is called God's beloved (Isaiah 41:8; 2 Chronicles 20:7), and this is what is prescribed for all Israel by Moses (Deuteronomy 6:5). It is the standard that all should aspire to—although not even all the wise attain it (*MT* loc. cit.).

"Allowances have to be made," Kenneth Seeskin writes, "for children or people unable to comprehend the true meaning of the commandments." But half measures are no substitute here, any more than they are in human loving: "The purpose of the commandments is to get us to the point where we change our outlook on what constitutes benefit or harm. . . . Maimonides' ideal is that of a person who deals with everyday matters but only because inwardly her heart is turned toward God."[28] We see clearly here why service out of fear can never be more than a form of training, as if for a child. Love, for Maimonides, Seeskin explains, "as for most religious thinkers, is more than attraction or obsession." It is because love demands knowledge that Maimonides can dismiss not just the thinking but the very piety of those whose God is a projection of their hopes and fears (1.77ab). For it is impossible to love a fantasy:

> You can become infatuated with it or, like Ponce de Leon, spend your whole life searching for it; but insofar as the object is an illusion, it is not really an object of love. Nor is there love in a relationship that is dominated by expectation of reward or fear of punishment. A despot who becomes violently angry and demands total obedience may be treated with care or respect, but again one hesitates to call these responses love. Love in the sense intended by Deuteronomy 6:5 is a virtue. . . . According to the rabbinic interpretation, "with all your heart" means that the heart should not be divided; "with all your soul" means, even at the cost of your life; "with all your might" means even at the cost of your property (B. Berakhot 54a, 61b). . . . Whatever causes a person to accept death in order to sanctify the name of God, it cannot be an assessment of present and future risks.[29]

Seeskin cites Plato here, where Socrates tells the public assembly who are about to condemn him, "You are wrong if you think a man who is any good at all should calculate the risks of living or dying. He should just consider whether what he does is right or wrong, whether he is acting as a good man or a bad" (*Apology* 28b). Maimonides drives home his like point with a simple parable (*mashal*), told at unwonted length, comparing otherworldly hopes to the motives a child might have when bribed to learn Torah with promises of candy, nuts, figs, or honey. As the child grows, the rewards become new shoes or clothing and, later, promises of prestige as a judge or rabbi. All this, the Rambam writes, is deplorable, although human weaknesses may demand it. For minds fixate on such externals and all too readily miss the intrinsic worth of learning—or the life of the mitzvot.

Philo goes to the heart of the matter when he writes,

> With the manna and every boon God gives our race, one should take one's share and no more. That would be overreaching. Let the soul gather a day's portion for a day (Exodus 16:4), calling God, not oneself, the keeper of good things. . . . Day here stands for light, and the soul's light is learning. Many have lit up the soul against darkness and night . . . all the elementary lessons of so-called book learning—and even philosophy, when pursued with no higher aim than to parade one's superiority, or from an appetite for office under our rulers. But the man of virtue seeks the day for the day's sake and the light for the light's sake, the beautiful for the sake of the beautiful alone, not for something else. That is why God adds *that I may prove them, whether they will walk in my way or no* (16:4).[30] For God's law is to prize excellence for its own sake. The right rule is to test all who have an aspiration as one tests coins to see if they have been debased and seek the soul's good for the sake of some external thing, or like the tried and true distinguish and guard this treasure as the true property of thought and mind alone. The latter are privileged, since they are fed not with earthly things but with heavenly knowledge. (*Legum Allegoria* 3.167–68)

The life of the mitzvot, the Rambam urges, is not about getting into heaven (whatever that may prove to mean). It is a life precious in itself and lived for its own sake. The mitzvot at the heart of it bring one near to God. So it is childish and misguided to ask, "If I keep these commandments, what will be my reward?" Maimonides shoos readers away from eschatology and deflates the appetite for sensory rewards or superstitious fears of God as a wrathful martinet. It is not real courage, as Plato's Socrates argues (*Phaedo* 68–69), to choose lesser risks in place of greater; nor is it temperance to opt for greater pleasures in the hereafter over lesser ones in the here and now. As Saadiah argues, doubt is inherent in the human condition, given our finitude and ignorance. Fortitude and authenticity mean acting with integrity even in the face of doubt.[31]

For Maimonides, as Yehuda Gellman stresses, service out of love is disinterested: It means "commitment to the Torah and its precepts, walking in the ways of wisdom not for the sake of anything in the world [or even beyond it!]—neither in fear of some ill nor to inherit something good—but doing what is true because it is true" (*MT* Laws of Repentance 10.2).

We all begin, Maimonides concedes, following the Sages, by pursuing real goods for extrinsic ends, making the true goal a means to some specious end. But as we mature, we learn to act in love of God. Hence the Sages' talk of the progress from pursuing Torah for some external good toward cherishing it for its intrinsic worth, living by its precepts for their own sake (B. Pesaḥim 50b). This, for Maimonides, is progress from fear to love of God (*MT* Laws of Repentance 10.5).[32] Acts chosen in fear are infantile; the mature act out of love. The argument here should not be lost sight of: To serve God in hopes of a reward (or in fear of punishment or loss of a reward) is a phase to be outgrown. The Torah was not given to lead us to turn our lives (or those of others) into a meretricious exercise.

Kāmil is a key word in Maimonides' Arabic. The temptation in translating is to use the dictionary definition, 'perfect.' But semantically, connotations rule, governed chiefly by context. Much of the context in English is Christian, whence the presumption that only God is perfect. So it smacks of hubris to make perfection a human goal. As a result, we've generally translated *kāmil* in the *Guide* not in terms of perfection but, as the context and Maimonides' usage requires, in terms of maturity, betterment, or enlightenment or (in the final chapter of the *Guide*, where the talk is of goods worth having and worth having for their own sake) in terms of attainments. Our human goal is not apotheosis. When Maimonides fuses God's command to emulate His holiness (Leviticus 19:2) with Plato's call to *imitatio Dei* (*Theaetetus* 176b), he retains Plato's qualifying phrase: We should strive to become as like to God as we can. That is, as like as humanly possible. To Maimonides, that means, to fulfill ourselves as human beings by transcending our limitations, not pretending to God's absoluteness or absolute perfection. Human nature is capped by reason, the echo in us that answers to God's grace. So the perfection we are called to seek is realization of our humanity, crowned by reason.

Such fulfillment is the goal of what Gellman calls the educational program of the *Guide*. It blossoms when we shift in spirit from fear toward love—from anxious conformity in pursuit of a reward (or fear of losing one)—toward doing what is right because it is right and so acting in love of God.[33] A sense of helplessness may breed service out of fear, but free people need not beg God to fix their fate. They know themselves and are prepared to exercise their God-given strengths. So to see the links between freedom and responsibility is empowering. It fosters service out of love, in recognition of the intrinsic worth of life and the goods it affords.[34]

Gellman finds these thoughts plainly pronounced in the *MT*, where the sense of self they foster may prove most needed, in the Laws of Repentance. Maimonides here affirms "a radical human freedom." No fate or divine decree determines one's destiny. Everyone can turn toward good or evil and, by his own choices, become as saintly (*tzaddik*) as Moses or as vicious as Jeroboam (5.1–2; cf. 1.5; cf. B. Bava Batra 16a). The link to God of our rational intelligence that promises providence and immortality is sustained or even restored by turning toward God in love, not fear, or feelings of helplessness (5.7–9). The Prophets, Maimonides explains, have taught us the ways of penitence and have shown us how to break free of the toils of sin before those toils entangle us in ways increasingly difficult to escape (6.5). Thus David's plea for penitence:

> *Teach me, Lord, Thy way* (Psalms 86:11), i.e., "May my sins not bar me from the path of truth, where I will learn Thy way and the Oneness of Thy name." Likewise, when he prays for *a spirit that is free to sustain me* (51:14), he means, "Let my soul achieve what it longs for; do not let my sins prevent me from repenting; make me free to turn back and to recognize and know the way of truth." (*MT* Laws of Repentance 6.4)[35]

The help David sought, Gellman explains, is no ad hoc intervention. It was in his hand (cf. Psalms 16:8, as read by Maimonides at 3.125b). For agency is ours, so long as habit or policy has not let vice waylay or commandeer our character.[36]

In laying out his Thirteen Articles, as we can see, Maimonides' aim was not to legislate "who is a Jew." One becomes a Jew by birth or conversion, not by uttering or muttering a creed. That fact may help us see why the Rambam does not bring up these articles when he discusses what is expected of a convert and why he does not headline them in the Book of Knowledge.

If the Thirteen Articles have a confessional aspect, it's salient in the affirmation of God's absolute unity, the uniqueness of Mosaic prophecy, the irreplaceability of the Torah, and the vision of the Messianic Age as an era of Israel's restoration, not mere apocalyptic upheaval passively observed or passionately awaited. The features we observe in Maimonides' articles of belief bind it tightly to the ancient biblical and rabbinic idea of faith as loyalty, faithfulness that mirrors God's faithfulness and truth (Exodus 34:6) and trust in God's goodness and in goodness itself—not "belief in things unseen."[37]

What Maimonides tabled in *Perek Ḥelek*, then, are articles of belief. And belief, as Saadiah taught, seeks conviction. Mature or enlightened belief, as Maimonides sees it, depends on understanding (1.58b). Beliefs are not knowledge, but true beliefs point toward knowledge. Beliefs alone cannot bootstrap themselves into the judgment seat, and faith, for Maimonides, is not a source of knowledge but a moral wellspring of constancy. Faith here is not a self-sustaining updraft to a celestial aerie. Beliefs, like virtues, are stepping-stones, leading toward higher, clearer, and better understanding, allowing even the least intellectual of human beings a pathway toward a sense of God's transcendence and the responsibilities, moral and intellectual, that God's perfection calls for (and calls forth) in us. The function of Maimonides' list grows clear when we realize that every true belief points to an idea beyond it, much as the eyelets in a silver filigree, as Maimonides puts it, afford glimpses to the inquiring eye of the gold that lies within (1.6b–7a).

Conflict

Late in life, Maimonides' reluctance to dwell on bodily resurrection—let alone describe it circumstantially, as others were wont to do—led to serious criticism, and he was forced to defend himself. Joseph ben Judah, the first addressee of the *Guide*, traveling to Baghdad, heard criticism of his mentor on this score from the circle of the Gaon Samuel ben ʿAlī Ibn Dastūr (d. ca. 1197), the long-standing head of the rabbinical academy at Baghdad. Samuel found Maimonides' commitment to bodily resurrection, as Joel Kraemer puts it, "halfhearted."[38] Rivals to the religious authority Maimonides enjoyed saw what they took for a fatal weakness: Maimonides had listed resurrection among his Articles of Belief but had failed to mention it in the *MT*![39]

Samuel had wide influence, appointing judges not only in Iraq but in Iran and even Syria, where Maimonides, too, was influential. Like Maimonides, he wrote numerous rabbinical letters and responsa. He was even in correspondence with Fusṭāṭ and wrote a now lost commentary on the *MT*. But unlike Maimonides, as Kraemer notes, Samuel was an autocrat. Where Maimonides' rulings came from his council, Samuel's authority was hegemonical. Where Maimonides earned his living as a physician, Samuel, the Geniza documents reveal, exacted significant sums from the provinces (including Syria/Palestine, Yemen, and Iraq): "He had sixty slaves, armed with whips, to force the people into obedience. Whoever did not carry out orders was flogged. . . . Every Jew in Iraq paid a gold dinar annually to his treasury."[40] Indeed, Samuel sought to limit the jurisdiction of the Exilarch at Mosul, seeking to enhance his own revenues. Maimonides took the Exilarch's part; and the Exilarch, in turn, offered Joseph ben Judah the headship of the new yeshiva he had founded to rival that of the Gaon. Maimonides advised Joseph to decline the honor. But he was not reticent in his appraisal of Samuel, calling him a beggar and a miserable old man (*CM* Bekhorot 4.4). Samuel's lectures were thronged with students who hung on his every word. But the curriculum of his academy was strictly talmudic. It left little room for synoptic codes like al-Fāsī's and still less for the new *MT*—let alone the sciences that Maimonides found vital to theological depth and to a robust, critical grasp of the Torah itself.[41]

Joseph had written to his teacher in alarm at the disparagement he was hearing. Maimonides urged calm, perhaps hoping to avoid open conflict. One must not respond to unfair criticisms in kind, lest one twist oneself into a like perversity. He, too, he confessed, was prone to anger in his youth. But the Sages' cautions, inspired by the Psalms (16:8 as glossed at III 51, 125b), had helped him learn to control his temper, as one must when facing such criticism.[42] However, when Samuel, not satisfied with polite correspondence among Baghdad, Fusṭāṭ, and Yemen or public debate in Damascus and Baghdad, published a *Treatise on Resurrection*, Joseph answered passionately in his so-called *Silencing Epistle*, and Maimonides saw the need to clear the air with his own *Treatise on Resurrection*, taking up the issues Joseph had raised.[43]

Samuel, he found, was clearly out of his depth and might better have stayed with homiletics than try his hand in rhetorical tilting at philosophical topics he did not well understand. Despite his cautions to Joseph against infection by the ethos of his adversary, he, too, was drawn into a maelstrom of less than rigorous argumentation. Sensitive on that score and on the issue of resurrection itself, he warns sophisticated readers not to scrutinize his apologia too closely. It was written, he declares, for a popular audience: His critics had failed to see the line between philosophy and faith.[44] Samuel, and Joseph too, had blurred that line.

Sarah Stroumsa highlights a key instance: Both had confused the soul with the mind. It was the soul that theologians wished to reunite with the body. But it was the mind that philosophers deemed immortal—insofar as it held pure ideas.

The *Treatise*, Stroumsa observes, diverges not just in rigor but in tenor from Maimonides' usual style of patient explanation. David Hartman ascribes its vexed tone to Maimonides' "resentment at having had to retract his opinions." "On closer examination, however," Stroumsa writes, "it becomes obvious that he retracts nothing."[45] What made that possible was the critical distinction we've touched on between knowledge and belief. Plato had summed up the position with the sort of pithy economy that Maimonides admired: "As being is to becoming, so is truth to belief" (*Timaeus* 29c). Maimonides was clearly aggrieved at having to go through the motions for the Gaon and his Baghdad cohorts, as if replicating his family's days under threat from the Almohads. Philosophically, he had nothing to recant. But he did need to respond. He was writing, as Kraemer notes, in the same year that Suhrawardī was crucified.[46] Like any orthodox Muslim, Saladin held with bodily resurrection. So did most faithful Jews. But Maimonides had arguments for intellectual immortality; for resurrection, he had none.

His *Treatise on Resurrection*, in fact, contains nothing not already in the Mishnah commentary and *Mishneh Torah*. Yet it was, as Kraemer writes, "a masterful piece of rhetorical accommodation" written with one eye on the general public, its arguments "not scientific or demonstrative but rhetorical and persuasive, geared to the popular imagination."[47] Resurrection does inspire the pictorial imagination—just consider the paintings of Stanley Spencer or those of many an old master. But intellectualist philosophers do not live in a picture world, and it is not there that they conceive of the eternal life of reason.

Maimonides' repeated protestations that bodily resurrection is a bastion of belief are true, even sincere. But his *Treatise* touches the delicate topic of an afterlife in a cautionary spirit, resorting to what Edmund Burke and John Henry Newman called an "economy": He told the truth, but not the whole truth.[48] A popular audience would little reflect (nor long remember) that belief cannot measure up to knowledge. Beliefs, for Maimonides, even core beliefs, stand in for more challenging ideas. They are a first rung, as he saw it, for those whose thought has not risen above the plane of imagination (3.60b). The core Mosaic thesis remains: Death is not the ultimate. But the true self is the mind, the rational intellect, not the animal or vegetative soul, far too intimately and intricately integrated with the body ever to be sundered from it.

Before drawing a curtain on this episode, it is worth giving the last word to Averroes, who never had to leave Spain and so had both the privilege and the pain of dealing with the Almohads all through his adult life. Near the end of *The Incoherence of the Incoherence*, answering Ghazālī's charge that "the Philosophers deny bodily resurrection," Averroes writes,

> This problem is not found in any of the ancient philosophers, although resurrection has been talked of in diverse religions for at least a thousand years.... The first to mention it were the prophets of Israel after Moses, as is clear from the Psalms.... It is also affirmed in the New Testament.... It is a theory of the Sabians,[49] whose religion, as Ibn Ḥazm has it, is the oldest.
>
> Philosophers, specifically, naturally see this doctrine as most vital to uphold since it sustains the social order, on which our life as human beings depends, and through which we may attain the highest happiness proper to our humanity. For this belief is crucial in mankind's acquiring the moral and intellectual virtues, and the practical sciences. Man, they hold, cannot live in this world without those sciences, and cannot live in this world or win the next without the intellectual virtues. Neither is won or perfected without the practical virtues, which grow strong only by one's knowing and adoring God and performing the duties prescribed by the laws of the several religions—such as offerings, prayers and supplications, and other such pronouncements, rendering praise to God, angels, and prophets.
>
> Philosophers believe religious laws are exigent political arts, their principles drawn from natural reason and inspiration—especially those common to all religions.... One must not cavil, they hold, in positive or negative terms, at any of the broad principles of religion, e.g., whether or not it is obligatory to serve God ... or whether there is a higher bliss ... for all religions unite in affirming a life after death, although differing in its description.[50]

Of this expostulation by Averroes, Kraemer writes, "I know no passage quite like it by one of the Islamic philosophers that defines so clearly the attitude of Islamic philosophers to religion."[51] Maimonides, with his characteristic love of concision, puts the point in a single sentence: "The Torah lays down certain beliefs critical to civic life—like the belief that God is filled with wrath toward those who flout His authority—to strike fear and consternation into the hearts of the fractious" (3.61a).

Critique

No one could reach the heights of intellectual success, prestige, and influence that Maimonides won without drawing some hostility. A harsh critic was Rabbi Abraham ben David of Posquières (ca. 1125–1198), known as Rabad, a Provençal talmudist whose acerbic comments on the *MT* are printed alongside its text in traditional editions. His family hailed from Andalusia, and a grandfather had been knowledgeable in astronomy; Rabad's son became a major kabbalist known as Isaac the Blind. Rabad himself devoted his life to the Talmud. Imprisoned by a local lord who coveted his wealth, he was rescued by a count well disposed toward Jews. A charitable man and a generous teacher, Rabad was a prolific talmudic commentator and an author of responsa. He was prone to assert his own halakhic views, and where his admiring successors could find no rabbinic basis for them, they credited divine inspiration. Few of his works survive.

Rabad respected al-Fāsī's talmudic learning but criticized his code and especially that of Maimonides. Taking up the cudgels in defense of the authority of the Geonim, he disliked philosophical jurisprudence and abhorred Maimonides' seeking and finding rational footings for the halakhic edifice. To him, such efforts smacked of second-guessing: Human standards were far too subjective to assay laws of divine authority. Behind Rabad's objections to the *Yad* lay a penchant for legal positivism.[52] That made him hostile to the moral realism that Maimonides anchored in the axiom of God's goodness, the thesis that God and His justice are inseparable (1.19a; 3.35a), and his presumption that God made His norms amenable to human understanding and devised them in the interests of their recipients (2.24a).[53]

Rabad's many strictures on the *MT* often picked at points of detail. But he took special issue with Maimonides' condemnation of superstitions (2.24ab). For he saw some forms of divination as rabbinically sanctioned (cf. 3.80ab). Holding science at arm's length, Rabad declined to address texts in the *MT* dealing with matters astronomical, "not being a member of that guild," he wrote. To see Maimonides flaunting his knowledge of "this profane subject," he confessed, "pushes my patience past the breaking point." Knowledge of astronomy, he implies, is irrelevant to halakhic work. Maimonides clearly disagreed, as Saadiah had two centuries earlier.[54]

In the *MT* (Laws of Repentance 3.7), Maimonides had called God the unique ultimate Cause and Rock of the universe. Rock (*Tzur*), as Rabad well knew, is a familiar biblical epithet of God (Deuteronomy 32:15; Habakkuk 1:12; 2 Samuel 23:3). When applied to God, Maimonides explains (I 16), it means calling Him the world's active Source and Cause. So Moses, in his final song, calls God *the Rock whose work is perfect* (Deuteronomy 32:4). But Rabad, by a play on words, took *Tzur* to suggest *Tzayyar*, a draftsman, intimating that Maimonides had called God the framer, not the Creator of the cosmos.[55] The inuendo was captious and motivated by hostility, not by any close reading of the Rambam's text.

Resentment seethes when Rabad goes on to flail at Maimonides for rejecting God's corporeality: "Many men greater and better than he have held this view" (at *MT* Laws of Repentance 3.7).[56] In a passage suppressed in most copies of the *MT* but preserved in later commentaries, Rabad assailed Maimonides' gloss of God's promising to show Moses "His back" (I 54). To Maimonides, the reference is to God's work in nature (I 64), the wake or impact of God's creativity. What Moses saw, on the Rambam's reading, was the panoply of nature, in which a prepared mind can behold the wisdom and grace by which God governs the world, characteristics that Moses would need to emulate in leading his people, as his request to see God's ways (Exodus 33:13) clearly implies (1.45b, 65ab, 72a, 104a). But as Rabad would have it, Moses was given *a vision* granted no other prophet and rightly concealed from others—a thought "perhaps unfamiliar" to Maimonides. Moses, Rabad may have thought, was shown the figure of a demiurge of some sort, leaving the Cause of all causes unseen.[57] Science was irrelevant and alien, but rabbinic corporealism was worth fighting for.

Rabad was incensed that Maimonides had allegorized the Banquet awaiting the righteous in the hereafter and had failed to tell of the kiddush cup to be passed at the climax of that feast and its coming to rest in King David's hand.[58] Of the Rambam's treatment of the afterlife, he wrote, "The words of that man seem to me to say, in effect, that there is no resurrection of bodies but only of souls. This, I swear, is not the view of the Sages, pronounced in Ketubot." In the passage Rabad cites, Rabbi Elazar denies an afterlife for the ignoramus (*'am ha-aretz*); his prooftext: *The dead live not* (Isaiah 26:14). Resolving that seeming tautology, Rabbi Elazar took the verse to mean that the ignorant—in effect, already dead—will enjoy no future life. Rabbi Hiyya bar Yosef, indeed, expected the saintly "to burst forth and rise from their graves in Jerusalem"—fully clothed (B. Ketubot 111b). For Maimonides, such imagery was, at best, allegorical. Still, at *Perek Ḥelek*, he softened Rabbi Elazar's judgment: The *ʿam ha-aretz* intended here is not merely unlearned but a boor who lives oblivious to the Torah's precepts. Such a brute, Maimonides holds, has indeed robbed himself of his portion in the World to Come. For he lacks both implicit and explicit wisdom and has frayed the linkage of the mind with God by his neglect of the rational soul, the image of God in all of us.

The Abiding Presence of al-Andalus

With the horrors of the Almohad conquest behind him and his stature established far out of reach of their oppressive regime, it is natural to wonder why Maimonides, in his maturity, continued to call himself a Spaniard. It was natural, of course, to take on a name reflecting the land of one's origin. But for Maimonides, Andalusia was more than a locale. To him, the name evoked a way of life and thinking, a complex of values to which he saw himself as an active heir, in medicine and the sciences, in halakhah, and in philosophy.

Al-Andalus had been the home of great Hebrew poets like Samuel Hanagīd (993–1056), Moses Ibn Ezra (1055–1138), poet/philosophers like Judah Halevi (1075–1141) and Solomon Ibn Gabirol (1021–1058), philosopher exegetes like Abraham Ibn Ezra (1089–1167), and pietist philosophers like Baḥyā Ibn Pāqūdah (early twelfth century). The world of cosmopolitan Jewish learning in law, medicine, and the sciences, where Jewish scholars, thinkers, and doers worked in close and often fruitful (if at times fitful and fraught) commercial, political, and intellectual contact and collaboration with their Muslim peers, had been destroyed by the Almohad conquest. But long after he and his family were exiled from Cordoba, Maimonides sustained his attachment to the homeland of his childhood, his father's learning, and the humanistic traditions in which that learning and those sciences and arts had flourished and borne fruit.

His medical training, in the Arabic Galenic tradition of scientific medicine, took place in the West. His Jewish jurisprudence, set forth in his commentary on the Mishnah, was itself Andalusian, favoring what he saw as the more open, responsive, and up-to-date readings of Halakhah that his father, Maimon, had learned at the feet of Ibn Migash, himself the disciple and successor of al-Fāsī at Lucena. And the Rambam's outlook in philosophy and the sciences, then sheltered under the wings of philosophy, was also Andalusian.

Maimonides credits the physicians from whom he learned—chiefly in Fez, it seems. Medicine, as he thought of it, was pretty straightforward: a scientific art far less fraught with problems than metaphysics (1.40a) but also an empiric practice. And it was in the West that he was able to lay the foundations in experience that enabled him to become an accomplished clinician. Even when well known and established as a physician, he made a point of consulting with others and seeking clinical information about important past cases. He makes reference to a medical experiment that he observed, testing the effects of a purgative—although we must note that neither ancient nor medieval medicine made use of experimental controls.

The idea of health, to him, seemed pretty clear. But the means to it rest on appraisals of an individual case, a luxury not typically available in law, where fairness and balance depend on uniformly applied rules and universal principles (3.74b). In medicine, as in any art or science, theory cannot stand alone. Balance matters here, just as it does in law, and Maimonides tells what he learned from a son of Ibn Zuhr about the importance of medical experience in tracing the efficacy of varied remedies and treatments.[59]

Medical training in his time was typically by way of apprenticeship and assistantship, often with a family member. Ibn Zuhr's family, for example, was to boast five generations of physicians, and generations of Maimonides' heirs went on to serve as physicians. Even Avicenna, son of a high official in the last days of the Samānid dynasty in Bukhara, proud to be self-taught, had clinical guidance in advancing from texts to cases—although he won his medical reputation by his contributions in hard cases that had defeated others. Experience was a critical ingredient here, as it remains today. And the floorboards of Maimonides' medical experience were laid down and aligned in the West.

Despite an account from Leo Africanus, it seems unlikely that the Rambam studied under Ibn Zuhr. But we know that he admired the senior physician and prized the information he gleaned from his son. Ibn Zuhr's empiric openness to folk remedies, however, had to be reconciled with Maimonides' naturalism: He rejected the efficacy of charms, which Ibn Zuhr tended to accept, evidently on empirical grounds. But given the seeming tolerance of such things by the usually more rationalistic Rabbi Meir (M. Shabbat 6.10), Maimonides met Ibn Zuhr halfway, forbidding the use of charms unless the patient believed in their efficacy (3.80b), an early suggestion of the placebo effect.

Jewish jurisprudence in the East did have its philosophical practitioners, the great exegete and philologist Saadiah Gaon foremost among them. Maimonides welcomes Saadiah's defense of free will and personal responsibility—although attributing such an outlook, in good part, to the fact that earlier Jewish thinkers happened to have encountered Muʿtazilism first during the days of its prominence. Truth be told, however, free will and human moral responsibility as well as moral realism were prominent givens in the ancient biblical canon and in the rabbinic tradition.

The Geonim, heads of the rabbinic academies during the centuries following the completion of the Talmud, "had dominated the Jewish world from the eighth century to the eleventh." But the authority of their schools, now located in Baghdad, had suffered "an extended decline," as Moshe Halbertal explains,[60] their writings grown obscure and hard to follow—much as the Talmud itself had tended to close in upon itself, turning its once fluent interchanges among the Sages into an increasingly closed world dependent on a shared universe of discourse. The work of the brilliant scholars of al-Andalus had begun to eclipse the Geonic tradition, all too focused on the past. The Jewish jurists of Western lands, using logic, philology, and the sciences, sought a coherent message in the welter of talmudic voices and focused on present practice and future theory. So although the Geonim saw their authority as permanent and binding on Jews everywhere, Maimonides regarded their achievements as more limited and local than the rabbinic rulings to which they appealed.[61]

His own comprehensive code, the *Mishneh Torah*, was an open challenge to the (often piecemeal) work of earlier talmudists. Completed in 1178, after a decade's intensive effort, the work drew the ire of Samuel ben ʿAlī, the eager heir to the authority of the Geonim, igniting a bitter controversy. One telling bone of contention: Was it permitted to sail on the Sabbath on great rivers like the Tigris, the Euphrates, or the Nile? Samuel ruled against it; Maimonides held that it was allowed, recalling Sabbath sailings on the Seville River near his birthplace in Cordoba. Authority, he argued, did not reside in an inherited office. There were geonim (eminences) in the West as well as Iraq. Or was halakhic authority, he asked with unmasked irony, just a matter of geography?

The struggle with Samuel might be read as a jurisdictional dispute or a mere power struggle. But the pull of practice cannot be ignored. Maimonides knew well how powerful familiar usages can be (1.34b; 3.69b–70a). But he did clearly see a kind of hubris in the claims of the Geonim. Unquestionably, he identified with the usages of al-Andalus, some of them, perhaps, fondly remembered. But Andalusian precedent also seemed rational to him, in part by its linkage with other facets of rationality that he had come to appreciate from that lost world.

We've noted the Rambam's keen desire to tailor his writing to his reader's needs. And that focus on fit, evident in his care with terminology in his writings on medicine and law, is all the more prominent in the *Guide*, where his concern is to help those who find themselves caught in a dilemma between Scripture's seeming naïveté and the vaunted certitude of the sciences. We see his drive for clarity in the Mishnah commentary and his titling it *K. al-Sirāj*, the Book of the Lamp. We see it again in the method and pattern of exposition he chooses in his legal code and in the telling epigram he chose for it from the Psalms: *Then shall I be unabashed to scrutinize all Thy commandments* (119:6). The aim of Halakhah, as he saw it, is to set out a way of life for Israelites to live by, not a sea to drown in, nor a cloistered existence in which study, by way of sublimation, becomes a substitute for the life itself that the Torah and the laws elaborated from it seek to sanctify.

Although a consummate master of the Babylonian Talmud, Maimonides had a special attachment to the less frequently consulted Jerusalem Talmud, partly because it more often states the reasons for the Sages' findings and rulings, partly because its exposition is tighter and less digressive, and partly, it seems, because he found its reasoning and its rulings often (but not always) more compelling. Maimonides' love of clarity goes hand in hand with the love of light and enlightenment that he associated with the world he had lost in Andalusia. Kraemer cites a case in point: The Sages had abolished the daily reading of the Decalogue in the liturgy. Why? It was, as Maimonides learned from the Jerusalem Talmud and explains in his Mishnah commentary, because "heretics" (early Christians) had been claiming that only the Ten Commandments were the Law God gave Israel at Sinai.

Another factor, called to my attention by my friend Ophir Ospovat, would have favored the Jerusalem Talmud in the Rambam's eyes: The Bavli, as the Babylonian Talmud is called, is rife with demons and demonology. But such figures appear very rarely in the Yerushalmi. Clarity was the Rambam's goal in the sciences, as it was in law and jurisprudence. And in all these realms, clarity, to him, meant intelligibility, meeting the tests of reason. His scientific studies had begun with astrology. But in time, he rejected it "with revulsion," as Kraemer puts it[62]—for its pagan roots, its unscientific core, and the doorways it opened to fatalism and the shrinking and shirking of personal and communal responsibility.

Love of logic is the obvious contrast. For logic is the focus of one of his earliest books, where we can see him feeling his way to an understanding of the rules of reasoning, which he is keen to elucidate and share with others. We can see in the love of logic one reason for Maimonides' abiding respect for Fārābī, "the Second Teacher." He developed a similar attachment to mathematics, and astronomy as well, which he, like the ancients, saw as an integral part of mathematics (2.13b). In astronomy, he charted his progress from the days when he knew no more than an ox or an ass[63] to his later mature and confident mastery, when he not only felt able to cite significant works in the field but could praise the precision of Ptolemaic predictions of eclipses, argue that the astronomer's task was not to map the heavens but to construct mathematical models that would save the observational phenomena—and able, even, to broach speculative proposals of his own, reducing the celestial spheres to four, with a view to linking the Philosophers' cosmological scheme to the four creatures of Ezekiel's vision and the four elements of Aristotelian terrestrial physics.

His little book on the terms (and methods!) of logic, written when he was in his early twenties, apparently for an Arabic-speaking Muslim patron, is extant and casts light on the growth of his thoughts about epistemology, given the epistemic force of logic in the quest for truth. As for astronomy, the Rambam's interest led him on to geometry and optics, evident in his revision of a work by one of the "Party Kings," the learned monarch of Saragossa, al-Mu'taman (fl. 1081) called *Al-Istikmāl* (The Quest for Perfection)—a good expression of Maimonides' own quest as he sought to broaden and deepen his understanding. His mastery of geometry, plane and solid, grew from his close work with this text.

In an early work on the Hebrew calendar (1157/58), written before he turned twenty, Maimonides put to work the knowledge of astronomy he had won thus far. Here, as in his book on logic and later in the *Guide*, he had used the *risālah* form, addressing the reader and seeking to tailor his instruction to that reader's needs even as he acknowledged this particular reader's limited background and wished he could write in this domain at a more advanced level. By 1166, when writing On the Sanctification of the New Moon in *CM*, he felt free to write more technically for an audience he expected to be more advanced. In the *Guide* itself, he would unlimber a sophisticated technique of resolving the tension he saw between the intellectually ready and the unready.

The great problem in astronomy in Maimonides' day lay in the issues that provoked what Ali Sabra calls the Andalusian Revolt regarding the Ptolemaic system.[64] We can see Ibn Rushd, among others, struggling to explain the apparent retrograde motion of the planets and finally giving up yet hoping someone one day would solve the problem.[65] Maimonides, like Ibn Rushd, rejected epicycles and eccentrics. For the posit of such entities played hob with the Aristotelian physics and cosmology that he and other experts of the day accepted:

> You know the topics in astronomy that you read with me and mastered in the *Almagest*. But there was no time to go further with you. As you know, the system matches what we observe only if we add epicycles or eccentrics, or both. But I need to note here that neither hypothesis makes any sense. They contradict all the physics we know. (II 24, 2.51b)

Even so, Maimonides knew and freely acknowledged that these posits allowed one to use Ptolemaic assumptions to predict an eclipse down to the minute:

> They state precisely when the darkness begins and how long the occultation lasts. How are the retrograde motion and other motions of a planet conceivable without positing an epicycle? (2.53b)

Maimonides' solution, at least as a stopgap, was a bold excursion into "instrumentalism":

> The object in astronomy is [not to draw a picture of the heavens but] to propose a model allowing for uniform, invariant revolutions . . . neither slowing nor speeding, on a course consistent with observation . . . striving to keep to a minimum the number of spheres and the complexity of their movements. (II 11, 2.22a; cf. II 24)

Rather than discard Ptolemaic astronomy, Maimonides admires its fine mathematical models and their impressive power to save the phenomena. The deep inconsistencies with Aristotelian physics of the epicycles and eccentrics invoked to repair Ptolemaic models will in time, he trusts, give way to new models—although he, like Averroes and other parties to the "Andalusian Revolt" in astronomy, had no inkling of just how radical a revision would be called for, leading in the end to the fall of geocentrism and the dissolution of the spheres.

There is a certain humility in Maimonides' respect for science when it reaches beyond the world we know best: "Only God," he writes, "knows the truth about the heavens—their natures, form and substance, motions and causal connections fully. He gave mankind the power to know the world below. It is our world. We are placed here and are part of it" (2.54a). As he confesses, "Of all things celestial, man has just this modicum of mathematics. You can see how far it goes. I say, as the Torah puts it lyrically, *The heavens are the heavens of the* L*ORD*, *but the earth He gave to the sons of man*" (loc. cit., quoting Psalms 115:16). Yet despite his disclaimer, the progress Maimonides expects in astronomy (2.42b) is scientific, not, say, astrological or fanciful. Hence his dismissal of the ancient and all-too-appealing idea of the music of the spheres (II 8).

The entire cosmology of the spheres and incorporeal intellects, upon which he will rest his reading of the Account of the Chariot, is, he must confess, "with few exceptions . . . speculative and conjectural" (II 22). He does freely employ it, finding it, for now, the least problematic option. But like Rāzī and Averroes, he knows that there has been and will continue to be progress in the sciences, including astronomy. So when the anatomy of the heavens is worked out (and even the seeming retrograde motion of the heavens is explained), the stout commitment we have already cited will stand firm: "In intellectual matters, one must follow where the argument leads and believe what is soundly proven" (2.19a).

We can see that commitment vividly in his handling of the battle day of the ancient Israelites at Gibeon, when Scripture reports *The sun stood in midheaven and did not haste to set the like of a full day* (Joshua 10:13). "I think . . . ," he writes, "it seemed the longest day of the year. . . . That day at Gibeon seemed to them the longest day of summer there" (2.77b). There's quite a contrast between his outlook here and that of, say, Church authorities in their dealings with Galileo. Maimonides gladly absorbs what natural science discovers. He has no mind to curb its work, which he holds sacred (II 38; III 28, 60b–61a). His watchword, drawn from the Talmud: "The sages of the nations of the world prevail" (B. Pesaḥim 94b at 2.19a).

He rejected the views of the occasionalist kalām, finding their methods suppositious—although he shared their theistic goals. They had, he charged, eliminated nature (1.97b) and our ways of probing it scientifically (see 2.50b) and working with it technologically, using pumps, for example, and the machinery of the Banū Shākir (1.107b). His aim is to accept the best science of his day, which he identifies as Andalusian (2.19b).

We can see the draw of naturalism in his reading of the biblical story of Elijah's revival of the son of the woman of Tzarefat (1 Kings 17:17). Perhaps the boy had not really died:

> Some Andalusians took it to mean that the boy's breath stopped and was undetectable, as in apoplexy or failure to breathe at birth. Sometimes one cannot tell if a patient is dead or alive and the doubt persists for one or two days. (I 42; 1.47b)

Respect for evidence and reason and for their collaboration in science and philosophy is powerful not just in Maimonides' thinking about logic and mathematics, natural science and cosmology, but in his metaphysics and theology as well.[66] That Andalusian outlook holds the key to his philosophical work in the *Guide to the Perplexed*. For the *Guide* looks to the idea of emanation pioneered by Plotinus and advanced by Fārābī and Avicenna to address the problems of creation and revelation, divine governance, and knowledge that the *Guide* confronts. Here, too, the learning and the literature of Andalusia play vital roles: At the pinnacle of Maimonides' ladder of human aspiration lies consummation of the soul's quest in the sustained intellectual love of God, which he reads as our ultimate goal in life, the highest end to be sought in all human quests, and the true test of the divine inspiration of any system of law. Such thinking is hardly Andalusian alone, of course. But its treatment as the cynosure of human aspirations was introduced in the West by al-Baṭalyawsī (1052–1127), the Andalusian grammarian (who is known to have debated with Ibn Bājjah regarding logic and grammar) whose philosophical *Book of Circles* was twice translated into Hebrew and whose *Book of Questions* Maimonides and many other Jews could read in Arabic. The work was known to Baḥyā Ibn Pāqūdah, Isaac Abravanel and Ibn Ṭufayl. Maimonides agrees with Baṭalyawsī (and Fārābī) that religion teaches the same truths by persuasion and imagination that philosophy pursues by way of proof and argument. Like other theistic philosophers, he turns to the images of spiritual ascent that Baṭalyawsī helped make at home in the West. And Baṭalyawsī, like Maimonides, believes that philosophy demands a grounding in the moral virtues if conceptual understanding is to proceed freely and responsibly. Summing up his outlook and giving it a name, Maimonides writes, "The Andalusians among our people all hold to the Philosophers' tenets and favor their views, so long as they do not contradict biblical principles" (1.94a).

PART II

The Work of the *Guide*

SIX

Defining the Issues

Rubrics

The first thing to know on reading any philosophically charged book is what problem or problems it means to address. Yet Maimonides does not state the problems the *Guide* will tackle. Instead, he offers a brief, if vivid, phenomenology of the dilemma he expects an educated, religiously committed reader to face in trying to square biblical texts and rabbinic discourse with what he knows rationally (1.3a). Even the anthropomorphisms so prominent in the Torah and Midrash are not yet cited. Rather, the problem areas are tagged with rubrics pointing to two domains the Sages had roped off: *Maʿaseh Bereshit*, the biblical account of creation, and *Maʿaseh Merkavah*, Ezekiel's account of his vision by the riverbank among the exiles in Babylon.

The account of creation, the Sages say, named by the opening words of Genesis, *In the beginning* (be-reshit), may not be expounded (*dorshin*) to two persons. Ezekiel's vision, named for the chariot thought to feature in it, "even to one—unless he be wise and understands it for himself" (B. Ḥagigah 11b, 13a). The two domains set off-limits by the Sages for all but the most private teaching are the very terrain to which Maimonides offers a guide, even as he admits that "laying out all these things in a book teaches thousands in effect" (1.4a): "God knows," he writes (at 1.9b), "I have had constant grave concerns about setting down the things I mean to set down in this work. They do belong under wraps.... How, then, can I break precedent and commit such things to writing? I rely on two warrants: first, the Sages' saying at a like pass, *The time has come to act for the LORD*... (Psalms 119:126, at B. Berakhot 63a), and their words: '—and all thy deeds, for the sake of Heaven'" (M. Avot 2.17). Chastened by the Sages' concerns, Maimonides, as Leo Strauss notes, avoids calling the *Guide* a book—although here he comes close. He calls it a *maqālah*, a discourse, using a word that connotes speech. The *Guide* does take the tone of a private conversation, and Maimonides, like other authors of his day, regularly speaks of his reader's hearing his case. But would it not be jejune to expect to sidestep rabbinic cautions just by pretending a substantial written work will not be read as a book? Maimonides knows that many will read it and urges them to study it closely and read its chapters against one another—as one would read not just any book but a book of moment (1.8b).[1] He anticipates, with some dread, that commentaries on it will be written (1.9a).

He had thought closely and clearly about what he was about and does not pretend his subject lies outside the dangerous domain. But ever reliant on precedent, he boldly cites the example of Judah the Patriarch a thousand years before: In deciding to codify the Oral Law in the Mishnah, Rabbi (as he is called) had seized upon a line from the Psalms to justify his undertaking. Where the psalmist desperately urged God to act, Rabbi had audaciously reversed the syntax: The time had come *for him* to act *for the LORD*—even if that meant breaching the tradition that the Oral Law must remain oral (B. Giṭṭin 60b). He must codify the growing body of Jewish case law, lest the content or context of rabbinical decisions be forgotten or the complex dynamic of priorities among the laws embedded in the Sages' teachings and precedents remain unconciliated and grow unsettled in the crisis of the age.

In his own times of exile and oppression, Maimonides invokes Rabbi's precedent to address the new crisis posed by the challenge of Greco-Arabic philosophy (1.9b). It was not Halakhah now that was at risk but Aggadah, the imaginative vehicle of the Torah's philosophical import and impact. The tools for decoding the ancient spiritual and intellectual message of Scripture and its midrashic embroidery were now long and deeply buried, in Maimonides' view. The deeper themes of the Prophetic books, as he calls them, and the discourse of the Sages might drop out of sight and out of reach altogether, sinking into the crevasse between philosophy and dogma. The new crisis seemed to leave him no choice but to forge ahead.

The perplexity the *Guide* aims to address stems from study of philosophy and the sciences. The religiously committed reader for whom Maimonides wrote the work faces a special kind of cognitive dissonance between received tradition and what reason may seem to teach. Reflecting on the affirmations and obligations that give the Torah substance, such a reader faces a quandary: Should he dismiss text and tradition as hopelessly primitive or restrain his reason, bracket what he knows of philosophy and science, and blanket the canon to insulate it from critical inquiry?

Maimonides aims not to evade but to confront such questions, confident that reason and science will not conflict with the truths God teaches in the Torah. His goal is not to reconcile "faith with reason," as if faith had no stake in reason or reason had no place in faith, but to uncover the deep harmony of biblical and rational truths. Maimonides shows himself a philosopher here and a synthetic thinker, ready to surmount seeming disparities and to discover to others the deeper unities he has discovered for himself, underlying differences of idiom and convention, of method and of content. Maimonides trusts the truth. Deep study and reflection have convinced him that God will not betray that trust: Trust in God is trust in truth.

Where, then, do philosophy or the sciences sprung from it seem at odds with some religious idea? In mapping the terrain, Maimonides turns to the Sages, the resource and recourse of his halakhic work. For the rabbis were hardly unaware of the tensions that would come to concern him and later readers of sacred Scripture. Nor were they themselves immune to such concerns. That is why they tag the key issues so gingerly with allusions to the two biblical passages where they stand out most starkly: *Maʿaseh Bereshit*, the account of creation in Genesis; and *Maʿaseh Merkavah*, Ezekiel's account of his vision. Even in his younger years, Maimonides had identified *Maʿaseh Bereshit* with what Greek philosophers called Physics and *Maʿaseh Merkavah* with Metaphysics (*CM* at Ḥagigah 1.8, 2.1). He calls the one "natural science" and the other "divine science." Knowledge of the mysteries resident in those two domains, he says, is an ornament to those who possess it but best unshared with those foreign to such inquiries (1.3b, citing *MT* Laws of the Foundations of the Torah 2.12, 4.13).

In his commentary on the Mishnah, he had explained why reticence was needed:[2] Taking the subject matter of Physics to be cosmology insofar as it touches on divinity, he argues that most people are not equipped to follow the relevant discussions; the ill prepared will only be thrown into doubt and confusion when the problems latent in that domain are broached. As for Metaphysics, only those capable of pursuing answers on their own should be given the hints they may need to guide them (B. Ḥagigah 13a). To others, if such topics are voiced directly and prosaically or obliquely and poetically, they will seem either vacuous or opaque (cf. 1.5b).

The domain of physics, as we've noted, reached far more broadly in Maimonides' day than what typically bears that name today. Classically, as the equivalent name "natural science" indicates, it concerned every aspect of nature: the elements and their compounds (animal, vegetable, and mineral), their changes and dispositions, and the causes of natural change. Maimonides is at home in these sciences. He applauds their progress (2.13b) and trusts in the efficacy of natural causes. Here, for him, Aristotelians hold the high ground. Where there are miracles, they would be woven into nature's fabric (1.85b–86a).[3] The Aristotelian approach, he writes, "forms a system that fits the facts" (2.42a). Whatever it says "about the sublunary world down to the earth's core is sound and undisputed" (2.49b).[4] Things grow more problematic, however, where terrestrial or celestial nature somehow makes contact with the divine.

Paramount in the Sages' concerns about cosmology, as their rubric *Maʿaseh Bereshit* announces, is the question of creation. It stands out vividly against the backdrop of Greek philosophy, where the world's eternity was regularly assumed and any origin for the cosmos, when the question did arise, was routinely denied. Was there a creation event? How was it possible? Under the heading of *Maʿaseh Bereshit*, where Physics touches its metaphysical boundaries, questions about causality, causal uniformity, miracles, God's will, and providence line up behind the central question of creation.

Divine science, too, broaches its questions at the borderlands of finitude with the Infinite. Yes, as Aristotle said, metaphysics—First Philosophy, as he called it—concerns being in the broadest possible terms, as Maimonides explains (*CM* at Ḥagigah 2.1). But more pointedly and specifically, it regards God's existence: Can it be proven? If so, how, without making God a part of nature or an artifact, a figment answerable only to the imagination? What are we to make of divine attributes? How are we to understand the notion of God's knowledge or the sharing of His wisdom and perfection with lesser beings? What is the soul, how does it relate to God, and how is its yearning for immortality to be met?

Just as questions about creation stand at the pinnacle of cosmological inquiry, questions about revelation, for Maimonides, are salient in the broad domain of metaphysics, with Ezekiel's all-too-graphic account of his epiphany a paradigm case. Here, as in grappling with questions about creation and divine governance, Maimonides prizes the Philosophers' idea of emanation, using it even to schematize the real relations he finds symbolized in the creatures Ezekiel reports that he beheld in his striking account of his vision. Maimonides will acknowledge that the Philosophers' carousel of celestial spheres—with their incorporeal intellects driving, steering, and somehow precipitating them into material reality—is highly conjectural and speculative (2.50a). And he will disallow the music of the cosmic calliope that some had thought ought in principle to be heard (II 8). But he retains the idea of emanation as the key to all the riddles that he will probe in the *Guide*, from the problems of creation and revelation to the problem of evil, the questions arising from the specificity of God's laws, and the mysteries of divine knowledge, human immortality, and God's providence over nature and human life.

The mystery of nature's linkage to divinity confronts us in the Torah's opening words, as the Sages freely confess:

> Given its immensity and sublimity and our incapacity to grasp such ultimates themselves, the profundities that divine wisdom saw we need were broached to us obliquely and poetically—in words quite baffling. As the Sages say: "It is impossible to convey to flesh and blood the power of the Creative Act, so Scripture baldly tells you, *In the beginning God created* . . ." (Midrash Sh'nei Ketuvim, Batei Midrashot 4)—putting you on notice that these things are ineffable. (1.5a)

The Rabbis' sensitivity to the problematics of creation contrasts sharply with naive readings. Genesis reveals nothing about how God created. It does affirm that He saw goodness in His work but says nothing about what creating is. By Maimonides' time, questions about that were many: Did God bring something from nothing? Aristotelians considered that impossible, even illogical. Or did God simply (or not so simply) call chaos to order? Did matter once exist on its own, not yet given form? Was there a start to time? Or does creation, paradoxically, imply a time "before which" there was no time? If creation was possible for God, didn't Aristotle teach that all possibility is grounded in matter (III Introduction, Premise 24)? If so, how was creation absolute? All these, Maimonides held, are legitimate questions deserving an answer but too fraught for straightforward exposition, as one might teach some topic in mathematics (cf. 1.40a).

Still, they must be explored and taught. When the Sages say better not to be born than ask, "What is above? What is below? What lies ahead, or behind?" (M. Ḥagigah 2.1), they meant their warning for the unready. To address such questions safely, one needs critical prerequisites (1.36a–38b). That is why they spoke, in the same context, of the need to safeguard the Master's Glory. The gift of reason is God's Glory. The ill prepared fail to honor it when they pursue profundities that they are intellectually unready to explore. Only the foolhardy attempt Everest unprepared.

The *Guide* will lay out a pathway of approach to the two great realms of inquiry subtended by the headings *Maʿaseh Bereshit* and *Maʿaseh Merkavah*. The object is safe access for those who are well equipped and ready, who need only subtle hints to pursue their inquiries, as the Sages urged. So the *Guide* must be subtly constructed. The reader's work will be more like piecing together a vast jigsaw puzzle than like, say, shelving books in a library under separate "magisteria" or tracing the genealogy of ideas. Maimonides' explorations showed him a harmony between nature and Scripture. Both are God's work. But creation and revelation use different languages. The project of the *Guide* is to find ways of fitting together the insights gained from both to frame a picture unfair to neither source of human understanding.

Caution and Credence

Superficial readings of a received text can stock quite a warehouse of unexamined dogmas. Set aside or raised high on some doxastic pedestal, such beliefs are hardly assured to mesh with experience, or even with one another. Always at risk of toppling at some trauma or of being swept away by a skeptical broom, they may remain uninterpreted, or they may be interpreted fancifully, homiletically, or superstitiously; personally or impersonally; superficially debunked or merely dismissed with laughter. Believers, pious or scientistic, may take heroic pride in their wealth of beliefs, a special kind of hubris judging faith by weight, or skepticism by its airiness: The more one takes on, the higher and holier one's piety; the more one discards, the loftier one's bearing. But credulity is not piety, and dismissal is not knowledge.

Maimonides' eye is on those who equate piety with credence when he writes, "Belief is not what you say but what you think. . . . There are plenty of dolts who have their creed by rote with no idea of what it means" (1.56b). Faith subverts itself when it turns to credulity. For a willingness to believe just *anything* undercuts, undermines, and in the end empties itself once it becomes, like the traveler at the outset of the *Golden Ass* of Apuleius, ready to believe, even before hearing, just what one is told.

Incoherence frames no judgment, so it is not faith, no matter how warmly wrapped in rhetoric or armored in vehemence (1.58b). And we must bracket carefully whatever cannot square with what is known, by experience or the sciences, including logic and our human grasp of human nature (1.5b, 34ab, 50b; 3.9a, 70ab). There's a matching caution for would-be skeptics. For doubt, well placed, is even-handed, as critical of denial as of affirmation. Hence Maimonides' warnings that eagerness "to discredit things not disproved but possible" renders one liable to every sort of dangerous and dispiriting delusion (1.35b). Naive readers, for this reason, stand outside Maimonides' ideal audience in the *Guide* (1.3a).

Living in a Darwinian world, we are used to historical modes of explanation. But the Sages, as we've noted, were sensitive to the stark absoluteness of the account of creation in Genesis, and Maimonides' philosophically astute contemporaries were keenly aware of issues here, since almost all philosophers in the Greek tradition, and their most accomplished Muslim followers, held creation to be impossible. Aristotle thought philosophy had left myth behind when thinkers first began to ask what things are made of rather than how they came to be. For that new line of questioning led on to real metaphysics, asking what it is for a thing to be rather than where things came from or where they're likely to end up. Aristotelians, including the Neoplatonic Aristotelians who took the name Philosopher as their own, held the world's eternity to be the only tenable view. Creation seemed to imply that nothing had become something, that events might occur with no earlier event behind them, and that God arbitrarily chose a moment as the beginning—and only then became a Creator.

Doubts about creation and direct denials hark back to the origins of Greek philosophy. Parmenides had raised the issue when he wondered *how* any first event could have occurred (as if out of nowhere)—and if a beginning is presumed, *why* at just this moment rather than some other: "How and whence did it arise?" the goddess asks in Parmenides' poem. "I'll not let you to say or think, 'From nothing,' for nothing is not and cannot be said or thought. And if it did arise from nothing, what need could drive it to come later and not sooner?"[5] Aristotle did not share Parmenides' monism and brilliantly refuted his Eleatic predecessor's denial of change (cf. 1.57b). But he saw a deep truth in Parmenides' exclusion of nonbeing. So he denied the reality of the void (Maimonides will follow him here) and rejected the absolute origination or annihilation of anything: All change presumed some prior change. Here Maimonides begged to differ.

Aristotelian faith in an unbroken causal sequence and philosophers' resultant denials of creation reflect the commitment to rational explanation that lies at the root of natural science. A chief reason for Aristotle's admiration of his pre-Socratic predecessors was their move away from myths of origin and toward modes of explanation that seek to understand things by probing their natures rather than picturing their origins. But more was at stake in denials of creation than a conflict of science with myth. There was a deep religious difference too. For Aristotle and his followers saw the world itself as divine and expected it to share in the eternity of the divine.

Confronting Christian challenges, Proclus (fifth century) framed eighteen arguments against creation, elaborating Aristotelian themes and echoing Parmenides' questions of *why* and *how*. If God is a creator, Proclus asked, shouldn't the creative act, and its product, be eternal? Was God idle and alone before creation? Why would He suddenly set to work to make a world? And if the world did begin a finite time ago, why just now? For there was, by hypothesis, nothing as yet to differentiate one potential first moment from another.

To the *Falāsifa* as a school, the idea of creation seemed empty at best. Maimonides disagrees. But he does not think creation can be demonstrated. Like Ibn Ṭufayl (and Galen before him) and like Aquinas later on—and Kant long afterward—Maimonides sees impressive arguments on both sides of the issue. It was in behalf of creation, as he sees it, that the Mutakallimūn had sacrificed nature and made God the sole cause of all events. So intense was their campaign to prove the world began that in the end, they made every atom and accident the immediate work of God's will.

But the Philosophers, Maimonides argues, failed to prove the world eternal. Their arguments may sound plausible, but they lacked rigor, as Aristotle well knew—for it was he who taught us how to distinguish proof from mere persuasion (II 15). Where real proof is wanting, Maimonides explains, the Peripatetics taught that we should choose the least problematic option (II 3, 15). And on such grounds, Maimonides sees good reasons to choose creation, quite apart from its centrality in the tradition of Moses and Abraham: Based on the fact that not everything must be as it is, making natural facts irreducible to logical necessities, Maimonides finds creation more probable than eternity (2.39, 49a–50b). He also judges it preferable theologically to belief in an eternal world, since the idea of creation preserves God's will rather than reduce divine agency to an automatism—or an algorithm.[6]

The one move Maimonides does not make in behalf of creation is to appeal to Scripture. For the Torah's truth lies at the heart of what he seeks to establish. Maimonides will not argue in a circle by appealing to authority. The Torah itself sets the example when it cites the wisdom of its laws as showing the nations of the world how close the lives of Israelites are to their God: The appeal is not to revelation in behalf of the law but to the wisdom of the law as warrant of its divine inspiration (Deuteronomy 4:6–8; see 2.24a, 3.68b). Only after showing that the Philosophers have no proof of their eternalism does Maimonides cite the conviction of Abraham and Moses (2.50a–51a).

Questions about creation breed a host of kindred questions: How could an incorporeal God create a corporeal world? How could such a God affect, let alone govern, this world? Students of philosophy today hear like doubts about "the really hard problem" of consciousness and its relation to the body and other physical realities: How can a body affect or be affected by thought? Thoughts are not described, let alone explained, in the language of physics—or biochemistry, genetics, neurophysiology, or any of the sciences that have fanned out from what Aristotelians once called Physics.

The Sages pair thoughts of Ezekiel's vision with the first verses of Genesis because revelation, like creation, stands at the boundary of finitude with the Infinite. 'How can an infinite God be known by a finite mind?', 'How can an incorporeal God even know nature, let alone govern it?', 'How can God's infinite perfection scale its demands to human needs and limitations?', 'What are we to make of the troubles and disappointments, pain, suffering, and death so prominent in the world we live in?' Our world is bounded by limits, spatial in an Aristotelian cosmos, temporal biblically, qualitative in the potentials of all natural beings, and even existential. For all determinate beings are contingent. God alone is a necessary being (1.60b–61a; 3.22b, 26b, 42a).

Far less philosophical background was needed to prompt one to shy at Ezekiel's theophany than at the first lines of Genesis. The exiled prophet says he saw an enthroned figure and four "living beings" with quadruple animal/human faces, triple pairs of wings, straight-fused legs, an unearthly glow, and an unworldly mode of locomotion. Ezekiel's vision has drawn fantasy elaborations and excursions from ancient mystics down to Erich von Däniken's space fantasies. Ezekiel did seem to say that he had seen God. Yet God Himself had said, *My face shall not be seen* (Exodus 33:23)?[7] Doesn't the Torah use the word *kadosh* (Leviticus 19:2; Isaiah 6:3, cf. 55:8–9) to point to God's transcendence? Doesn't it vigorously combat any reduction of God to graphic or plastic representation (Exodus 20:4)?

Genesis declined to portray the Creator. It offers no description, discloses no divine motive for the creative act, and (unlike many a mythic theogony) offers no backstory. But this very chastity tempted those who loved a mystery. The Sages, who so relished the chance to work out precise parameters for the Torah's prescriptions and who loved to encrust biblical narratives with their homilies, here drew a curtain, barring public exposition of the mysteries of creation and revelation. Only *in camera* could these verses be expounded. The two hedged-off domains, as Maimonides saw clearly, include much that we, like the Greeks, call philosophy: Physics, here construed to mean cosmology theologically considered, will embrace questions of natural causality and human agency and their relations to divine causation. It will regard the duration as well as the origin of our world. Metaphysics will extend from questions of God's Self-revelation to touch on legal and moral philosophy and the interplay, in both, of reason, nature, history, and culture. As the questions proliferate, *Maʿaseh Bereshit* shades into *Maʿaseh Merkavah*.[8]

Ezekiel's vision, arresting in its concreteness, has a bluntness to it much like what the Sages found so challenging in the account of creation. Their worries begin with embarrassment that the prophet's vision is so graphic, as if in counterpoint to the self-restraint of Genesis. Did Ezekiel really say that on the banks of the river Kevar he saw God? That would be troubling enough. But a host of further problems lie just beneath the surface. Creation and revelation focus the

Sages' concerns, but neither can be isolated from questions about God's knowledge and governance and our human efforts to know (and be known by) God. Questions about creation do broaden naturally to questions about providence (or "governance," as Maimonides also calls it). But questions about Ezekiel's vision also lead to questions about prophecy itself: What is revelation? How is it possible for a transcendent God to connect with a human mind? How can a human being know God, let alone speak with Him—or learn what He expects of us? How does God's boundlessness accommodate itself to our limits intellectually, morally, culturally, historically? Where do prophets get their rhetoric and tropes? How does Perfection take prescriptive shape in laws, moral norms, even ceremonial details? How can we tell authentic prophecy from error or imposture—or firsthand inspiration from what is ersatz or derivative? How does prophecy differ from ordinary experience or from dreams, mystical and trancelike states, even hallucinations? What makes prophetic experience so vivid yet often so obscure in meaning?

If the world is God's work, it is also His expression, itself a revelation—in a way, a work of art. What, then, can we know of God from nature? How does nature's nonverbal message jibe with Scripture's more explicit themes? And what are we to make of those areas where we find nature troubling or disappointing? If God is infinite, why are all things else determinate? If God is good, why are His creatures vulnerable, fallible, even evil? Again, if the Torah is a revelation, it is also God's creation: What can be said of the rationality of its laws as they interact with human minds and cultures? Where does ethical naturalism end and natural law begin? All these questions fall within the ambit of the *Guide*.

The domain intended by the Sages' talk of the Account of Creation and the Account of the Chariot, Maimonides had said in the *Mishneh Torah*, is the Pardes, the Park or Garden of speculation that four of the greatest talmudic sages entered. Only one of the four, Rabbi Akiva, emerged unscathed (1.35b). Hence the warning signs the Sages posted. They saw dangers in cosmological and metaphysical inquiries. Madness, apostasy, even death lay among the hazards of this pleasure park. But Akiva stands among the greatest of the rabbis (1.35b; 2.68b), renowned for his learning and insight; ardent in support of Bar Kokhva's rebellion against Rome; a paragon of creative, humane, and rational exegesis; unwavering in his love of God and Israel, even in his excruciating martyrdom. So the tale of the Pardes is a warning—but also a challenge.

The difficulty Maimonides faced in writing the *Guide* mirrors the dilemma he sees facing his intended reader. Thoughtful and educated contemporaries, like their counterparts today, faced tensions between their religious commitments and their scientific and philosophical knowledge. Should they dismiss the ideas of creation and revelation and bracket the biblical commandments, practical and spiritual, hold Scripture obsolete, primitive, or unscientific? Or should they turn science inside out, as the Mutakallimūn had done, rejecting nature for religion's sake? Should they compartmentalize, relegating the biblical narrative, fondly perhaps, to the realm of myth; observe the old prescriptions as traditions, clutched nostalgically, since they help bind the community together, even if they are fundamentally incomprehensible; hold piety apart from science, inviolable but ultimately irrelevant, a thing of exotic beauty, perhaps, yet always somehow suspect?

No educated and intellectually honest person in Maimonides' day, as in ours, could scrub the intellectual authority and practical effectiveness of science. But religion, to most thoughtful people, then as now, meant far more than tradition and community. It meant far more than "faith" kept apart for special use but not to be touched intellectually on a daily basis. Religion, for many, in Maimonides' day, as it is for many in our own, was the chief source of meaning and repository of value. Without it, one faced not just anomie—seen aplenty today—but emptiness. Atheism was nihilism, and bracketing Scripture was the gateway to atheism.

The crisis was acute in Maimonides' time, like its counterpart today, with Darwin drafted as the poster child of denial. Aristotelians, owners of the most cogent system of reasoning and science known in Maimonides' day, called creation demonstrably untrue. Muslims, whose hands held both the sword of state and the purse of high office, denied that Moses was God's consummate prophet. Christians had long dismissed Jewish ritual laws as onerous and otiose.[9] Biblical miracles, to the scientifically informed, seemed arbitrary and unaccountable disruptions of the natural order.

So the seas were no less choppy then than now. Nature is where we live, even if heaven funds our inspiration and illuminates our hopes. But it is at the interface of heaven and earth that Maimonides finds the questions that give pause to a religious reader who has studied the sciences and philosophy. Philosophers working in the Greek tradition and their followers and commentators—Muslims,

Christians, and Jews among them—revere the argument, clarity, and rigor that are the pride of philosophy. But could loyal Jews find confidence and comfort in the ideas and practices of the Torah or the vast corpus the Rabbis built up to elucidate its teachings and protect its prescriptions? The religiously committed but well-educated reader in Maimonides' day faced a species of diglossia not unfamiliar now, and the challenge, then as now, had to be faced if the pious did not mean simply to stop up the ears and blindfold the eyes of the brightest and most dedicated among them—or leave them disaffected and confused.

Most rabbinical scholars seemed ill prepared to meet the challenges of central philosophical concern to Maimonides: "If you told one of the self-professed sages of Israel that God sends an angel that enters a woman's womb and forms the fetus there, he would be awestruck and take it as a mark of God's greatness and power—and wisdom—although convinced that an angel is a body of raging fire one-third the size of the entire world" (2.17a). Innocent of both science and poetry, how were such rabbis to see, let alone explain, that 'angel' figuratively names the powers by which God regulates nature's course?

Wouldn't it be irresponsible, given the unpreparedness of so many, to bypass the Talmud's warnings and confront readers with problems they were ill equipped to handle? Maimonides' frequent cautions about the dangers of haste (1.9a, 13b; 3.31a, 40ab, 135a) reflect his sensitivity to the risks. Ghazālī, a century back, had faced like problems and knew the challenges from personal experience. He himself had gone through a skeptical crisis. For he was not one, he wrote, to embrace blind faith. Critical review of the spiritual and intellectual options had shown him where he must lodge his trust. But the glass of faith, once broken, he wrote, could not be patched up or pasted back together. It had to be melted down and formed anew. In seeking to guide others past naïveté and toward what he saw as deeper truths, he had written more than one book labeled esoteric. One work ascribed to him, filled with Neoplatonic readings of Islamic thoughts, bears the title *K. al-Maḍnūn al-Ṣaghīr* (or more fully, The Little Book to be Kept from those Unsuited to It). But such a title naturally seemed more a banner than a barrier.

Maimonides saw the hazards of the Pardes. But there was treasure too, rare and precious, even necessary, or the Torah would not have broached these topics—as it did, so prominently. Clearly, a strategy was needed, a way of screening the readership to ensure that the *Guide* helped those who needed help without endangering the naive, safely aiding the adept toward critical appropriation of the Torah's deeper thoughts, helping them see for themselves (for, as the Rabbis saw, this is not something one can do for someone else) and discover how to integrate their religion with what they knew of science and philosophy. As Maimonides wrote, citing the Sages, "You can bring up pearls from the seabed if you know how to swim—but if not, you'll drown" (1.37b). He had found a way to bind himself to the mast and hear the Siren song of philosophy without capsizing or crashing on the rocks. Now in the *Guide*, beyond that private joy, he must find ways of introducing to others the song he had heard, if they could master it and not be mastered by it. His strategy for winnowing serious readers from dilettantes, dabblers, and dogmatists began in his use of the *risālah* form for the *Guide*.

Rasā'il

Thematically organized writing does not come naturally. It must be learned. We can see that in the rambling, associative prose of Cato, who bares his Roman teeth by resisting Greek thematic structuring of his thoughts. We see it, too, in the digressive, associative, repetitious linkages of the Talmud, with its fictive exchanges between named and unnamed interlocutors, treating men who lived generations apart as though they were debating in the same room. It was by reading Greek works in translation that Arabic authors learned to cut their discourse at the joints and marshal their thoughts using Plato's analytic and synthetic toolbox (*Phaedrus* 265d–66b). The methods they learned are silhouetted in the plan of many an Arabic work—and not least in Maimonides' Code, written in mishnaic Hebrew, its sharply delineated structure marked and celebrated graphically by Renaissance calligraphers in the illuminated manuscripts of its fourteen volumes. Why, then, did Maimonides, a master of thematic organization, compose his major philosophical work in a far more informal mode? We can see the beginnings of an answer in the intimacy of the essay form.

As Menachem Kellner likes to tell his students, "*MT* is a work largely of Jewish content (Halakhah) written in a Greek mode. The *Guide* is a work of philosophic content written in a midrashic mode." What is midrashic in the *Guide* is its informal structure and its conversational tone. Yet the conversation here is no dialogue overheard among the ancient Sages but Maimonides' engagement, as if face to face, with his reader in the kind of one-on-one colloquy that the ancient rabbis picture when they warn against public broadcast of the mysteries of *Maʿaseh Bereshit* and *Maʿaseh Merkavah*. The vehicle Maimonides finds for that guiding but never merely directive exchange is the *risālah* form.

Poetry was the lifeblood of Arabic literature before the coming of Islam. The assonance, rhymes, and rhythms of pre-Islamic poetry, like its sense of drama and its earthy images, reecho in the rhymed prose, ecstatic oaths, and monitory tales of the Qurʾān. But learning that clarity means more than sonority of sound and vividness of image brought Arabic writing to its maturity. In the young Islamic Empire, the new class of administrators, secretaries—*kuttāb*, as they were called, literally writers—created a prose literature at home in the familiar form of a report or letter (*risālah*, pl. *rasāʾil*). In Arabic, as in the surviving writings of Epicurus in Greek or of Pliny and Seneca in Latin, letters morphed into essays. Variable in length and topic, the Arabic essay was more intimate than a sermon and less formally structured than a treatise. A *risālah* can be more modest and more useful than more systematic works. The genre appealed to Maimonides for the *Guide*, in good part because it let him shape the work to the reader's anticipated needs.

Kindī in the ninth century wrote many a philosophical *risālah*. In one, "On How to Banish Sorrow," his notional addressee (and dedicatee) has asked him, as a philosophically informed physician, for help in dealing with anxiety and grief. Kindī offers a variety of strategies, drawing on the *consolatio* literature of Greek antiquity: One must loosen one's worldly attachments and seek more lasting, intellectual objects. Worldly things, he argues in a Platonizing mode, are elusive and will be lost in the end (3.133a). Ideas are the real treasure. Readily won, they cannot be lost but indeed will bring the immortality that is the mind's true goal, shelter, and respite in the world that is our true home.

The Ikhwān al-Ṣafāʾ, or Sincere Brethren of Basra (tenth century), jointly wrote an encyclopedic body of fifty-two *rasāʾil* on the sciences (including mathematics), philosophy, and religion. Aiming to be both edifying and entertaining, the essays repeatedly address the reader, warmly urging him to join the authors in their spiritual quest. One of the suite is fictional rather than expository. The authors had decided, when it came to the animal kingdom, to emulate the classic Sanskrit fables of the *Panchatantra*, which they knew in translation, and (for the first time in Arabic) give the animals full speaking parts. Their Aesopian fable, *The Case of the Animals vs. Man*, like others of their *rasā'il*, is well known to Maimonides and echoed in the *Guide.*

Ghazālī had also used the *risālah* form, welcome to him for its openings to intimate, hortatory address. And Ibn Ṭufayl clearly valued it for letting him define what he saw as his reader's needs and escape the seeming immodesty of publishing his thoughts on delicate topics like creation and the beatific experience. He sets out his agenda in letter form before commencing his philosophical tale; and once his story has reached its climax, he engages both his reader and an imagined critic in fictive dialogue, addressing questions that he thinks deserve an answer.[10] Maimonides, too, will embed miniature dialogues in the *Guide* (e.g., at 2.40b–41a) and will frequently speak to his reader's background, capabilities, and presumptive needs. Addressing him toward the end of the *Guide*, he warmly calls him "son," offering fatherly advice and hoping he will attain the spiritual/intellectual fulfillment that awaits one at the summit of the pathway the *Guide* has marked out (3.124a).

Intimacy is a particular advantage of the *risālah* form, building a rapport between author and reader. In a way, that rapport meets one of the central concerns that Plato felt so keenly about written work as distinguished from living conversation. No text will have the spontaneity and immediacy of the spoken word. But by prequalifying his reader and identifying that reader's needs and the questions and quandaries he is expected to confront, Maimonides is able, in the *Guide*, to replicate much of the appositeness that conversation or a personal tutorial would be able to accomplish. So it is not surprising that the *Guide* makes use of the strengths afforded by the *risālah* form—frequent address to the needs, questions, and expectations of the reader, along with advice and encouragement. The conversational tone and fluid style of the work are enlivened with occasional anecdotes, personal reflections, appraisals, insights, and asides.[11] The salutation at the outset opens a letter dedicatory. The tone is personal, although Maimonides knows that the *Guide* will be published in manuscript and handled by many unknown readers (1.4, 9a). His warm praises of the addressee, common in a dedication, prequalify that broader readership. But behind this tactful listing of prerequisites and the later, more directive, stress on the need for time, discipline, and dedication to master the necessary subjects and methods stands the Rambam's striking contrast of dedicated inquiry with dilettantish Bible reading. The reader he hopes to address and expects to profit most from the *Guide* is motivated to learn and listen, having wondered about how to square serious religious commitments with scientific and philosophical engagement—a far cry from the dilettantish curiosity of a lazy and passive mind always ready to find more pressing concerns than the pursuit of ultimates (1.38ab). So Maimonides' focus in the opening pages of the *Guide* is on the tensions he expects to trap and trouble a serious reader's mind (1.6a). His goal is to release one from the traps and troubles that such a reader will inevitably confront. That goal is what sets the *Guide*'s agenda: to render reason and tradition (*ʿaql* and *naql*) allies rather than foes, despite their jostling commitments.

SEVEN

Problematics

A few examples might illustrate how Maimonides uses the informal structure of the *Guide* to open up his thinking to a reader suitably prepared while leaving others neither more nor less in the dark than they were when they ventured into these waters. One example involves the so-called lexicon of scriptural anthropomorphisms so prominent in Part I of the *Guide*. Another comes in a digression that interrupts that survey of biblical terms almost before it has begun, offering a bold and insightful reading of the story of Adam and Eve. In both cases, Maimonides sorts the ready from the unready by declining to state the problem addressed. The measure of his success lies in the widespread failure of many readers, even specialists, to name the problem he means to deal with in his "lexicon." We see this method at work again in his treatment of the far more readily identified problem of evil. Perhaps the Rambam feels he has shaken casual and dilettantish readers before the *Guide* has reached questions about prophecy and revelation in Part II, or the problem of evil, or those of divine knowledge and providence, or the warrants for the biblical commandments in Part III. But there is a subtle example of his use of understatement in his reflections on the logic and metaphysics of possibility and necessity first introduced in his engagement with kalām cosmology in Part I. Let's consider that example first.

Modalities

Study of kalām left a bitter taste in Maimonides' mouth, quite beyond the prolixity of kalām authors and the diatribes that often marred their work. Still, as the Sages taught, the wise can learn from everyone. From his encounter with kalām, Maimonides preserved three things: (1) His analysis of kalām occasionalism highlighted the centrality (and interdependence) of natural causation, human agency, scientific understanding, and practical effort in our private and public lives and in the arts and professions, ranging from weaving and ironwork to agriculture and animal husbandry, the building trades, the design of machinery, the making of needles—and his own work in medicine (1.61b, 62b, 107b; 3.40a, 43b; Eight Chapters 5).

(2) A kindred treasure lay in the realm of epistemology. Of the many weaknesses Maimonides found in the methods of the Mutakallimūn, beyond their penchant for theological wishful thinking, was their reliance on the imagination to trace the parameters of possibility: They thought anything imaginable was possible (I 73, Premise 10, 1.112b–116a; cf. 121a, 122a). That premise (and their calling the senses unreliable) licensed their erasure of nature, opening up the realm of possibility to bizarre fantasies like the notion that thought does not require life. But partly with the help of kalām thinking, Maimonides saw a complementary weakness in the views of the Philosophers: Their essentialism pressed them toward making all necessities necessities of logic, since things must be what they are and must behave and function as their essences require.

The same motives that led Maimonides to reach out to save nature (including human nature) from reduction to an occasionalist puppet show prompted him to salvage, with the help of the kalām, the recognition that not all necessities are formal necessities. Fārābī and Avicenna helped here: Fārābī by showing that no event is rendered necessary merely by the fact that it takes place—or by the truth that it will; and Avicenna by a related insight, his critical distinction of what is necessary in itself from what is made necessary by its causes. Even so, in the philosophies of both men, essentialism posed a formidable threat to divine and human freedom. For if things must be as they are, how is it possible for anything to change? If all is determined by the essences of things, how are human freedom and agency possible? And how is even creation not a matter of necessity? That last outcome may be a desideratum for eternalists, but even for them, it may seem to vitiate the very idea of God's creative act if, in the end, it makes that act as much a necessity as the truth of the Pythagorean theorem.

Reason, not imagination, Maimonides urged, must be the judge of what is possible or impossible, *pace* the Kalām. But reason gives wide scope to possibilities; not all are realized. Kalām arguments showed vividly (*pace* the Philosophers) that not all necessities are logical necessities. That thought helped Maimonides curb the logicism of the Philosophers. Granted, the imagination is too fallible and protean to provide a reliable test of possibility and the other modalities of necessity and impossibility. But the kalām challenge to essentialism, further advanced by Ghazālī, showed clearly that not all impossibilities are formal contradictions. Where occasionalism had abolished nature, Maimonides could restore it—by advancing the idea of natural necessities, ordained by God and woven into nature's fabric but not inherent in the laws of logic.

Natural causes, Maimonides reasoned, can bring about effects that are neither logically inevitable nor arbitrary expressions of divine caprice. Causal agents, including human agents, moved by their natures or desires, can act in the realm of nature. By opening a space between logical and natural necessity, moreover, Maimonides can conceive of creation as God's free act, not a mere implication of God's wisdom. Things might have been made differently than they were. Divine and human agency have scope to act and choose. Nature, as ordained by God, harbors necessities and possibilities of its own. To Maimonides, as to Ghazālī, that means miracles are possible. Natures can change, as Maimonides reasons they must have done while the world was aborning. And we human beings can initiate actions that do not just play out the natures we are given (II 17, 19–20). That leaves room in the natural world for the relevance of moral norms and imperatives, warnings, precautions, preparations, and even repentance.

Natural necessities distinct from necessities of logic subsist in the vital modal space that Maimonides' version of naturalism opens up. It is in this space that natural beings express, develop, and fulfill their identities and characters. The Mutakallimūn had not seen the need. But this realm of nature, distinct from the realm of logical necessity, is the site of all events known to our daily experience. It is here that we find the theater of human freedom and creativity. Kalām thoughts goaded Maimonides to build in that ground, once it was cleared of the ruins of kalām deference to the imagination, much as medieval builders built new structures by a creative bricolage, using the stones and columns of ruined palaces.

(3) Maimonides plants his pennant philosophically in another modal issue, again by hybridizing what he learned from the Philosophers with what he learned from the Kalām: Ghazālī had taught that the consummate monotheist sees God in all things. Now Maimonides knew well that God is not the only being, any more than He is the only cause. But the Rambam can appropriate Ghazālī's monistic flavored thought without succumbing to a stifling acosmism that would belie the very idea of creation that the Mutakallimūn had labored so boldly to protect. Again, he turns for help to Avicenna: If we want to say that God alone is real, what that must mean, Maimonides reasons, is that only in the Necessary Being is being absolute. Only in God is essence identical with existence. All contingent beings derive their share in reality from God (1.69a), as Maimonides had stressed at the start of his *MT.* He headlines the point in making Abraham's invocation of the universal God the epigram of each of the three parts of the *Guide*. In keeping with that thought, Maimonides sees the Tetragrammaton (coded into the opening words of the *MT*) as God's truest name. For rather than rely on some derivative epithet like 'King,' or 'Lord,' or even the generic term 'God,' the Tetragrammaton signifies God's absoluteness as the Necessary Being (I 63)—and so the Author of all those beings whose essence is not their existence.

That core idea that God is a being of a different order holds true to Plato's marking off the boundary, permeable by divine generosity, between Being and becoming. And it puts an Aristotelian spin on Ghazālī's saying that the truest monotheist sees God in all things. For as Maimonides studies the world through the lens of natural science, he can say in tones at once scientific and celebratory that the more we know of nature, the more we see of God in the active expression of His wisdom and grace. Finite beings share in the reality and the powers that God gives them. But in God alone is being absolute.

Maimonides' patient, if testy, exposition of kalām cosmology reveals how occasionalism, by dissolving and discarding natural causality (and even the substantial forms that give material things their stable character), sacrifices the sciences and practical arts, medicine included, on the altar of a God fancied to be the sole actor in the universe. Keen to defend the act of creation, kalām occasionalists had pressed an idea of constant creation that made every event

God's immediate act, erasing natural causality in general and voluntary action specifically,[1] dissolving nature and turning experience into a shimmering tapestry of illusion. Maimonides' alternative: to accept the risk of following where argument and experience lead. Intellectual honesty is at stake, but so is trust in God as the guarantor of truth and of human reason as our avenue to truth—so long as reason is rightly understood and wisely and patiently used. The Mutakallimūn had built a world around their theological agenda. But ironically, in the process, they had neutered the very deity they meant to serve. For dissolving nature voids God's grace as the Creator who gave things not only their being but their powers to act—and human beings, specifically, our powers to choose.

Even so, kalām argumentation glints with another treasure to be salvaged from the wreck of the kalām vessel, the so-called argument from determination, most familiar to us in the Principle of Sufficient Reason: If a thing exists that need not have existed, something must have determined its existence over nonexistence (1.120b–121a).[2] The argument is scriptural at root, harking back to the reasoning implicit in the biblical account of creation. So Maimonides can rightly claim it as lost property, husbanded by the Mutakallimūn—not materially advanced over what is left unstated in Genesis but made explicit and opened up to generalization.

Maimonides had found inadequate the use of the principle as deployed by the Kalām. But he bolsters and refurbishes the reasoning with thoughts gleaned from Avicenna's exclusion of an infinite regress of causes: All causality will then indeed lead back to a Self-sufficing Source. For Maimonides, this First Cause is no mere Prime Mover, as it was for strict Aristotelians like Averroes. Rather, it is an ultimate Cause in every sense, the Source of purpose, of form—being itself—and the Goal of all activity. For the form imparted to things from above is, in a Neoplatonic world, the essence that gives a being its purpose and efficacy (I 69 and 2.3b–4a, Premises 19 and 20), the power to act and pursue a goal. All these powers are gifts of God. So is even the matter of things, the otherness that permits natural beings to exist in their own right apart from God. God need no longer be the Creator that somehow magically conjures things into existence and acts upon them only from without. For emanation is the source of the essences of things, and by giving natural beings their natures, God gave them all their powers to act for themselves and for one another.

Jacob's Ladder

Maimonides works obliquely but early on to introduce the hierarchy that is the subtext in his "lexicon" of biblical anthropomorphisms. This, by quoting the account of Jacob's dream of a ladder to the heavens (Genesis 28:12–17), contrasting it with lines from Proverbs warning against the wiles of a married harlot (7:1, 6–21). He reads both passages as symbolically freighted. But many of the particulars in Proverbs 7 he sees as literary embellishments, corroborative detail not meant to symbolize anything, whereas every element in the account of Jacob's dream bears symbolic weight (1.7b–8a). The two passages are quoted as if merely to contrast two modes of exegesis, matched to two modes of scriptural poetics—one fine grained, the other broader in its use of the imagination. But we are cautioned at the outset that nothing in the *Guide* is casual: "For the argument of the work is not laid out randomly but carefully and exactingly so as to omit no issue that needs clearing up. Nothing is out of place unless to shed light elsewhere" (1.8b).

We'll see no sharper instance of indirection in the *Guide* than when the "lexicon" camouflages the problem to be wrestled with by the simple expedient of leaving the issue addressed unstated and unnamed. To many a reader, the survey of biblical terms applied to God that fills much of the work's first seventy chapters seems little more than an extended "refutation" of anthropomorphism. Calling Maimonides "the foremost opponent of anthropomorphism in the Jewish tradition," Yair Lorberbaum writes,

> Most of his *Guide of the Perplexed*, along with large portions of his other writings, was devoted to developing and refining arguments and exegetical devices to be used for removing any anthropomorphism from the Bible and from Midrashic and Talmudic literature.[3]

But was Maimonides' purpose in the *Guide*—and in the "lexicon" in particular—"removing" anthropomorphism? If so, where is the argument? These early chapters do not argue that anthropomorphism is false but assume that it is. We can see why Maimonides prequalifies his reader at the outset (1.3a) as a committed Jew with some exposure to philosophy—and why he returns to that point as the "lexicon" draws to a close (1.89a). Only a tyro would fail to notice that no argument is offered against anthropomorphism in the early chapters of the *Guide*. A philosopher would not miss the difference between what is argued and what is assumed and would be awaiting the argument, on the lookout for the real thrust of whatever point is subtended by the lexicon itself, since the analysis of the terms singled out is driven by the assumption that anthropomorphism is false. We get a hint of Maimonides' true quarry when we confront his stunning claim that *all* predicates are inapplicable to God, since God *has* no proper attributes, a thesis broader and far more radical than rejection of anthropomorphism or corporealism (see 1.42a, 51a, 54a, I 50–54).

Maimonides shares his distaste for anthropomorphism with the same outlook evident in the classic Aramaic rendering of the Torah ascribed to Onkelos, known as the Proselyte. The actual author of this Targum may well have lived in the fourth/fifth century, but the historic Onkelos flourished in the early second century and was linked to Rabbi Akiva's disciples. The Targum circulated under Onkelos' name held near canonical status, and Maimonides deeply respects its periphrastic renderings of biblical anthropomorphisms. Widely used in the synagogue and in domestic study, it retains its ancient authority down to the present day. So Maimonides hardly needed an extended survey of biblical anthropomorphisms to privilege a deanthropomorphizing reading of Scripture. That was well established in "Onkelos" and in the Targum ascribed to Jonathan ben Uzziel, which he also quotes. The naive and undiscerning, he urges, have no excuse for not following sound thinkers and the patterns of reading established by such works as theirs (1.44ab).

But a translation, be it ever so hermeneutical, left little room for a translator to step aside in midcourse to explain his reasoning. Addressing an especially challenging passage, the verse in Exodus (24:10) that seems to speak of something as *clear as sapphire* seen *under the feet* of God, Maimonides commends Onkelos for avoiding the suggestion that the Torah assigns feet to God. The feet, as Onkelos read the verse, belonged to a throne seen by the elders—and it was not *God's* throne at all. Maimonides recalls to his reader the scene as rendered in the Aramaic:

> Onkelos, as you know, took the feet to be those of the throne and renders the phrase "under the throne of His Glory." You can see and admire how far he kept from corporealism or anything even remotely suggesting it. He does not say "under His throne." For treating the throne as God's and taking "throne"

> in its base sense would imply God's sitting on it, entailing His corporeality. So he makes it the throne of God's Glory, the Shekhinah, a created light. (I 28)

But after commending Onkelos' handling of the text, Maimonides adds,

> You have seen Onkelos' gloss. But that is as far as it goes. He excludes anthropomorphism but does not enlighten us about what the elders perceived or what it symbolized. That is what he does consistently. He does not explain a passage but simply bars anthropomorphism, since God's incorporeality is demonstrable and critical to belief. Sure of this, he translated accordingly. But symbols are contentious. They might mean this or that. It can be very obscure, and understanding these symbols is not critical to the faith, nor are they readily grasped by the masses. So he does not broach the subject. But in keeping with this work's purpose, I do need to offer a gloss. (1.31ab)

The finding (or making) of meanings is Maimonides' meat and much to the purpose in the *Guide*. But some body of assumptions is needed to construe or construct meanings. The meaning Maimonides finds for the biblical reference to a sapphire-like surface seen by the elders (the "pavement," as the term is often rendered today) reflects the Greco-Arabic hybrid of science and philosophy that Maimonides brings to his task—the cosmology of the spheres that, with all its flaws, was the most advanced available to him. He admits that the scheme is conjectural (2.50a) and is well aware of its limitations. But he does find it vitally useful.

Prophets, he explains, find themselves compelled to speak about their experience and can speak only in human language: Inevitably, they turn to poetry, boldly but obliquely reaching with their words for the Transcendent (1.52b–53a). Their images are bubbles, tropes that deconstruct when tested against one another. Yet a prophet's words, even as they betray their own inadequacy, point beyond themselves toward what no visionary has seen and what language cannot capture: Their very obliquity bespeaks transcendence.

Teaching us to read biblical prophecy as inspired poetry, Maimonides argues that the Sages, too, read it as such and freely followed, adopting and adapting biblical imagery (1.51a–53a). The Torah's images, he finds, point to a being whose absoluteness leaves all humans speechless: "With God, the more you negate, the closer you come" (1.72b). That sounds risky. Is the outcome emptiness? Years before he wrote the *Guide*, Maimonides called it our highest goal to know God (Eight Chapters 5). He still proclaims that goal as the *Guide* approaches its climax (2.79a and III 51). But has he declared God unknowable? God Himself said that His face cannot be seen. Has Maimonides left his reader marooned on an island of apophasis with nothing to sustain him but an austere agnosticism or worse? Franz Rosenzweig clearly thought so. Negative theology, he wrote,

> dismembered and abolished the existing assertions about God's "attributes," until the negative of all these attributes remained behind as God's essence. Thus God could be defined only by his complete indefinability. This path leads from Aught to Nought; at its end atheism and mysticism can shake hands.[4]

It might not be terrible if atheism and mysticism did learn to shake hands. But it's hardly clear that Maimonides' denial of divine attributes presages a deeper denial. Wolfson, as Daniel Davies points out, offers ample evidence that Maimonides' negative theology points to God's perfection.[5] That, after all, was its goal, clearly stated by the Rambam himself. As A. H. Armstrong wrote in reflecting on the enduring worth of Plotinus, whose metaphysics was a key source for Maimonides, "The only form of the 'negative theology' which seems to be of permanent value is that which I have called the 'negative theology of positive transcendence,' the 'analogical method.'"[6]

Maimonides does avoid talk of God's essence.[7] That is critical in what he means to teach: that God has no essence distinct from His existence. The Identity of a necessary being cannot be parsed or parted. That is part of what it means to call God undefinable and say that He acts, but not by "faculties" or "powers" (1.52a). It is part of what it means to say that God, in the strongest sense, is one. Maimonides holds that God's every act is an expression of Himself. God's life and knowledge, creativity, will, and wisdom are no different from Himself. Were God divisible, even conceptually, he argues, He would be a contingent being, like the objects of His creation, and there would be no contradiction in denying His reality, as there is none in denying that of any finite thing.

The worry about negative theology is hardly new. It was voiced by Gersonides and Thomas and anticipated by Ghazālī, who compared the press toward transcendence to peeling an onion and finding only emptiness within. Yet as

Ghazālī and the rest well knew, once one tastes the idea of God's absoluteness, it grows hard to speak of God in ordinary terms. Qualities only qualify. That fact attests to the boldness of prophetic poesy. In showing how the prophets of Israel faced this difficulty, Maimonides teaches us how to read them and understand how their anthropomorphisms point higher. Here we glimpse the purpose of the "lexicon": It prepares us for the apophasis to come, when Maimonides will argue not just for God's incorporeality but for the larger thesis, of which incorporeality is a corollary or special case: the impropriety of attribute language altogether.

The lexicon does its work in addressing the worry that negative theology leaves nothing to be said of God: It shows how biblical anthropomorphisms point beyond themselves and allows a sophisticated reader to learn from the Torah the direction in which God's reality is rightly sought. It also illustrates what Maimonides means in telling his disciple to read the chapters of the *Guide* against one another (1.8b). For it reveals that the early mention of Jacob's ladder was not casually chosen—and that we have not really read the *Guide* until we've read it more than once. For the antidote to apophasis lies in the lexicon's subtext.

The lexicon opens with the words *tzelem* and *demut*, 'image' and 'likeness'—fraught terms, since the Torah affirms that mankind was made in God's image and likeness. Using Saadiah's lexicographic method to resolve biblical imagery, Maimonides surveys the canon for passages allowing or excluding the senses of each term targeted. Thus, in the *Guide*'s first chapter, he cites a verse in the Psalms (102:7) where the psalmist likens himself to *a pelican in the desert*: "Not that he has wings and feathers like a pelican, but that he is as desolate" (1.12b–13a). Clearly *likeness*, then, can have a sense beyond physical resemblance. *Tavnit*, Maimonides argues (I 3), connotes structure. So it's never biblically applied to God. But *temunah* has three senses: one physical, one nested in the imagination, and one conceptual. It's that third sense that is applied to God (at Numbers 12:8): Moses saw no picture but attained true, conceptual knowledge of God (1.15a).

Similarly with seeing and beholding: Maimonides distinguishes a sensory from an intellectual sense. Kohelet says that his heart *hath seen much wisdom* (Ecclesiastes 1:16). Some seeing, then, would be conceptual; wisdom is not seen visually. Place, we learn (I 8), can mean location. But it can also mean rank or status—including ontic status. So when we read *Blessed be the glory of the Lord from His place* (Ezekiel 3:12), we need not take the words spatially but as alluding to God's "exalted standing in the order of being." Maimonides carefully notes that he has not yet argued for God's unique ontic standing (1.18b). Exegetically, it suffices to note that *place* can mean rank. Literally, the Hebrew word *makom* means standing. To elucidate just what such terms can mean in God's case is the real function of the "lexicon."

Throne is a key word in the *Guide*, given the prominence of the throne beheld in Ezekiel's vision. A throne symbolized majesty, and a throne's stability symbolizes the legitimacy of a monarch's rule (I 9, cf. 1.90ab). We have not yet heard it argued that God has no body and so needs no chair. But Maimonides can promise that such an argument will come. For now, he suggests that just as the Temple stands for God's majesty, the heavens can be called His throne. For the heavens bespeak God's reality and betoken His majesty and power, their exaltation and stability emblematic of His sovereignty. Just as the stability of a monarch's throne bespeaks the justice that anchors his claim to legitimacy, the image of God's throne is emblematic of His justice, which Maimonides says is inseparable from God Himself (1.19a; 3.35a, 130a).

We begin to see a trend here. Biblical mention of rising or falling can refer to rank and status, not just to spatial position (I 10). Sitting can have a physical sense, but it can also indicate stability in social or political terms—or in a higher sense (I 11). *Standing* may be a matter of posture, but it can also signify completion or permanence (I 13). *Rising* and related words (I 12–13, 15) have not only spatial but social and ontic senses. And these terms turn us back to thoughts of Jacob's ladder (1.22ab).

God is called a rock biblically. But this rock is also called the Author of creation. So it's pretty clear that 'rock' need not always refer to an inert object (I 16). As applied to Abraham, 'rock' takes the sense of 'source' (Isaiah 51:1), and when applied to God, the reference is plainly not to anything lifeless or inert. That is why God can be called *the Rock whose work is perfect* (Deuteronomy 32:4) or *the rock that begat thee* (32:18). The Torah itself enriches the semantic reach of the word, making it mean something dynamic and creative, although unseen. The metaphor here both empties itself and yields meanings that point beyond what we might see as the base sense.[8]

Language about nearing or touching (I 18) once again proves to have moral, social, and intellectual/spiritual senses, as shown in passages that clearly exclude a physical sense. Talk of filling (I 19) similarly reaches beyond the physical base sense of such terms. Likewise *high*, *come*, and *go* (I 20, 21, 22). Motion is not what's implied when we say, 'Night came.' And *dwell* (I 25), as used in the Torah, bears metaphorical as well as spatial senses. For when Job curses the day he was born, he says, *darkness dwell upon it* (3:5). Here dwelling is notional, not physical.

Opening up the pattern of prophetic poesy captured in the rabbinic dictum that he takes as a general rule, that "Torah speaks in human language,"[9] Maimonides invites an inductive inference:

> That means that what applies to God is whatever people in general can absorb and conceive of without reflection. So He is described in physical terms to signify that He exists. For to the masses, at first blush, only bodies exist. What is not a body, or of a body, to them is not real. Similarly, anything we take to be a perfection is ascribed to Him, so as to indicate His supreme and absolute perfection, unmarred by any defect; and nothing popularly thought a lack or defect is ascribed to Him: He is not said to eat, drink, sleep, fall ill, do wrong, or anything of the sort. But whatever the masses consider a perfection is ascribed to Him, even if it is such only in us. For in Him our supposed perfections would be utter defects. (1.29a)

Analyzing the language biblically applied to God and discounting the surface sense of the imagery called for by the Torah's need to use human language, Maimonides has plotted points that orient an axis, ontological and axiological. Language anchored in the physical world affords a prophet the only terms available in addressing his fellow human beings. Biblical usages are skewed by the need to accommodate human notions of perfection—that is, of what counts as real and good. But in the range of senses that Maimonides finds in the terms applied to God biblically, calibrating levels of value or reality, God can always be sought at the upper extreme.

Like Plato, Maimonides sees a hierarchy, ontic and axiological, with the phases of awareness matching the rungs of reality and value. None of this should seem surprising: Where Plato finds that what is most good must be real, the Torah teaches that what is most real must be good. The congruence of being and value guides Maimonides in ranking the senses of biblical anthropomorphisms: They rise from the physical to the realm of images in human fancy, to the social and moral, and on to the conceptual. We can track their course, and piety demands that any language applied to God in the Torah must be taken in the highest of the senses charted: ideal rather than physical.

The work of the lexicon, then, is to mark the direction in which divinity is to be sought. Maimonides sees a system in the Torah's imagery. And behind that system, as the biblical metaphors interact and deconstruct one another, the ontological/axiological hierarchy shines through: God's perfection is absolute; human perfections, relative—sorely lacking beside God's, in whom they would be mere imperfections, eclipsed by His infinite perfection. For the complexity demanded by our embodiment binds our every attainment to concomitant imperfections. Once we see this, knowledge and love, working in tandem, can trace an upward path. For knowledge, as such, is of truth, and love can find no higher object than God, who is truth and perfection Itself.

Sophisticated readers may sense a tension between Maimonides' speaking of God in intellectual terms and his speaking of God as an absolute beyond our grasp. But here we see a key to that conundrum: The rise from the physical to the ideal orients us toward God's perfection. But if, as Plotinus held, there is anything more perfect than Intelligence, it is there that God must be sought. The Matter/Form axis orients us. But if there are higher reaches, that is where God lives and acts. Whatever we learn that presses our idea of God yet higher toward transcendence, Maimonides urges, points to the heights of Truth itself (I 53, 57, 59.). So the tension dissolves between talk of God in intellectual terms and talk of God in terms of the pure transcendence honored by negative theology. Wolfson, then, is not just projecting onto Maimonides his own deep study of Spinoza when he speaks of God's infinite perfections. For whatever perfections are real, God must possess them. That, *pace* Rosenzweig, is what negative theology teaches. And Spinoza understood Maimonides here more deeply than did his, or Maimonides', critics.

The best name for the axis the lexicon plots, the dimension metaphorically named by talk of 'up' or 'down,' is perfection, denoting both reality and value on the biblical (and Platonic) assumption that the two not only go hand in hand but are identical: Being is good (3.17a, 19a). Here is the key to Maimonides' thesis that evil is no real thing but is sheer or relative lack (3.45a, 46a). And here is the Maimonidean key to ethics. For where God's perfection is absolute, our goal is vested in our humanity: We seek perfection in ourselves as human beings and (since each human being, like God, is unique) in our individuality. Here, too, lies the epistemic key to our welfare and to realizing the intellectual affinity that links us to God. For knowledge traces and tracks the pathway of perfection.

Jacob's ladder is the symbol of the ontic/axiological hierarchy for Maimonides.[10] Like Plato's Divided Line in the *Republic* (VI 508b–11e), its footings are in this world, but it leads toward higher rungs of reality, goodness, and truth, its Summit surmounted by God's ultimate Reality. The same ladder matches the Ladder of Love in Plato's *Symposium* (209–11). For the human intellect is seated here on earth, but its gaze is upward. Reality and perfection, once glimpsed, evoke love and provoke the climb toward the summit that God's perfection invites and commands (Deuteronomy 6:5).

The intellectual/spiritual aspiration of our love powers our climbing the ladder of human perfections in pursuit of the goodness, beauty, joy, truth, holiness, and reality that fuse in God. Lives spent in that pursuit do, in a way, already attain its goal. Hence Maimonides' thesis that no harm befalls those who commune with God (I 23–24, III 17–18). The claim, as I read it, is not the naive or superstitious notion that pain and suffering cannot touch the innocent. Maimonides knows all too well, as we all do, that such claims are false, if harm and suffering are seen in worldly terms. But real harm, for him, is loss of our link with God. Physical goods and ills are real enough in their way. But theirs is not the coin in which true worth is weighed (III 12, cf. I 30). The view is classic and lies at the heart of the Socratic philosophy propounded by Plato. For Maimonides too, cultivation of the mind is the supreme human duty, since it is reason that links us to God, making cultivation of the mind our highest calling, a calling, indeed, enjoined by God. It is in those terms, I believe, that one must understand Maimonides' thesis that the wise cannot be harmed—and the moral corollary that Plato drew from his Socratic version of that idea, that it is better to suffer evils than to commit them (*Apology* 30cd).

Fact and Value

Scarcely has Maimonides begun his review of biblical anthropomorphisms than he uses the informality of the *risālah* form to interrupt his survey of terms to tell of an objection he once heard from a "sophisticated man" to the story of Adam and Eve (I 2). The vehemence of his response shows how captious he found the cavil he reports. But it also exposes a deeper issue, introduced as if in an aside but hardly extraneous to the work of the *Guide*. The Torah, he cautions, was not given to be a sounding board for just any thoughts that may cross one's mind and seem clever at the time. And the seeming digression about the tale of the loss of Eden introduces another point critical to touch on at the outset: Part of what we learn when we read the Torah seriously is that the mitzvot are not arbitrary impositions. The moral imperatives discernible through the fine fabric of the mitzvot bespeak objective values that reason can discern.

Reason, we've just been told in chapter 1, is God's image in us. So it seems natural enough to segue to the story of Adam and Eve. But were the *Guide* laid out in geometrical form, the thesis of its second chapter would be a scholium: If human reason is God's image, what can we say of our judgments—and specifically, our value judgments, where so often we fail? If, as Genesis may seem to relate, Adam and Eve gained moral knowledge by disobeying God's command and eating of the tree of knowledge of good and evil, the objector asked, how was their new knowledge a punishment? Isn't moral discernment the great human distinction? How is this story different from saying that someone was punished for some egregious wrong by being made a star in the sky? Man, the objector assumed, was not originally meant to have reason but to be like any other animal. Yet by disobeying God's command, he won our highest attainment. Is that a punishment? Was humanity's distinction the meed of disobedience? Such was the objection. Maimonides notes that he has only paraphrased it, perhaps preferring not to open his work with tales of titans and their mythic punishments—although he will later cite many pagan myths and practices to shed light on a variety of biblical laws (III 29–30, 37, 41).

The response he says he gave may sound harsh. He calls the querulous critic hasty, foreshadowing his criticism of Israel's nobles, whose epiphany, he will say, was tarnished by their haste in pursuing a vision for which they were unready (I 5). The critic spoke to the plain sense of Genesis as he saw it. But his reading held too close to the surface, as the Arabic term for the plain meaning (*ẓāhir*) suggests: The Torah, Maimonides argues, should not be read as a work of literature or history that one might browse in "between having a drink and making love" (I 2).

Maimonides wants to alert readers to the spirit in which to read the Torah: not casually, picking at some surface feature and trying to score points about the mythic thinking of ancient authors or that of their first audience to show off one's wit or sophistication. A surface reading is an *external* reading (as *ẓāhir* also implies). The objector treats the text as though it were some archaic artifact held up to the light for scrutiny but bearing no present significance, unless as evidence of the mentality of a bygone era. On the contrary, Maimonides cautions, this book was given as a guide to "every generation, from first to last" (I 2, 1.13b). Its message is not time bound but perennial, and so also immediate—although that message does not always lie right on the surface. How does that thought apply to the story of Adam and Eve?

The account of Adam and Eve in Genesis, as Maimonides reads it, does not record an event, "the Fall." It is meant, rather, to typify the human condition. The Torah does not relate that Adam and Eve fell through sin (inherited by all their seed). Nor does it portray the birth of reason. Adam and Eve, as archetypal humans, had reason from the start, as the Sages held and as Genesis presumes. They were human; reason was part of their *fiṭra*, Maimonides argues, using the Arabic term for one's core endowment of talents and capabilities. Like humanity at large, whom they represent, they received reason from God by emanation (*fayḍ*). We know this, Maimonides argues, when Genesis tells us that God created humans in His image and likeness. Human rationality is confirmed by God's giving precepts to Adam and Eve. For without reason, one is not morally responsible, as human beings are (1.14a).

Maimonides' treatment of the narrative, as Pines reads it, turns on the fact/value distinction: By reason, the first couple could distinguish true from false. Disobedience led to their talk of good and bad—matters of convention. So Maimonides would be a relativist. But Maimonides is, in fact, an outspoken moral realist. We see that in the virtue ethics of the Eight Chapters, all through the *MT*, and perhaps most vividly in his broad effort in the *Guide* to show how all the Torah's commandments are warranted by the three aims that he holds prove it to be a divinely given law: to improve human life materially, to better human character morally, and to help its recipients toward the intellectual/spiritual enlightenment that is our raison d'être and our highest goal (II 40, III 26–27, 36–49).[11]

What, then, of Maimonides' saying that reason discriminates truth from falsehood, whereas fair and foul, good and evil, are matters of convention (1.14a)? We catch sight of an answer when we recall that it was moral knowledge that Maimonides pled in affirming that humans had reason from the start.

Reason, as Maimonides understands it, evidently does have the capacity to make moral judgments and to make them soundly, or God would not have given the archetypal human couple morally freighted responsibilities. Maimonides does not agree that reason—including moral reason—came from the forbidden fruit. The literalism that distances the critic from the biblical text shows up sharply: Knowledge, we know, does not grow on trees. Were the biblical author and the original audience of Genesis innocent of that fact? Has cultural arrogance so blinded the reader of this "primitive text" as to render its wisdom opaque to him?

If there is moral knowledge, then its purview is of moral facts. So just what does Maimonides take the first couple's eating of the fruit of the tree of knowledge of good and evil to represent? Genesis, we can say, contrasts the human condition as we know it with an imagined virtuality: Reason, God's image within us, accesses truths—including moral truths. But our embodiment gives us appetites, which are blown up and distorted by the imagination to the scale and perversity of passions, projecting ever more fantastic images of gratification, anger, fear, vengeance, social acceptance, fame, éclat, or self-importance. Imagination, when it plays this role, Maimonides will say, is the true Evil Inclination (2.26b). So the serpent, emblematic of the Saṭan and the Evil Inclination, represents the suborning of reason at the prompting of imagination.

Genesis, as Maimonides reads it, indicts the senses and the appetites they serve. Man, as he retells the story (not just Eve), saw *that the tree was good to eat and a delight to the eyes* (3:6). Willful passions are pinioned when the serpent promises that this fruit will make the couple godlike—"as rulers," as Maimonides reads the verse (1.13b). The sway of convention is suggested by their discovery of their nakedness (3:7). Convention, like appetite, has good uses. But error rears its head when sense, appetite, and passion, egged on by imagination, usurp the role of reason. Maimonides knows that conventions can be civilizing. But he also sees that a false or shallow sense of propriety can usurp reason's moral role—by allegiance to a corrupt cause, perhaps, or shamefaced or eager conformity.

What Maimonides sees in the Torah's story of the Garden is not a fall from reason and fact to mere value judgments but our all-too-human penchant to let personal (or social!) preferences, masquerading as moral truths, take God-given reason's place. There are moral truths; and reason can discern them, enabling us to distinguish right from wrong, good from evil, fair from foul. But too often what we present to ourselves or propose to others as right or good is what sense, appetite, passion, or convention falsely label as such. Sin feeds on the imposture. It becomes systemic and worse when we think ourselves not just the judges but the arbiters of right: lords, as Maimonides reads the serpent's promise (or gods, as the serpent falsely promises in the Torah's bolder diction), as though our passions and preferences, or those that we make our own, were sufficient tests or indeed criteria of moral truth.

Before opening his response to the bit of biblical criticism he takes as his argument's springboard arising from a would-be critic's attempt to read the Bible as literature, Maimonides explains that *elohim* need not mean God. It can mean angels or authorities. He endorses Onkelos' choice of that last sense in the serpent's promise that once Eve and Adam taste this fruit, they will be *like* elohim, *knowing good and evil* (3:5). The serpent, of course, spoke with forked tongue: What the couple heard was that they would become like God. But they were already like God, made in His image and likeness. The delusion, born of moral liberty, was that we are not mere judges but arbiters of value. The serpent's deceit lies in the notion (also timeless!) that our desires and perceptions (including socially mediated perceptions) are self-certifying, as though reason made us not just discoverers but creators of moral truths.[12]

Resolving the Torah's poetry, Maimonides sees the forbidden fruit as a token of moral arrogance, the delusion that we rule in the moral realm. Maimonides lays that bit of self-aggrandizement not at the serpent's missing feet but at the swift feet of imagination. The human imperative is not Nietzsche's call to become gods: We are not morally omnipotent. Our choices are not self-justifying. We are called to pursue what is good and right just as we are called on to recognize any truth. The contrast that Maimonides finds dramatized in the Torah's narrative of Eden is not between facts and values but between objectively constituted and subjectively compromised value judgments. Reason gives us moral competence, but we are not infallible. Our penchant to displace moral truths in favor of attitudes that masquerade as such truths puts us, in a way, as Maimonides suggests (1.14b), not on a par with God but on all fours with the beasts. Yet the Tree of Life still stands and is, indeed, within our reach (*MT* Laws of Repentance 5.1). Genesis has told us not what we once were and how we have fallen but what we really are and may yet become.[13]

Had Job Been Wise . . .

The Achilles heel of theism is widely seen to be the problem of evil, classically posed in the Epicurean dilemma: If there is a God who is wise and caring, powerful and benevolent, why is there evil? Innocents suffer natural evils in diseases, earthquakes and tsunamis, cyclones and tornadoes like the storm wind that swept away Job's children. Moral evils include the cruelties that human beings inflict on innocent victims. Job suffers evils of both kinds: A blameless man has lost his property, his children, and his health. Only his life and his sanity are spared, leaving him the moral strength to reject his wife's counsel to curse God and die (Job 2:6, 9–10).

"Naked came I from my mother's womb," he says, then gnomically, *"and naked shall I return thither. The LORD gave, and the LORD hath taken. Blessed be the name of the LORD." In all this, Job did not sin or reproach God* (Job 1:21–22). Job curses the day he was born (3:1), yet he does not give up on life. He answers his wife's counsels of despair with simple reasoning: *"Shall we accept the good from God and not the evil?"* (2:13). Holding fast to his integrity (2:3), he will not deny God's goodness *or* give up his claim to innocence, despite the friends who tell him that somehow he must deserve his plight. Insistently, he demands of God, often in the language of a legal brief, that He reveal why he must suffer as he does—and why evildoers prosper (21:7–22). Similar complaints are frequently heard in the Psalms, often in the form of prayers. For the Psalms, too, presume that God is real and just. Hence the questioning: If there is no God, the Epicurean dilemma may retain its teeth but has little to take hold of.

The Epicurean dilemma is meant to prove that there are no caring gods. Epicurus was not an atheist. But he held that the gods, being blessed and immortal, know no trouble and cause none. They live in pleasant fellowship in the spaces between nature's infinite worlds. They are not creators or lawgivers and do not judge or sanction human conduct (3.31b). Hence, as noted, the force of the rabbinic word *apikoros*, not an atheist per se but a denier of providence.

Theists confronting the Epicurean dilemma may deny or delimit God's knowledge or powers (3.31b–32a, 39ab). More readily, they deny that evils prevail. Muʿtazilites, for example, expected undeserved sufferings to be requited in this life or in the hereafter. Some Christians see suffering as the human default condition: Born in sin, we deserve suffering in this world and damnation in the hereafter—unless saved by a faith granted by God's grace. To Jewish thinkers, that familiar view seems alien to God's love. Maimonides knows a comparable outlook in Ashʿarite Islam. Rather than deem mankind damnable by nature, Ashʿarites hold that justice is God's to dispense: It is not for us to judge Him; we are His chattels, and "there is no injustice to a chattel." Maimonides thanks God that such views did not take hold among his Jewish predecessors (3.34b)—not that they saw through the moral and theological flaws in such thinking but because the theologians his Jewish predecessors encountered first happened to be Muʿtazilite defenders of God's justice and human freedom (1.94b).

Maimonides abhors Rāzī's thought that evils outweigh goods in this life (3.18a). But Saadiah used the same thesis to infer the necessity of an afterlife on the Muʿtazilite grounds that God morally must requite all undeserved suffering. Rather than blame Saadiah directly, Maimonides ascribes to vulgar opinion the notion that this life holds more ills than good, a thought echoed in popular poetry and rhetoric, where it's easy to flatter an audience by playing on their sympathy or self-pity and to dress up cynicism in the garb of realism. But popular pessimism denies more than God's love and justice. It fosters a deadly fatalism. For it's easily taken to imply that effort is futile. When disheartenment turns to resentment, cynicism has subverted the idea that creation is an act of grace.

Maimonides tends to avoid naming Saadiah when disagreeing with him, but Saadiah was much influenced by Muʿtazilism, and Maimonides scorns Saadiah's Muʿtazilite notions—not least the thought that even animal sufferings will be requited in the hereafter (3.35b). Saadiah did hold that evildoers must be punished after death. For plainly, not every crime is requited in this life. Maimonides upholds immortality, but he sidesteps thoughts of infernal punishment, as we've seen (3.35a). He shows a strong distaste, seconded by logic, for expecting recompense for the gift of life. When we bless God for sustaining us to meet life's joyous moments, we accept the Torah's premise: Being is good (Genesis 1:4, etc., 3.17a). But if so, life's ills cannot outweigh the good: Pain and loss, error and depravity, are evils. But what makes them evils is the prior good they prey upon (3.17ab).

At the Sages' notion of the "Sufferings of Love," the notion that God torments those He loves so as to justify their disproportionate reward in the hereafter, Maimonides puts his foot down. Sages or no Sages, the notion is unbiblical and untrue. For it impugns God's justice (3.35ab). Even outsize rewards cannot justify undeserved suffering.

To be fair, Saadiah ascribes the thesis of the sufferings of love to Elihu, the last of Job's mortal interlocutors, treating it, in effect, as a human answer—respectable, since the Sages affirm it, doubtless as a comfort in facing the rigors of Israel's persecution. But Saadiah finds higher ground in God's speech from the storm wind, an answer that strikes closer to home for Maimonides: Providence regards all things, not humanity alone; still less, everyone who fancies himself the hero of the piece (3.18b, 20b). The truth is that general providence does typically override particular providence (3.74b).

The metaphysical response to the Epicurean dilemma is to deny the reality of evil. In a sense, Maimonides does that. But only in a sense. Evil, for him, is lack, and lack is not a thing but a privation (I 7, I 73.7, III 8). He voices this view in glossing the figure of the Saṭan in Job. Saadiah, unwilling to entertain any notion of a fallen angel, saw the Adversary (*ha-Saṭan* in Hebrew) as a mortal critic of Job's. Maimonides needs no such expedient. He inclines to agree with those of the Sages who thought Job's story allegorical, but like Saadiah (and unlike many of the Sages), he holds fast to the book's premise that innocents do suffer: "Whether or not Job existed, cases like his trouble every thoughtful person.... Either way, whether or not Job existed, the prologue (Job 1:6–12)—the Saṭan's speech, God's reply, and His giving Job into the Saṭan's hands—is entirely symbolic, of course, as any sensible person can see" (3.44b).

In decoding the symbolism of the Book of Job, Maimonides takes a hint from the talmudic sage Resh Lakish: The Saṭan personifies sin and death (3.46b), although Job, by hypothesis, was free of sin—at least of any sin that would warrant the magnitude of his suffering. The key for Maimonides is that the Saṭan is not numbered among "the sons of God"—but does "accompany" them (3.46ab). The figure, then, represents a concomitant of creation: Far from a prince or principle of evil, he stands for matter—which is not itself evil but the foothold of privation. Here, Maimonides says, the Philosophers lost sight of the basis that their own scheme provides for comprehending evil: Troubled by what they saw as the lack of moral order in the world, they denied God's knowledge of particulars. But they should have seen that matter gave them all that they needed if their aim was to account for vice and vulnerability (3.30ab) without imputing ill or impotence to God.

To affirm that evil is no positive reality but mere privation is not to deny that there is suffering or that it is an evil—any more than to treat sin and wrongdoing as the fruit of error, as Maimonides does (3.17b), is to deny that sins and crimes are evils. Maimonides does deny the dominance of evils in this life. We need not pretend that every outcome is for the best but only recognize that ills do not predominate. There are, the Rambam affirms, transcendent goods that outweigh the risks and disabilities attendant on our finitude. The peak of such goods, justifying our embodiment, even with all the ills it entrains, is the chance of knowing God, if one makes the most of one's endowment, physical, moral, and intellectual. Not everyone will reach that peak. But Maimonides finds it presaged in the Book of Job itself. For Job had asked repeatedly for God to address him, and in the end, that prayer is answered.

It is that rare epiphany—and the possibility it represents (*MT* Laws of Repentance 5.1)—that for Maimonides justifies our embodiment and its risks. That is how the Rambam reads Job's saying, *By my ears had I heard tell of Thee, but now my eyes see Thee. Therefore do I loathe and repent of dust and ashes* (42:5–6). Job does not merely recant. He recognizes the lack of real worth in all that he once lived for, as compared with the chance of knowing God. It was "while still unenlightened, knowing God only by faith, as the pious masses do," that Job fell into doubt. For faith, despite the familiar protestations in its behalf, lacks the certitude of experience—and, not least, the highest experience, where reason encounters its Original: "As long as Job knew God secondhand and not rationally, he pictured presumed felicities like health, wealth, and offspring as the ultimate goal. That is why he fell into perplexity" (3.48b–49a).

The epiphany that Maimonides finds to have answered Job's complaint was mirrored in his own experience by his discovery, in the depths of his despair at his brother David's loss, that the chance of enlightenment is the light that's worth the candle of our own embodiment, with its attendant and inevitable suffering and ultimate loss and death. It is in this sense that the Book of Job is, as Raphael Jospe suggests, a tiny biblical mirror reflecting and, in turn, reflected in the *Guide* and in the experience of its author of grief and loss and their overcoming in the discovery of the purpose God gave our lives.[14]

The Epicurean dilemma, as Maimonides sees keenly, rests on Epicurean premises, mistaking health, wealth, and other externals for ultimate goods. Maimonides agrees that there are goods here. He knows that pains are hateful, if necessary, at times—surgery, say, or bitter-tasting medicines, or sacrifices for a greater good. He knows that pleasures are welcome and has no quarrel with pleasures if they are just, lawful, wholesome, and conducive to our higher end. It's not as if God hates the body, he explains (Eight Chapters 4–5). But pleasure, or even the blessing of children, is not the be-all and end-all of human life. What sets up the Epicurean dilemma, reducing human lives and choices to an animal level and skewing the weighting of life's goals, is the presumption that pleasures are the sole good and pains the ultimate evil (1.18a; 2.79a; 3.13a–14a, 38a).

Maimonides knows that one cannot reach for higher thoughts "when in pain, famished, parched, or extremely hot or cold" (3.60a). Of Job's case, he writes, "No one can bear bodily torment without resentment or complaint at the wrong of it, whether voiced or unspoken in one's heart" (3.46a; Eight Chapters, 7). Hedonic ends can be real goods. But they are not the true coin of value. To know God is the real gold. And we must not discount the joys attendant on, conducive to, or constitutive in the quest—in acts of kindness, moments of discovery, and the sharing of their fruits, even to our cost, even at the risk of death (II 37).

As early as his Letter on the Persecution, Maimonides cites the line *Job spoke without knowledge* (Job 34:35). He returns to that thought in the *Guide*, calling it "the most striking and remarkable facet of the story" that Job is not described as wise:

> It does not say that he was wise, discerning, or insightful but just describes him as a man of good character and upright deeds. Had he been wise, his plight would not have been obscure to him. (3.45b)

Job himself confesses his prior lack of insight. Caught up in the toils of life before his enlightenment, he failed to fathom human vulnerability. A more reflective mind might have seen that our bodies are at once the butt of circumstance and our springboard of moral and epistemic opportunity. Had it not been for his pain, bodily and spiritual, Job might have seen how it is that general providence may override our personal claims. But he'd have needed scientific study to see that, in nature's larger scheme, change—including destruction, even at the elemental level—and death, too, are critical to life's persistence.

If we turn from natural science to the broader scope of metaphysics, we can see yet more of what Job might have known: Recognizing that ills are privations shows that sufferings are consequences of finitude, concomitants of creation. That shows just how wrongheaded is the parity, imposed in the kalām, between having and lacking a trait (1.111ab, Premise 7). That kalām equation opens the door to the theistic subjectivism of the Ashʿarites. The metaphysics Maimonides finds in the Torah rests on the recognition that all being is good, and God creates only being (3.17a). So evil can only be the privation attendant on finitude. But if, as the Mutakallimūn claim (with a notable Muʿtazilite exception), having and lacking stand on a par, nothing precludes the transvaluation of values that God is allowed by Ashʿarite moral voluntarism: God can commit what we might see as evil acts, but in so doing, He does no wrong, since He alone is the arbiter of justice. Ours not to judge.

Vulgar complaints about life's balance of joys and sorrows gain volume in popular poetry and have traction in the work of philosophers like Rāzī. But Maimonides can counter: If the composition of our bodies entails one's inevitable ultimate dissolution, the ongoing dance of the elements, sustained by God's goodness and grace, ensures that the cosmos will endure; life will go on (II 29). Complaints about life's agonies, moreover, too often elide the ills for which we humans are responsible. Beyond the evils "one suffers through the nature of generation and corruption" (3.19a), there are those that some inflict on others. Maimonides, like the Torah, sees a plane of communal responsibility here. Hence God's universal (Noaḥidic) command, *Establish judges and magistrates in all thy gates* (Deuteronomy 16:18). "No fool is more fatuous," he writes, "than one who claims that it is humane to abolish punishment. That would be the height of inhumanity and the ruin of civil order" (3.75b). Like human freedom, the charge to curb crime and wrongdoing comes from God. As the Torah says of the Mosaic law, *It is not in heaven* (Deuteronomy 30:12, as cited at 2.84b). Maimonides' commitment as a jurist shines through here—as it does again when he presses the distinction, motivated by his moral realism, between asylum for a runaway slave and its denial to an escaped felon (3.86ab).

Most of the ills we complain of, Maimonides urges, are such that we bring them upon ourselves (3.20ab). His outlook here is therapeutic: He sees vices as illnesses, counsels moderation, and urges one to distinguish necessities from superfluities: Passions, when flattered, grow insatiable. So do appetites if unbridled: "If you set your heart on silver dishes, gold would be nicer. Others have crystal. Why not emerald or sapphire, if you could get it!" Thoughts of such excesses provoke an anger in Maimonides:

> Every foul-minded boor cannot stop pining and grieving for lack of the luxuries others have, all too often risking grave dangers like sea voyages or royal service to win such superfluities. But when stricken by any misfortune in the course that he has taken, he bemoans God's judgment and decree, blames fate, and rails at fickle fortune for denying him the wealth to buy wine enough to keep him ever drunk and girls decked out in gold and jewels to excite him beyond his capacities—as if the whole object of existence were the pleasure of such scum! This delusion of the vulgar even leads them to believe the Creator powerless in the world He created, for making it subject by nature to what they fancy are such dreadful evils, since nature does not cater to the pleasure of every base profligate or gratify his vice to his wicked heart's content—seeking to fill a demand that, as I explained, has no limit. (3.20b–21a)

It was sea travel that had cost his brother David's life; and royal service is a fair description of the life that he himself had chosen, its risks all too palpable, as his conflict with Zuta; his visibility as a prominent Jew, hardly immune to the shifting sands of palace politics; and the experience with Ibn Maʿīsha's charges make all too plain. It remains foolish to blame God for the consequences of one's own choices (3.36a)—a fortiori for the concomitants of life itself. Here again, as in telling of his disappointment with the kalām, we catch reflections of Maimonides' own struggle in trying to fathom David's loss and his thoughts about the facts of his own and his people's condition.

Protective of God's honor and good name, Maimonides calls it "a bastion of the Torah" that no wrong can be ascribed to God:

> Any weal or woe that befalls people, individually or collectively, is deserved, by a justice utterly fair. If a thorn pierces someone's hand and he pulls it straight out, it was a punishment; the least pleasure one enjoys was a due reward. As it says, *All His ways are justice* (Deuteronomy 32:4)—although we do not always know just how. (3.34b–35a)

That last phrase smacks of Ashʿarite quietude or Stoic resignation, and the argument itself is redolent of kalām reasoning, as if pursuing some variant of kalām determinism, where our every move seems scripted. So it helps to notice the use of words like "bastion" (*qāʿida*, pl. *qawāʿid*) here, suggesting that the thesis advanced calls for some exegesis. Given Maimonides' acceptance of the premise of the Book of Job, it seems pretty clear that he does not intend his talk of punishment and reward in this case in strictly moral terms. Perhaps he reads the Torah's axiom of God's justice on a more cosmic plane in making his strong claim. The famous surviving fragment of Anaximander's words about nature's stability suggests how that might work:

> The Source of coming to be for existing things is that into which destruction too occurs, "by necessity; for they pay penalty and retribution to each other for their injustice, at the assessment of Time"—as he puts it so poetically. (DK 12A9 ap. Simplicius)

Metaphorically speaking, the elements aggress against one another. But in nature's cyclicity, a key Aristotelian doctrine that Maimonides repeatedly affirms (1.21a, 3.5b, 7b, 18b, 23b, 100a, 101b, 119b), no element ever ultimately overwhelms another. The retribution that time exacts repays the debts accrued. So nature endures.[15]

If we see *Maʿaseh Bereshit* and *Maʿaseh Merkavah* as posing (and addressing) critical questions about God's governance, we can see how much Maimonides learned from Aristotle's works and their commentaries. Aristotle saw the world as sustained by the recycling of its elements, and Maimonides profits from Aristotle's seeing the birth of one thing in the death of another: Nature, like the heavens, moves cyclically. So death, and harm too, belong to an ongoing cosmic continuity and rhythm that set before us the mechanics of God's pledge to creation (Genesis 8:22). Matter does give a foothold to evil: Our embodiment is the portal of our vulnerability and the root of every moral and intellectual weakness. But it also grounds our individuality, the base from which our every aspiration springs. As the enduring substrate of all natural change, matter, then, is not just the basis of vulnerability but also the receptacle (to use Plato's term) of the grace by which God blesses the world with sustained vitality and the promise of futurity.

Emanation

Maimonides found at hand in the work of the Philosophers his answer to the problems posed by creation, providence, divine knowledge, revelation, and the presence of evil. The key lay in the idea of emanation framed by Plotinus and his followers, including Fārābī and Avicenna. What a committed monotheist needed was not a polemic like Ghazālī's, exploiting the Philosophers' tools for use against their thinking, but a way of putting to work the core concepts and arguments of the philosophical tradition to draw out its deep affinities with Scripture—and the skill and insight to make the necessary adjustments to allow the use of the idea of emanation in understanding and explaining how God creates and rules the world and enlightens human minds.

It is hardly the case that one word settled everything. That's not how jigsaw puzzles work. There's a price to pay for any move one makes as a philosopher: Arguments have costs in premises and implications. Maimonides' aim is truth. He hopes to reveal the harmony of biblical truths with those grasped by reason's encounter with the natural world. But such a harmony, like any truth, must be discovered and worked out, not presumed. When a text seems to clash with what reason and experience teach, the necessary adjustments must be disciplined by intellectual honesty and synthetic intelligence if one hopes to avoid the trap of wishful thinking. The failed project of the kalām offered Maimonides a vivid object lesson: If the Torah is taken to be true and capable of recognition as such by a critical intelligence, the discrepancies must be worked out between its seeming sense and what we otherwise know. That project calls for deeper probing of biblical language, just as Saadiah taught.[16] Anthropomorphisms must be allegorized. For they jarringly belie the core given—God's perfection. But where proof positive does not discredit Scripture's teachings, Maimonides reasons, we should hold fast. The Sages knew that we cannot follow in God's footsteps if God is a flaming fire. But it remains to be learned just what the Torah means by its bold and vivid imagery when it calls us to follow in God's footsteps.

Emanation, the gift of form, clearly offered a more promising model of the world's dependence on God than did the image of a divine fiat that Mutakallimūn seemed unable to open up into anything more than an abracadabra moment. But use of the idea of emanation demands accommodation to a Platonizing ontology and a sister epistemology: Ideas must be real outside the mind if they are to make their presence felt within the mind or to fund the making and governance of a world.

Even before Plotinus, Philo had found worth and insight in the Torah's image of God's creating and ruling by a word. God has no vocal cords, is not literally a king, and does not work His will by giving orders. Following up on Stoic thoughts, but laying aside Stoic materialism, Philo resolved the Torah's images of the power of language by treating God's word, the *logos*, as God's wisdom and plan, His thought made manifest—immanent in the laws of nature, but explicit in the Torah, which is understood as God's law of nature made applicable in the lives of the recipients of the Mosaic revelation.

Maimonides does not know Philo, but he does know Plato, and he knows Neoplatonism well from the summaries of Plotinus' *Enneads* 4–6 in the so-called *Theology of Aristotle*, made available in Arabic in Kindī's circle in the ninth century. He also knows Proclus' *Liber de Causis* from its Arabic version, the *Discourse on the Pure Good*. And, of course, he knows Fārābī, his trusted guide in logic, the anatomy of the sciences, and the metaphysics of emanation. Emanation, the Neoplatonists held, gives things their reality through the gift of forms, the essences that make things what they are.[17] And form, on reaching consciousness, is insight: An informed mind is a fulfilled mind, not just capable of knowing but actually aware.

Plato had told his own creation story in the *Timaeus*, well known in Arabic from the translated text of Galen's summary. Plato's creator god, the Demiurge or Craftsman, is good and "can harbor no jealousy" (*Timaeus* 29e). So he does not withhold reality from lesser beings but shares it, allowing such beings all that they are capable of accepting and achieving. Maimonides echoes that thought when he affirms the principle of plenitude: "God's whole purpose was to give being to all that can be in the world we know" (3.55b).

Nothing, Aristotle had argued, can make itself real, as if to lift itself by its bootstraps. A mind, he'd said, cannot just think by thinking it must think. Such notions prompt only a regressive tailspin. Minds get the help they need from the Active Intellect—its gift, a counterpart in the world of thought to the light that makes things visible. The ideas imparted allow one to frame concepts that experience alone could never validate.[18] Neoplatonists built on that reasoning: The Active Intellect bestows the forms that make things real, but it also empowers minds to marry their inner rationality to the objective rationality informing all things. Scientific knowledge is born of that union.

It is in just such an intellectual link that Maimonides finds the nexus of God's absoluteness to worldly finitude. Human reason, when realized in a knowing subject, rises to an ideal world (1.63ab). So it is rightly called our link to God, a link clearest in our moments of discovery and shining brightest in the overwhelming enlightenment of prophecy. But throughout nature, the forms known to our understanding show us God's plan, enabling us to see the world as an expression of God's will and wisdom. We see here how an incorporeal God can create and rule the world we know. Matter, poles apart from God's infinite perfection, is the locus of God's expression. It is not a thing, ultimately. Rather, it is the otherness counterpoised against God's oneness, an openness or receptivity answering to the expression of God's idea. Matter is needy, lustful, ever hungry for new forms, lapping up yet limiting and refracting the flow of good from God. Matter is the complement and beneficiary of God's creative grace, the multicolored shadow of His light.

In conceiving of emanation, Plotinus rendered dynamic Plato's seemingly static image of the nexus of things to the eternal Forms. Plato had called that relation participation or imitation, modeling it on notions of class membership or suggesting a kind of artistic mimesis, even emulation. Plotinus added life to Plato's picture by capturing the dynamism of the Stoic idea of *tonos*, the vibrant energizing of the cosmos by its divine spirit. He stripped away the Stoic premise of the physicality of the word, since what the notion of the logos stands for in reality is an idea. Plotinus, then, restored the Source to its Platonic heights, beyond embodied nature: What flows from above is form. The same ideas that give things their reality and their powers bestow the intellectual vibrancy that informs a mind and energizes all rational awareness.

Plotinus gave his students an idea of how emanation imparts form by explaining that one candle may light another without loss of its own light. Guiding that metaphor were thoughts of teaching: One person can *inform* another without loss of understanding. The pedagogic power of such imagery lay in the fact that the source of being itself was intellectual. The flow of water from a spring or of light from the sun were apt and appealing Platonic images. For light brings knowledge, and a spring gives life. What emanation gives is form. On that account, we can see how it is that without physical contact, God gives being to nature: The gift is intellectual.

Flow, the metaphor for emanation favored by Maimonides and other Neoplatonizing monotheists, vividly evokes visions of a spring or fountain. But any metaphor lives mainly in the pictorial imagination. That sets it further from, not closer to, the reality reason reaches for. Hence the compounding of the metaphor: What flows may be called water, but sunlight is a brighter image for a flow that is, in truth, intellectual. It is in thought that Maimonides, retracing the footsteps of the Neoplatonists, sees the active, expressive, creative work and life of God.

Plotinian images of the gift of form as the spread of sunlight or of water from a boundless wellspring, a fount whose center is everywhere, resonate with the Torah's images of God's bounty, and Maimonides is keenly alive to the resonances: "The biblical use . . . of images of flow for God's act is found in His saying . . . *the fount of living waters* (Jeremiah 2:13)—referring to the flow of life—that is, being, which is life, of course. Likewise, when it says, *With Thee is the fount of life* (Psalms 36:10), the reference is to the emanation of being. The balance of the line, *In Thy light do we see light*, means the same: 'It is by the intelligence, flowing from Thee, that we think, reason, find our way, make inferences, and gain our awareness of reason itself'" (2.26b). Of the imagery of emanation as the Torah's way of signifying God's act, Maimonides writes, "There is no finer comparison for the act of an incorporeal being, since we have no term adequate to what this act really is" (2.26a).

Emanation, then, was a precious idea, its poetic power not only Greek but biblical. And although Maimonides did not know Philo, he did know, besides the Neoplatonic authors, comparable moves by the Peripatetic Alexander of Aphrodisias, notably in *On the Cosmos*, a work well known in Arabic and often cited and echoed in the *Guide*. Here, too, the power permeating nature was intellectual, not physical.[19] The beauty of emanation for Maimonides was precisely here: If the reality of things lay in their forms, as Plato taught, the mystery of creation could be solved: God creates by giving form, with no mechanical link to nature, as if He were a blacksmith at the forge hammering out the firmament.

Maimonides puts the idea of emanation to work when he contrasts the creativity of an inventor against our learning stepwise how, say, a water clock works.

The inventor's idea does not come from studying the clock. On the contrary, the inventor's idea establishes the design (3.43b).[20] Similarly, in glossing a line from the Psalms, *Will He who plants the ear not hear and He who forms the eye not see?* (94:9), Maimonides explains that the verse presents God not as a learner but as a designer—at work eminently, as the scholastics will put it: The psalmist's God knows the need and worth of eyes and ears just as a smith must know something of sewing to make a decent needle (3.40a).

Seeing creation as emanation, Maimonides confronts the hoary question, 'Whom did God address in saying, *Let us make man in our own image* (Genesis 1:26)?' His answer is Platonic. Glossing the Sages' remark that "the Holy One does nothing without consulting His *pamalya* on high" (B. Sanhedrin 38b, J. Soṭah 5.6, 25b), he hears in their reference to God's retinue an echo of Plato's thought that the Demiurge, to fashion so fair a world, would consult an eternal plan (*Timaeus* 29a). The word "consult" excites Maimonides here, since it links the Sages' thoughts to Plato's (2.16b–17a). In governance, as in creation, the angels of biblical and rabbinic parlance are Platonic forms and natural forces. These are the "messengers" through which God rules. The forms and the celestial intelligences that bear them execute God's commands. Here lies the sense Maimonides will invoke in seeking to unriddle the symbolism of Ezekiel's vision, which he takes to speak of the interface of celestial with terrestrial physics.

Rich as they were, the metaphor of flow and the confluence of metaphors in the ideas of life-giving water and the light that makes sight possible and indeed makes itself visible remain only metaphors.[21] Despite their power—in part because of that power—like any metaphor, they may mislead. Plotinus' favored term for emanation was *prohodos*, a procession. Yet it was critical to him that emanation was not a temporal process but an intellectual dynamic, no more adequately described in terms of motion, we might say, than the metaphor of "flow" as applied to an alternating current means that matter moves from one end of an electric cord to the other.

Proclus, a geometer in philosophy where Plotinus was a poet, cut closer to the bone in his choice of imagery. Emanation, for him, was less like the flow of light or water than like the flow of theorems from axioms. His talk of emanation as implication made explicit what the images of light or water flow only suggest: that God's necessary existence makes the world a derivative necessity (see 2.18a).

Does that imagery of dual necessities render the world and God, then, counterparts, co-eternal, even coexistent deities? Neoplatonists like Proclus and Simplicius, beset by Christian critics, had doggedly defended the world's eternity—and its divinity—long before Maimonides was born. Their conclusions, welcome as they were to pagan philosophers, horrified scriptural monotheists—for whom creation both links the world to God and divides it from Him. To Neoplatonists like Fārābī and Avicenna, the division implicit in the idea of creation seemed too sharp. They, like the pagan Greek philosophers, saw a timeless link in the world's dependence on God: Narratives of creation, whether in Scripture or in Plato, were at best relics of mythic thinking. Hence Ghazālī's verdict: These philosophers were atheists *malgré eux*, for what need had an eternal world of a transcendent God? Yet Ghazālī, too, had turned to emanation to describe God's link to nature. It was too precious an idea to discard.

Maimonides, like Ibn Ṭufayl, demurred at Ghazālī's charges: Emanation did not make the Philosophers atheists. But like Ghazālī, he did not agree that the world was eternal or accept the specious compromise of *formatio mundi*, which still seemed to exempt matter from God's creation and control, rendering the act of creation less than absolute and God's governance and providence less than perfect. Maimonides found a valuable expedient, favored by Ghazālī and before him by the Jewish philosopher/poet Ibn Gabirol, in overlaying emanation with the idea of God's will, preserving the voluntarism critical in the idea of creation, lest God become a mere mechanism—or worse, an algorithm.

Matter

Matter, for Neoplatonists, was the first reality to emanate from God.[22] Matter itself in its primal sense was not yet bodily. It was the original otherness, the eternal reflex and recipient of God's generosity. Plato had used the language of numbers to ply the strait between the Absolute and relativity. So if God was the One, what came next would be the Two, "the Indefinite Dyad of the Great and Small,"[23] the first version of what we now call matter—or space. For space is the same as matter where nature is a plenum. Sprung from God's generosity, the very fullness of the One that makes room for others, matter was the first fruit of emanation, not temporally but in the order of being. Such otherness was form to what lay below it, but it was matter relative to the absoluteness of the One. For Neoplatonic monotheists like Ibn Gabirol, it was here that the work or play of divine volition must be sought. And it was here that Maimonides found the sheer otherness of prime matter that was given the specificity of form in the Aristotelian elements. God, he reasoned, created prime matter from nothing (see 2.36a; cf. the "sapphire" of Ezekiel's vision, 2.56b, 3.7b–8a, 10a).

Where Ibn Gabirol had relied on thoughts of God's will and the idea of relative matter, Halevi spoke of God's creative, commanding word, again an expression of God's creative grace and volition. The God of Scripture would act not out of necessity but in freedom. It was in that spirit that Ghazālī had championed creation, to avoid collapsing God's will into His wisdom and thus making the act of creation a matter of necessity. Maimonides fords the same stream, his commitment to God's will bound up with his creationism, lest God's creative/emanative act collapse into an automatism rather than be recognized as an act of grace (3.131a).

The goal sought is won if matter, as a first hypostasis, represents what we see as the willful aspect of God, and emanation is no mere mechanism like the flow of water from a spring or light from the sun, let alone the flow of theorems from axioms. Maimonides relies on the volitional reading of emanation when he affirms that God need not create all that can possibly exist (cf. 2.49ab); when he rejects the view he finds in the Philosophers that anyone wise enough and well trained enough will become a prophet (2.73ab), insisting that God can withhold the prophetic gift at will; and when, in broader terms, he links matter (the seat of the imagination) with what our limited understanding will see in terms of chance.[24]

Matter, for Maimonides, was the far shore lapped by the waves of emanation. Here ideas were absorbed and reached the limits of their efficacy. Matter gave Maimonides his answer to Job's complaints against natural and moral evil. Job suffered not for any wrong he had done but simply, or not so simply, as any embodied being will suffer that is vulnerable to injury and loss. The material siting of imagination in the brain enables Maimonides to explain why dreams project the shapes they do, as images reconfigured from experience representing our appetites and passions or bodying forth the concepts and aspirations of a higher reason. It is the dependence of (almost all) prophecy on the imagination, as Maimonides sees it, that prompts the Sages to call dreaming the sixtieth part of prophecy. And the same matter that makes our bodies vulnerable to the illnesses he treats as a physician allows Maimonides to make sense of the Torah's accommodations of human weaknesses, moral, intellectual, historical, and cultural. It is matter that explains why and how there should be such friable, fallible creatures as we are. For part of God's generosity in allowing us our brief moment in being was to give us bodies. Properly cared for and with good fortune, our bodies can be the springboard enabling us to train ourselves to pursue the moral improvement that allows human reason to reach toward knowing God and so find its way back to the Source that gave us life.

Matter was a problem for emanationists. For creation, to them, meant the gift of form. Yet matter was in the mix from the outset, whether emanation was temporal or atemporal, since matter was the otherness without which only God would exist. That is why Plato came to speak of the Indefinite Dyad and Proclus acknowledged matter as the first offspring of the ontic fecundity of the One. Maimonides accepts this idea (1.31b). Where Plato had called matter "the receptacle," suggesting its identity with (never empty) space and its metaphoric femininity vis-à-vis the active efficacy of the forms, Maimonides uses like imagery in the *Guide*: Matter was the married harlot of Proverbs 7, always hungry for new "mates," ever changing by taking on new forms. But even when he finds the root of evil in matter's inevitable lack, Maimonides sees the hallmark of God's goodness. For the neediness reflecting what matter lacks underlies the continual recycling of the elements and of all material things that promises ongoing life for the cosmos, a mark of God's sustaining grace.

To a creative mind, problems are opportunities; and to Maimonides, matter gave an answer to our inevitable questions about evil, as we've seen: Our embodiment explains our vulnerability and the fallibility at the root of human wrongdoing. Matter underlies all desire and all error. For imagination, working in the space between reason and sensation, can rearrange and so distort sensations, memories, and emotions, enlarging natural appetites and passions to monstrous proportions, constructing fantasies and phantoms, and even prompting us to think actual truths impossible and veritable impossibilities real (1.115a; 2.100b). So Maimonides finds good reason to call imagination the true *yetzer ha-raʿ*, the fact behind the imagery of an Evil Inclination (2.26b). Yet imagination is also the key he finds, aided by Fārābī's thoughts, to crucial questions about prophecy. For if emanation explained the flow of insight to the inspired mind, only the imagination could body forth in language, symbols, rituals, laws, and institutions the pure concepts imparted by the Active Intellect, making them accessible to those who do not think conceptually but who live their lives, in good part, on the plane of sensory representations.

Even in venturing to explain how forms animate the natural world, Maimonides turns to matter, albeit of a special kind, reading into Ezekiel's vision the cosmology of the spheres and the incorporeal intelligences that drive them and shed their influences on the world below. He knows that this scheme of the Philosophers is "speculative and conjectural" (2.41b–42b, 50a) and that (Ptolemaic) astronomy affords no proper map of the heavens but, at best, a mathematical model devised to save the phenomena (2.22b, 51a). He also knows all too well the pagan background of the Neoplatonic astral system (3.62a, 63b, 65b, 83b). Yet he boldly ventures to find the animating principles of nature in the four living creatures of Ezekiel's vision, linking them to the fire, water, earth, and air of the terrestrial world. He qualifies his exposition of Ezekiel's vision with a candid confession:

> My thoughts here reflect my own intuition and surmise. No divine inspiration has come to teach me what these things mean. Nor have I drawn my beliefs about this from any teacher. I take my lead from the biblical text, the Sages' discussions, and the premises reason tells me must hold. But I could be wrong; the intent might be quite otherwise. (3.2b)

Maimonides' reading of Ezekiel's vision as symbolizing the structures that link divinity to the natural world via the heavens and the incorporeal intelligences is, indeed, speculative. But he cannot avoid treating the crucial index case of *Maʿaseh Merkavah*. After seven chapters on Ezekiel's vision, he writes,

> But after this chapter you should not expect to hear another word from me about this, direct or indirect. I have said all that can be said about it and even gone somewhat overboard. So let us turn to other matters now. (3.11a)

The Rambam seems almost relieved to move on, having made clear that what Ezekiel saw was not God and that what compromised this prophet's vision was his difficulty in rising above the physical realm, the home turf of the imagination. For Ezekiel's roadblock here was not unlike the difficulty that long before had compromised the vision of the intellectually unready nobles of Israel (1.16b).

Maimonides' effort to link nature with Ezekiel's living creatures, and so with God, not surprisingly proved unsuccessful. The incorporeal intellects—offspring of Aristotle's effort to save the pagan pantheon as astral gods even when those gods are demoted by monotheists to the rank of angels or sublimated by philosophers as lively and intelligent Platonic forms—can no longer do the work once assigned to them, powering and steering the celestial carousel. Indeed, they never could. For even with its calliope silenced (II 8), the Neoplatonizing vision of nature's mechanism is disabled by the same difficulty as Descartes' attempt to press the pineal gland into service as the link between mind and body. Indeed, the effort to yoke these incorporeals to embodied nature fails for the same reason that Spinoza pinpointed in Descartes' case: If there are only minds and bodies, there is no quasi-physical, quasi-spiritual substance to connect them. Any cog or pinion that could have purchase in either world would itself be either physical or spiritual and would therefore gain no traction in the other.

So even before the crystalline spheres that once moored the stars and planets were shattered by the astronomy of Galileo, Copernicus, and Kepler and before the new physics of Newton obviated any need for epicycles or eccentrics, the notion of a sort of matter (quintessence) that somehow transcends the mutability of terrestrial elements and yet remains visible and retains the mechanical properties of an engine in motion is no more help in linking God to nature than is Descartes' (medieval) notion of a highly rarefied "animal spirit," a sort of living vapor touching and touched by the incorporeal mind and thus capable of linking souls to bodies. The physical cannot physically harness the incorporeal, and the incorporeal does not spiritually bow or kneel to shoulder a physical yoke. Only an idea can link divinity to nature, as the Neoplatonists understood, or could have understood once they were ready to set aside astral piety. Only the pure Good, to give it its most generic name, could shed life and awareness on matter. Philo saw this, and so did Maimonides, when not answering a call of duty to gloss Ezekiel's visions. It was not some mediating substance that was needed but a far more basic thought, still accessible to us in the quiver of ideas that Maimonides left behind: that God Himself governs nature, through no delegate or surrogate, just as He inspires human understanding by ideas, subject to discovery by human minds when we do our intellectual work and do it well.

Creation and Evolution

Maimonides admired the rigor the Philosophers used in their efforts to establish the theological desiderata he shares with them and with the kalām—the existence, unity, and incorporeality of God. But he contents himself with a disjunctive argument: The world is either eternal or created. If it is created *ex nihilo*, as he takes the Torah to affirm, the Creator must be one and incorporeal, lest (as Saadiah explains) God be made just another natural being still needing a cause to determine its existence and character. But even if the cosmos be eternal, Maimonides held, the Philosophers can still show its Cause to be one and incorporeal, since only an infinite power could sustain the unceasing ordered motion of the spheres that underlies all terrestrial processes in an Aristotelian universe.

Following Alexander's advice that when faced with inconclusive arguments, one should choose the path least beset with difficulties (2.12a), Maimonides finds creation both more probable than its alternative and preferable to it (2.5a, 34b, 37a, 44a, 49b): preferable theologically, since it does not strip God of volition; more probable, in recognizing that not every possibility is realized, since much in nature might have been otherwise, and the cosmos does not seem to be wholly ordered by some insuperable and internal natural necessity. Maimonides' latter argument here harks back to Philoponus, and like him, Maimonides looks to the heavens for corroboration: The stars, he argues, need not be situated as they are. Besides that, the stars' light, in their putatively transparent spheres, bespeaks compositeness (2.39a, 49ab)—and thus contingency. For as the Philosophers had shown, no composite can be a necessary being (2.4a, premises 21–25). How, then, could the heavens be eternal?

Creation is controversial and may remain so, as Maimonides sees the question. It is, he grants, no more demonstrable than the world's eternity. But creation is not disproven. It remains a live option. Had it been refuted, he concedes, the scriptural account of creation could as readily be allegorized as its anthropomorphism. This Fārābī and Avicenna had done in dealing with the references to creation in Islamic scripture. But because the arguments against creation fail to reach demonstrative pitch, allegorization is unneeded, and good reasons remain for retaining creation, since the alternatives bear deeper difficulties, failing to preserve God's freedom and straitjacketing nature in necessity.

The Mutakallimūn had sacrificed nature to God's will—with collateral damage to His wisdom. But the Philosophers, for their part, had reduced will in God to wisdom. In effect, they had made all things necessary, conflating natural with logical necessity and turning science, in principle, a priori. The idea of creation, by contrast, preserves God's will, leaves room for empiricism and discovery in the natural sciences, and safeguards the open future. For as Fārābī showed, even divine omniscience does not import a necessity of its own into what is known. If events are necessary, it is their causes that make them so, not their being known, whether by an accurate prognosticator, or by God, or by the truth of the fact that they will take place. God's knowledge and power do not, in fact, preclude His imparting powers of action to natural beings or powers of choice to human minds. Rabbi Akiva stated the point clearly when he said, "All is overseen but choice is delegated" (M. Avot 3.14).

Rather than read Maimonides' openness to the Philosophers' eternalism as a surrender, Menachem Kellner and David Gillis see it as testimony to the universalism of the *Guide*.[25] The Rambam's irenic move in allowing, *pace* Ghazālī, that eternalists, too, can be theists parallels Ibn Ṭufayl's portrayal of Ḥayy Ibn Yaqẓān's discovery that God's reality follows whether or not he presumes the world to have had a beginning. Maimonides' stance here shows a spirit of pluralism and tolerance worlds apart from the Almohad rigorism that left no room among the living for any human subject failing their test of piety. For those who stood and, in a way, still stand in the light of Sinai, divine freedom (and thus creation) shines brightly. But to others, Maimonides knows, eternal emanation still bespeaks a single Source of good and being, even if they have not heard, with Mosaic help, all the implications of the first two precepts that Israel heard at Sinai, proclaiming God's uniqueness—and thus pressing the distinction between eternity and creation.

Once Maimonides has made his best (admittedly dialectical) case for creation, he need no longer hold open an eternalist option. Since the Philosophers have no cogent case against it, creation is not an exploded myth. So in retelling the story of Abraham as the founder of monotheism, Maimonides ascribes to him the view that God created all the world, the stars and spheres included, the bodies that the Philosophers thought eternal and that pagans worshipped as divine (3.63ab). Maimonides shows his hard-won confidence in creation when he qualifies his credence in the Philosophers' cosmology. Their sublunary physics, he grants, is sound. But for the celestial world, he reserves judgment. And like Halevi, he's especially skeptical about just how emanation might precipitate the spheres (2.33a, 48b–49a, 54a). The Philosophers' speculations turned all too conjectural here. Just as the eternal heavens harbor residues of star worship (2.39a), Neoplatonic eternalism seems to have set matter beyond God's reach, leaving inexplicable the rise of a particolored world from divine simplicity.[26] For that God must have and exercise will and choice.

God's Knowledge and Providence

The problems of divine knowledge and providence are linked, Maimonides explains (III 16), and their solutions are linked as well, in thoughts of emanation (3.36a): It is through the ideal forms of things that God both knows and governs. So Maimonides can sail past the Philosophers' notion that God's knowledge, being universal, cannot embrace particulars (3.31a), and he can rebut Aristotelian denials of personal providence: If the substance of things lies in the forms that give them being, God can govern through those essences. For they are the forms shed from above, giving things their natures and capacities—and giving every human being the rational soul common to our species but unique in each one of us, the mind linking each human being to God, ours to cultivate and realize, not to neglect (1.133b–134a).

Maimonides must curb his deep respect for Alexander here. The Stoics had framed a brief for providence, coining the Greek term *pronoia* (*providentia* was Cicero's calque). Stoic gods practiced Stoic virtues: They were caring, concerned, and responsible. But Alexander had rebutted the Stoic faith in personal providence. The view of providence that Maimonides fathers upon Aristotle is, in fact, Alexander's, its provenance marked by Alexander's typology of the rival views on the subject (3.30b, 32a). Aristotelians had no qualms about general providence, affirmed in Aristotle's thesis that nature does nothing in vain, the idea at the heart of the teleology that David Novak calls "Aristotle's greatest contribution in the history of human thought."[27]

That Aristotelian teleology loomed large for Maimonides, alongside and parallel to its biblical counterparts, enshrined in the ideas that all God's ways are justice (Deuteronomy 32:4) and that *God is good to all; His mercies, upon all His works* (Psalms 145:9). But is there a tension between general and individual providence? Personal providence seemed arbitrary to Peripatetics, and Alexander combated the notion in his critique of Stoicism. Here was a critical issue under the rubric of *Maʿaseh Merkavah*. For individual providence is crucial in biblical and rabbinic ideas of God's governance.[28] Help was at hand in a precious text by the Christian philosopher Yaḥyā b. ʿAdī.

Addressing the concerns of a Jewish correspondent regarding Alexander's critique of the Stoic faith in personal providence, Yaḥyā turned to a response by Proclus.[29] Alexander had laid out three views on providence (cf. III 17): Democritus and Epicurus denied it altogether; others, including Plato, Proclus writes, held that God oversees all things, great and small, "general and particular"; Aristotle took a middle ground. As the accredited Peripatetic spokesman of his generation, Alexander defended what he took to be the Peripatetic stance: that God attends to the species of things, but not to the particulars. Yaḥyā, urging a deep harmony between Aristotle and Plato, proposed that providence reaches all things, but in varying degrees. What prompted Alexander's doubts, he explains, was physicality. For matter precludes permanence in changeable particulars.

Proclus had argued, with Yaḥyā and then Maimonides in his train, that the One, "immutable and indivisible," knows all things—"mankind and the sun . . . and every particular. Nothing escapes It." Proclus, not uncharacteristically, turned to geometry to flesh out his thought: The center "causes" the circle, and (as emanation suggests) "the entire circle is present (virtually) in the center." Similarly, "every number exists as an individual in the monad"—for all numbers are composed of units. All things, similarly, are present in the One—in their ideas. If the center knew the circle, Proclus reasons, its knowledge would be central, not divided like the points of the circumference. Knowledge in the One is undivided in this way: "Just as it gives being to all things, it knows all things, in its Oneness." But the objects known are not muddled together just because they are known in a unity.[30] The One knows as befits its unity, and its providence, too, must be one within it: Were its knowledge somehow at a remove, that knowledge would, in effect, escape it. But its knowledge is, in fact, Itself (cf. 3.44a). So the One knows all things in its unity, and it can exercise its providence in the same way, even over things many and contingent: Objects may be divided, temporal, corporeal, or unstable. But knowledge of them in the One is "incorporeal, timeless, undivided, beyond all contrariety." For knowledge follows the character of the knower, and the same holds true of providence.[31]

Doubts about God's knowledge of and providence over particulars below the sphere of the moon, Yaḥyā explains, reflect our human concerns with human fates and, centrally, with those fates that seem undeserved (cf. 3.30a). He finds three reasons in Proclus that help explain why life may seem unjust: (1) Some misjudge the true character of the goods and ills that really matter (cf. III 12); (2) souls may be seduced by worldly interests and maroon themselves among material things, bound by the very attachments that make them vulnerable; and (3) souls face worldly challenges even as they learn to surmount such challenges.

Just as Maimonides agrees with Proclus that God's unity and timelessness are unaffected by the multiplicity and mutability of the things He knows, we can see the impact on his thinking of Proclus' response to Alexander: (1) The Epicurean dilemma embeds false values in its premises. Pleasures and pains do matter, but they are not rightly our ultimate concern (III 17). Our highest good is to know God, as Job learned in the end (3.49a). Ancillary goods are those that contribute to that end. (2) Pleasures and passions all too often deflect us from our true quest—thus Maimonides' ad hominem against the popular complaints voiced by Rāzī (3.18a). Worldly attachments can injure and trap us. We win safety insofar as our thoughts remain with God (3.127b–128a). (3) Proclus did make a (Stoic-tinged) suggestion that sufferings can elevate and educate the soul.[32] That thought cannot but appeal to Yaḥyā, given the ideal of martyrdom in Christian sacred history. Maimonides, less keen to celebrate martyrdom,[33] turns the thought in a more positive direction when he affirms that Israelites were inured to freedom and hardened for battle by their forty-year desert sojourn (3.70b). Yes, sufferings can be of value. But they are no more the true coin of real worth than pleasures are.

Looking to the core rubrics of the *Guide*, then, we find that emanation is the idea that enables Maimonides to offer explanations of creation and providence, inspiration and enlightenment, the suffering of innocents, and even the possibility of error. The imagery of flow connects biblical poetry to Platonic imagery. Sunlight, the natural light and warmth that permeates the world, becomes the symbol of God's rule and law:

Without speech or word, their voice unheard,
Their ray extends through all the earth . . .
The L*ORD's law is perfect,*

> *Renewing the soul . . .*
> *Giving wisdom to the simple.* (Psalms 19:4–8)

God's Law, as Maimonides reads the lines, informs and perfects the mind, giving wisdom to the innocent and moral strength to the simple hearted. The Torah gives life because it is a law of life (Deuteronomy 30:20). So the images of life and light fuse in verses that Maimonides holds precious (2.26b), where enlightenment becomes the stuff of life:

> *For with Thee is the Fount of Life—*
> *By Thy light do we see light!* (36:10)

PART III

Esoterics

Maimonides knows that not every reader—certainly not a casual reader (I 34, 38ab)—can profit on the intellectual route the *Guide* maps out, let alone travel it safely. So there's more to the choice of the *risālah* form than the rapport invited by a letter—or built up in correspondence. Indeed, Maimonides' extant letters are typically more formal and courtly in style than the *Guide*. Why the frequent digressions here? Why are terms defined so long after they're introduced? Why are arguments deferred long after their conclusions have been posited? Why do key premises remain unstated, and why are the key problems left unnamed? These are marks of esoteric writing.

Many readers today know that the *Guide* has long been called an esoteric work, meant, as Maimonides writes, "to reveal but also conceal" (1.3b). The *risālah* form gave him effective means of protecting the unready from intellectual risks they were ill equipped to handle. It is because this form welcomes obliquity that he wrote the *Guide* as an essay—and not, say, as a commentary like his exposition of the Mishnah, or a catalog like his Book of the Commandments, or a thematic treatise like his code, the *Mishneh Torah*. Hints dropped, as if casually, in a digression or an aside, a foreshadowing, a striking gloss, or a telling nexus of biblical and rabbinic texts are meant to be picked up by a reader who is on the qui vive but glossed over by readers not alive to the issues the *Guide* will address.

It is appropriate to realize that Maimonides' *Guide* is an esoteric work in the sense that much of what he means to teach one here is not present on the surface. Unlike many a modern author, Maimonides does not just lay all his cards on the table. And unlike many an ancient or medieval author, he does not ease readers into his argument with an introduction stating the problem(s) he means to address, spelling out his premises, and announcing the conclusions for which he will argue. We should, however, free the idea of the esoteric from notions of the hermetic and occult.

Lucian, a second-century writer known for his satirical handling of philosophies and philosophers, is the first on record to use the term esoteric. He applied it humorously to distinguish Aristotle's more technical lecture courses, those with prerequisites, as set apart from his more popularly targeted "evening walks," called exoteric by Aristotelians.[1] By a quirk of fate, it was the esoteric works that survived to form the bulk of Aristotle's work known today. These were the originally unpublished conspectuses of his lecture courses, densely packed texts filled with cross-references and occasional words of encouragement to the students, like his urging genteel students not to be squeamish about the dissections expected of them, since there was beauty even here, in slimy sea creatures.[2] Few of Aristotle's published writings survive today, but Lucian could joke that in Aristotle, one got two philosophers for the price of one.[3] It was not long, however, before the term esoteric was applied to the secret teachings of the Pythagoreans, who were organized as a religious cult and a political movement. The aura of secrecy soon masked the Aristotelian reference of the word. So the first sense of 'esoteric' in the *OED* speaks of the closely held teachings of an inner circle; the second means private, secret, or undisclosed.

'Hermetic' begins in an allusion to Hermes Trismegistus ("Thrice Greatest Hermes"), a figure identified with the Egyptian god Thoth (and the legendary Islamic prophet Idrīs), a fictive wellspring of magical and alchemical lore. So 'hermetic' refers to ideas and practices presumed arcane, transmitted within a closed circle of initiates. The notion persists when a container is termed "hermetically sealed"—simply (or metaphorically) airtight. The word occult originally applied to anything hidden—as in astronomy, say. But it came to refer, as the *OED* puts it, to "those ancient or medieval reputed sciences (or their modern representatives) held to involve the knowledge or use of agencies of a secret and mysterious nature (as magic, alchemy, astrology, theosophy, and the like)."

But Maimonides abhorred superstition in any form. Materials of the sort now signposted as "Occult" in a bookstore he called *hadhyān*, ravings. He inveighed against "amulet writers" and "their idiotic books," bearing promises of wonders, "fictions unfit for a grown man to hear, let alone believe!" (1.78b–79a; cf. 81a and *MT* Laws of Tefillin and Mezuzot 5.4). He denounced astrology for its pagan roots, scientific pretensions, and fatalistic subtext.[4] The *Guide* was not offered as an occult work.

Does it address a closed circle? On the contrary, Maimonides expects that thousands might read it (1.4a)—as they have done and continue to do. He does write for a well-prepared reader who faces the kind of cognitive dissonance that he describes and hopes to help, but others, too, he hopes may profit from the *Guide* if they are committed to "reaching for human perfection and seeking to banish the delusions that have dogged them from childhood" (1.29b). He knows that he cannot control the hands that will hold the work, but he asks readers to use the rule of charity and not press his words beyond the bourne of accepted tradition (1.9a). Real access will depend on intellectual seriousness. There will be some self-selection, of course. But the circle is not closed but open:

> Any beginner who is no thinker at all can profit, I'm sure, from some chapters in this work. An accomplished student of the Torah who is perplexed in the way that I've described will profit from every chapter and should be all the more thrilled and delighted to hear them. But the addleheads whose brains teem with the unsound notions and specious teachings that they take for solid science, the self-styled thinkers who know no science worthy of the name, will shy at many a chapter, alarmed when they fail to grasp its sense, or it begins to dawn on them how worthless is the dross they own, the false coin they've hoarded against hard times. (1.9ab)

The *Guide*, then, is not a hermetic work. Is there another way of understanding Maimonides' desire at once to reveal and conceal? We get a hint from his linking patience with prerequisites (1.5a) and highlighting images of haste and impatience in inquiry, which he compares to an unhealthy gluttony for honey (I 30, 33a–36a). For his main caution in the *Guide* is for readers who have an inkling of the issues to be addressed but lack the tools to deal with them.

EIGHT

The Esoteric Style

In a classic essay "On the Esoteric Style," David Margoliouth (1858–1940) introduces his English translation from the Greek and his Latin translation from the Arabic of Aristotle's *Poetics*.[1] The *Poetics*, he writes, "acknowledges itself an esoteric work," distinguished from Aristotle's (now mostly lost) published writings (1454b18). Unlike the "evening walks," these courses did have prerequisites. Intertextuality, as we now call it, was critical here, as it is in the *Guide*, where the portals unlatched open vistas on a varied terrain but also shed critical light on matters close at hand. That thought may help us see what is esoteric in the *Guide*. Maimonides expects the work to have a reader who is at home in the Torah and Midrash and the works of Aristotle and his commentators. But he is not averse to taking one by the hand and helping out with his own insightful readings of these texts. The problematic of the *Guide* springs from their interactions. It's in the dialogue among them that solutions may be looked for to the problems faced by readers of the *Guide*.

In Aristotle, the vital zones of intertextuality are not mere echoes of earlier sources but statements of (and allusions to) central themes. Here's one: Substances are distinguished from accidents by their self-sufficiency. A similar (relative) self-sufficiency distinguishes an organism from an organ, a *polis* from a neighborhood, a sentence from a phrase—and a drama from an episode. Organicity is critical in all of these. Naturalness is another major Aristotelian theme: Serious drama stands apart, say, from melodrama by invoking no deus ex machina (1454a36–38). A fortiori is nature of critical import in the framing of a hypothesis. So when Aristotle speaks of nature's artistry (*On the Parts of Animals* I 5, 645a), as I wrote years ago, his "artificer is immanent and thus allegorical." He retains Plato's image of artisanship: "There is no better description of a natural effect than as a product of design—yet the design is the work of natural causes."[2] It is not the mere appeal to magic that makes a deus ex machina a dramatic flaw but failure to motivate organically its appearance in a story's plot. Likewise in relating God to nature: The Torah, Maimonides stresses, calls natural causes God's acts or dictates (II 48). For ultimately that is what they are. Natural beings, including human beings, are not marionettes. They act through the powers vested in them.

Maimonides, like Aristotle, does not make God a deus ex machina. In grappling with questions about creation, revelation, or providence, he sees God's rule as no mere fiat. Rather, he seeks to unwrap the metaphors that Scripture and rabbinic parlance use in cushioning these mysteries at the interface of the Infinite and Transcendent with the finite and determinate. His exegeses will not leave unresolved the implicit imagery that represents God's rule as effectuated by His royal command. Angels, here, will be ideal forms/intelligences or natural forces, not flaming creatures dwarfing the world but obedient to God's command. Maimonides is not reticent but outspoken about this (2.17a)—not least in rebutting Galen's critique of the Torah, painting the God of Moses as nothing more than an all-powerful magician (2.21b). The thesis Maimonides draws out at all of these critical junctures is esoteric only because one must connect the dots to see it. Memory helps; mystery is irrelevant.

What is crucial about the "esoteric style," as Margoliouth explains, is that one needs to know the whole of a text (and its context) adequately to understand any part of it. Beyond that, "one feature of the esoteric style about which it is not easy to convince oneself," he adds, "is that the author by preference uses a word in different senses in the same paragraph or sentence."[3] For the reader is presumed to be familiar with—indeed, immersed in—the problematic the text addresses. A text situated in the living catena of a tradition does not need semantical rigidity but dances free of it. The body of literature linked by intertextual reference frames an array of meanings that obviates merely technical terminology. Concepts, themes, and arguments map the terrain. That fact is crucial in understanding the *Guide*—and critical for translators and interpreters of this work and others of its ilk, as Maimonides himself stressed.

The *Guide to the Perplexed* is esoteric in just the way that Margoliouth describes: One needs to read all of it before claiming serious understanding of any of it. That is why Maimonides urges one to read its text recursively, to study and engage with it, checking its chapters against one another (1.8b, 9a; 3.11a, 51b, 135a *ad fin.*). When we follow this advice, we can see delayed definitions, postponed premises, and deferred arguments move into the light and connect; the larger themes emerge, and the work gains a coherence lost on casual readers.

In an important passage written near the start of his distinguished career, Harry Wolfson describes the method of talmudic study that Jewish scholars brought to their reading and writing of philosophic texts:[4] Faced with a statement on any subject, he explains, the serious student will want to know what its author intends; why, if the thought seems too obvious, it needed to be stated at all; what underlying principle was invoked; how broadly a generalization should be taken and with what qualifications; what circumstances framed its articulation; how seeming tensions or contradictions were to be resolved; and how seeming irrelevancies might intersect to illuminate one another. Pilpul here bears fruit, when it ceases to be a game played for its own sake.

To Wolfson, the mode of reading he commends was "the very same kind of logic which underlies any sort of scientific research, and by which one is enabled to form hypotheses, to test them and to formulate general laws. . . . Just as the scientist proceeds on the assumption that there is a uniformity and continuity in nature so the Talmudic student proceeds on the assumption that there is a uniformity and continuity in human reasoning." The use of this approach by Jewish philosophers made it "well nigh impossible to understand their writings . . . unless we view them from this particular angle. . . . We must assume that their reasoning was sound, their method of expression precise and well-chosen. . . . In the case of Maimonides we have his own statement as to the care he exercised in the choice of terms, and the arrangement of his problems, declaring that what he has written in his work 'was not the suggestion of the moment; it is the result of deep study and great application' (Introduction, 8b)."[5]

Discernment remains critical, Wolfson stresses. Ingenuity and skill matter.[6] Maimonides offers related advice when he cautions against the kind of overinterpreting that can lead one to miss the point of a passage or the thrust of an argument or to trap one in "mad ravings," trying to force a fanciful reading onto recalcitrant facts. As David Novak puts it, pointing up the parallel Wolfson saw between exegetical and scientific work, whether interrogating nature or probing a serious text, "one should explain all that one can but explain away nothing."[7] In neither case is there any substitute for insight and good sense.

In the literature generated when the method is put to use that Wolfson describes, "owing to the intimacy of the circle to which it was addressed, arguments are often given in an abbreviated form in which the essential assumptions are entirely omitted or only alluded to, the intermediary steps suppressed or only hinted at, and what we get is only a resultant conclusion."[8] Still, there is no lock on the door. The intimacy of the *Guide* is not that of a closed circle but that of an open conversation, reflecting and reflecting on shared problematics but hedged about by concern for the unprepared. To repeat the warning that Maimonides echoes, Don't try swimming if you haven't learned how (1.37b).

The three literatures that matter most to Maimonides all demand the same recursive study: the Tanakh, abetted by its targumim; the Talmud, with its midrashic appanages; and the Aristotelian corpus, enlarged by its commentators and continuators. All three literatures are alive in school traditions. Torah study is emblematic of the mode of learning critical here: Students in a traditional setting learn the ancient text with their letters when hardly ready to probe its depths. But the more one reads and rereads as one's experience grows, the more one sees the relevance to life and thought of the Torah's narratives and precepts and the nexus of its themes (cf. 1.18b, 3.25a). The same is true of the Aristotelian and the rabbinic literature—and of the *Guide* itself. Maimonides does not begin by defining his terms or stating his premises. He lets his argument open up like a seed sending out its first shoots, leaves, and roots, with little hint of what it will become; but those who watch and study patiently, tracing the fibers and following the limbs and the roots that give it anchor, will not be surprised in the end by the tree that towers up from that beginning.

NINE

Not Philosophy?

Does the *Guide* bear a secret message? That contention is what provokes most questions today about its esotericism. Leo Strauss raised the issue in an essay first presented at a 1935 conference on Maimonides at Columbia University, published unaltered in a volume edited by Salo Baron in 1941, and reprinted as a chapter in *Persecution and the Art of Writing* (1952). Other chapters in that book apply like methods and assumptions in reading Fārābī, Halevi, and Spinoza. The book's core thesis, now a conclusion, now a premise, was that authors do not always mean what they say. That is surely true, and it was vital to say so when the Nazi Party had gained power in Germany and was brutally enforcing its dominance in all areas of life. It was salubrious to restate the point at midcentury, when positivism and scientism had muddied the intellectual waters and historicism had erased or obscured the complexity and subtlety of many a line of thought not considered "modern." Published against the dark backdrop of the Shoah and the persistent oppression of the Soviet Empire, *Persecution and the Art of Writing* was a ray of light. Conformity was much in the air even in societies that boasted of their openness. In much of the world, ideas were warped and expression stunted under the gray shroud of what we now, with Orwell's help, call doublethink.

Describing the living relevance of his experiment in the history of ideas, in words meant to sound tentative and hypothetical, Strauss wrote,

> We can easily imagine that a historian living in a totalitarian country, a generally respected and unsuspected member of the only party in existence, might be led by his investigations to doubt the soundness of the government-sponsored interpretation of the history of religion. Nobody would prevent him from publishing a passionate attack on what he would call the liberal view. He would of course have to state the liberal view before attacking it; he would make that statement in the quiet, unspectacular and somewhat boring manner which would seem to be but natural; he would use many technical terms, give many quotations and attach undue importance to insignificant details; he would seem to forget the holy war of mankind in the petty squabbles of pedants. Only when he reached the core of the argument would he write three or four sentences in that terse and lively style which is apt to arrest the attention of young men who think. That central passage would state the case of the adversaries more clearly, compellingly and mercilessly than it had ever been stated in the heyday of liberalism. . . . His reasonable young reader would for the first time catch a glimpse of the forbidden fruit.[1]

Now, Maimonides, be it said, was not a liberal. Nor did he live in a totalitarian society. The dynasts of his day could only wish they had the kind of control, technological at its base, that enabled totalitarian tyrannies like those of the Nazis or the Soviets in the twentieth century to inflict the deepest scar on the face of the modernity in which optimists take pride.[2] But Strauss casts Maimonides as a central figure in the kind of intellectual rebellion he envisions.

Today we can catch echoes of the cautious voices of the actual oppressed. We can read the once buried journals, scattered poems scratched on scraps of paper, prisoners' furtive archives, the carefully recorded registers of the Nazi death camps and ghettoes, the samizdat novels and epic chronicles smuggled from the Gulag, and the narratives, still suppressed in China, of the genocidal Great Leap Forward and the famine it produced, and what followed as the narrative of the Great Proletarian Cultural Revolution.

We are only beginning to see the shredded corners of the record of the tens of millions tortured and slain by Stalin and by Mao.[3] But we do possess the muted testimonies that Jewish intellectuals published, while they still could, in the early days of Hitler's Reich. We can read the protest, muffled between the lines, in the words they chose in translating key terms from Maimonides.[4] We even possess the now published words of holy souls who still struggled to bear witness (for a martyr is a witness) within the smoldering depths of the Shoah to some glint of God's light, words like those of Kalonymus Kalman Shapira, the Piaseczno Rebbe (1889–1943), left in aluminum milk canisters in Warsaw and unearthed in 1950, like archaeological treasures from a lost world and a never-to-be-forgotten hell.[5]

We can view the Unpainted Pictures Emil Nolde made at Seebüll after trying hard to be a loyal Nazi and a good anti-Semite. We know how Matisse survived in Vichy France, played the game, and painted, at times in code.[6] We know how Erich Auerbach survived the war years in Istanbul, alluding, in only slightly veiled terms in *Mimesis*, to what he called the real, grisly business of medieval knights. We know how Johan Huizinga broke up an academic conference in 1936 by refusing to shake hands with the delegate from Germany, how he was briefly imprisoned in 1942 after the German invasion of the Netherlands, released on grounds of ill health but forced to live out his last years away from major cities, and died in 1945, not living to witness the Allied victory over the Axis. We can view the works Soviet artists made in the earliest heady post-Revolution days in Russia, when still able to tell themselves that Bolshevism was a modernizing and therefore liberating movement, before Marc Chagall had to leave the Soviet state, and before Shostakovich had learned to dance with the bear and play the yurodivy to survive and let his music live.

Maimonides was not a protestor against the powers that be. He escaped the Almohads and was valued and honored by the Ayyūbids. But he did not soft pedal his keen sense of the situation that he and all Israelites lived in as *dhimmī*s. In his letter to the Jews of Yemen, he wrote poignantly of the indignities and humiliations Jews bore in durance to the dominant society and the repeated outbreaks of violence and hostilities they suffered as a powerless minority, seeking safety in silence. Israel's subjection among the nations, he writes in the *Guide*, was the true cause of the lapse of prophecy. For prophetic inspiration, as the Rabbis held, awaits a tranquil soul. Revelation is not received in lassitude or grief—but "what greater grief and lassitude could befall one than chattel slavery to vicious barbarians whose unreason joins with the full-blown passions of beasts"? (2.80a).

Maimonides' existential home was Jewish, not Islamic. He was a leader and a teacher of Jews, raised by his learning and insight to a position of intellectual prominence and juridical responsibility that reached far beyond his perch in Cairo. He took a dim view of the dearth of "real science" among many of the rabbis of his day (1.5b; 3.66a). But he had little cause to fear them. He did not muffle his criticisms of their naïveté, their legal positivism (III 25–26), or their ignorance, although he knew how their hostility toward his rationalism in law and his critical openness and creativity in philosophy could blacken his name and blunt the impact of his work.

Pressed on the matter of resurrection, he did resort to an economy, as we have seen. He read traditional affirmations of bodily resurrection as a symbolic surrogate for the more demanding but more defensible idea of incorporeal immortality. But did he conceal his core convictions in the *Guide*? Was his philosophic masterpiece a work of doublethink? There is no evidence of that and much to count against it. Maimonides was hardly an intellectual coward. His courage and independence of mind are salient in his rejection of divine attributes (I 36, 50–54, 60). Assigning real attributes to God, he urges, is close to corporealism, and worse, indeed, than idolatry (I 36). Imputed attributes are hard to keep from flying off as hypostases in their own right—God's wisdom or power, say, made new eternal entities alongside God Himself—or introducing a compositeness incompatible with God's necessary being (1.27b; 68, 86b; 69, 90b; 2.31b, 39a; cf. 3.26b). Maimonides' strict and radical monotheism gives new depth to the remark of the Sages in the Hagaddah of Passover that it was God Himself and no angel, seraph, or emissary that freed Israel from slavery in Egypt.

Those who predicate anthropomorphic attributes of God are, to Maimonides' way of thinking, in some ways worse than idolaters. For the idolater, he argues, does not confound his fetish with the Creator and Ruler of the universe but takes that artifact of human manufacture to be but the locus of the spirit he summons to invest it and mediate between him and his god. But those who assign attributes to God, even when the traits they assign are psychic rather than corporeal, worship projections of their own fancy. Their prayers are not addressed to God at all. What we humans picture as perfections, Maimonides reminds his reader, would be utter imperfections in God. It is as inapposite to call God merciful in any literal sense as to call Him chaste (1.36, 59b). Is this the language of a man seeking approval from traditional authorities?

A corporealist, Maimonides writes, is "worse than a pagan who takes idols for mediators or who deems them beneficent or maleficent" (1.44a). But to assign attributes to God Himself is not so different from making God a body bearing accidents (1.86b). It's best to see any "attributes" rightly assigned to God as human traits predicated by analogy with the wisdom and grace seen in God's work. God's attributes, then, are not "properties" of His but human notions derived from our discovery of wisdom and grace in God's creation and governance of nature (1.19a; 38, 45b, 83ab, 90b; 2.31b, 54a; 3.21a, 56a–57b, 69a).

That thought sails high above the plane of the Thirteen Articles. It's a higher truth, taught by the Torah, but rather subtler, say, than God's immutability, which Maimonides treats as a corollary of the incorporealism that children should be taught at their mother's knee (I 35; 1.41a). The Rambam is well aware that there are Jewish corporealists, and he is hardly unaware that most Jews who believe in God assign Him real attributes. But he rejects corporealism without compromise, and his dismissal of traditional attribute language is far from camouflaged or conciliatory. "Teaching," he says, "should not start with what is most difficult and abstruse" (1.37b). Yet his radical stance is hardly soft-pedaled or obscured when he spends pages of the *Guide* denouncing the notion that God has attributes or can be assigned predicates that describe Him as He really is.

Historians of philosophy regularly stumble over the dovecotes they lay out in hopes of pigeonholing great thinkers. There's a fine example in A. E. Taylor's finding a raft of "incoherencies" in Spinoza's *Ethics*.[7] The taxonomist begins with assumptions about compatibilities and incompatibilities. Then, where a philosopher has forged a creative synthesis overcoming or dissolving a perceived dichotomy, the critic labors to pry apart the synthesis. "Halevi and Maimonides," Strauss wrote, "took it for granted that being a Jew and being a philosopher are mutually exclusive."[8] The narrow and parochial outlook fathered on these two great thinkers is not theirs but Strauss': As "an adherent of the law," he wrote, Maimonides "cannot possibly be a philosopher, and consequently a book of his in which he explains his views concerning all important topics cannot possibly be a philosophic book" (39–43).

Maimonides blames such biases as these (like the loss of prophecy) on Israel's exile: "Mingling with the benighted, we absorbed their outlook. . . . Bred up in superstition, we found Philosophy foreign to our Torah" (2.24a). It was just such a presumption of alienness (redolent of Hegel's ethno-essentialism) that drove Strauss' analysis of the *Guide*. It underlay his role in the commissioning of Shlomo Pines to translate the work, and it underwrote both men's introductions to that translation and many of their papers.

The key to Strauss' analysis was his discovery, "which we stumbled upon by chance," of "the necessary connection between politics and metaphysics (theology)." Recognition of this nexus, Strauss wrote, "guarantees that the interpretation of the Jewish philosophy of the Middle Ages" must be grounded in political understanding: The medieval Jewish philosophical tradition, championed by Maimonides, Strauss argued (rightly I believe), was anchored at least as much in Plato's thinking as in Aristotle's. But that tradition "begins," he added, pressing his discovery, "not with the *Timaeus* or Aristotle's *Metaphysics*" but in "Platonic politics."[9] Politics was the key. That presumption, perhaps, might lend tolerance if not credence in a secular and scientistic age to the study of Maimonides' metaphysical and theological excursions and his diligent and insightful probing of rabbinical midrash and biblical narratives and imperatives for philosophical insights of a moral or indeed metaphysical (and thus theological) order. If politics held the reins, metaphysical talk might seem tolerable, or at least translatable. The ropes were tightened on the procrustean bed Strauss had framed in hopes of saving for posterity the Maimonidean work he had long admired: Surely the author of the *Guide* must have suspected that metaphysics is impossible[10] and that the synthesis his work projects is unworkable. He must have hidden hints of his awareness—confessions, in effect—within the work, letting sophisticated readers in on the secret.

"Maimonides and his medieval predecessors and successors," Strauss writes, "were not Enlighteners":

> They were not concerned with *spreading* light, with educating the *many* to rational knowledge. . . . They constantly impress upon the philosophers the duty to *keep* rationally recognized truth *secret* from the unchosen many. The *esoteric* character of philosophy was unconditionally established for them.[11]

Granted, Strauss admits, "men such as Maimonides cherished a *certain* enlightenment of all"—but they did not "propagate" their message.[12] To document his concession, Strauss cites I 35, where Maimonides urges that everyone should be taught that God is not corporeal or subject to changes or affections. But he ignores Maimonides' prominent placement, near the start of the *Guide*, of the biblical image of "a word well spoken" as a golden apple chased in silver, the eyelets in its filigree tracery inviting deeper examination by those ready to see beyond the surface (1.6b–7a).

Moses Maimonides, it is true, was not Moses Mendelssohn, nor did he live in the age of Mendelssohn. But the sharing of enlightenment was a vital motive to him, central to his life's work (see I 15, 103b *n.*, 2.23b, 66a). Maimonides' ideal of spreading enlightenment to those capable of it was central to his understanding of the festivals and sabbaths of Israel and runs all the way back to Abraham's persecution at his first proclamation of monotheism and the Patriarch's refusal to desist from argument on that subject. It extends to his reflections on the martyrdom of countless ancient Sages and the sacrifices and sufferings of his own contemporaries who refused to desist from teaching God's truth as they saw it. It extends further, to his vision of the Messianic Age, with which he closes the *Guide*, as an age of universal enlightenment, where polity reaches peace through universal knowledge of God (3.135b, citing Isaiah 35:5; and 11:9, cited at 3.17b).[13]

Sarah Stroumsa writes with admirable calm and balance about Strauss' approach:

> Leo Strauss has described the *Treatise on Resurrection* as "the most authentic commentary on the *Guide*" (73). . . . Assuming a sharp dichotomy between what philosophers like Maimonides believed and what they could explicitly say, Strauss sees the esoteric discourse as a characteristic trait of Maimonides' writings. Strauss's insights were immensely useful in understanding medieval philosophy, and for a time were also widely accepted. The pendulum of scholarly fashion, however, now swings in the other direction. This is due partly to the fact that Strauss's ideas were overused by Strauss himself. . . . Many readers today wince at the very suggestion of esoteric writing, and insist that, rather than scrutinize everything Maimonides says in search of its opposite meaning, we should listen to what he actually says. To be sure one should not treat Maimonides as a disciple of Strauss; and indeed, one should listen to what he actually says in his own voice. This, however, includes Maimonides' repeated and unambiguous announcements that he intends to speak in an esoteric way.[14]

Fashions need not concern us here. But given the outsize impact of Strauss' work, we owe it to readers to see if we can make sense of what Maimonides does say and what he means when he speaks of veiling his intent in the *Guide*.

Beyond his a priori premise as to the incompatibility of Judaism and philosophy, Strauss pegs his claim that the *Guide* is "not a philosophic book" (42–43) to the opening lines of III 16, where Maimonides faults "the Philosophers" for denying God's knowledge of particulars and hence denying individual providence. The philosophers whose views are rejected here are thus of a specific school, and Strauss' point turns on an equivocation. He knows well that "we use the word 'philosophy' in a rather broad sense" (42). Maimonides tends to use it as a proper name for the Philosophers' school, to refer to such "moderns" as Fārābī, Avicenna, Ibn Bājjah, and Ibn Ṭufayl, who embraced the title of philosopher and called their own synthetic approach *falsafa*, using the transliterated Greek term. (We capitalize the word when Maimonides uses it that way.[15]) But Maimonides also uses the term "philosophy" generically, to designate one who relies on reason in addressing basic questions, including those broached in the *Guide*.[16] He had pledged, as we've seen, to rely on reason and trust argument, and he urges his reader to do the same (1.95b–96b; cf. 2.19a, 47b; 3.16a)—and not trust wishful thinking of the sort he found so prominent and problematic in kalām.

Taking 'philosophy' in its generic sense, the *Guide* clearly is a philosophic work. That's manifest when Maimonides calls on his reader, soon after describing his own rejection of the methods of kalām, to choose between philosophy and apologetics: "Think it over now, dear inquirer. Would you not rather seek the truth and drop the dogma, wishful thinking, and awestruck deference to habit and cant?" (1.127b). One must be ready to "follow where the argument leads and believe what is soundly proven" (2.19a). There is no clearer declaration of a philosopher's faith in reason's guidance, and Maimonides holds fast to the rule he states here, flagging the points where his argument turns dialectical and falls short of apodeictic rigor. He expects the same of any would-be defender of received beliefs (1.96a; 2.50ab; II 15). He seeks and finds philosophy in the Torah, although its "mode of exposition" is not academic but presented "as revelation," relying on the poetic devices critical in any discourse that seeks to reach beyond the bourne of ordinary experience and is yet reliant on the usages of human language (2.33b).

Maimonides cannot have written a philosophic book, Strauss urges, because he "knew nothing of 'systems of philosophy'" (42). But in fact, just as he knows of multiple schools of kalām (1.104b), Maimonides knows of multiple philosophical schools (2.39b, 46b, 48a; 3.39a, 40b; cf. 1.96a). He singles out the

Aristotelian as the school to be taken most seriously (2.29a–30a). He knows Peripatetic philosophy best with the help of commentators like Themistius and Alexander of Aphrodisias. But the Philosophy he most respects and takes most seriously, even where he finds it wanting (for serious philosophers always have their reservations when they make critical study of a received and elaborate philosophical tradition), is the hybrid Neoplatonic Aristotelianism pursued when philosophers like Fārābī and Avicenna seek to reconcile scriptural monotheism with what they see as reason's most compelling discoveries and caveats. Like other scriptural monotheists, Maimonides recognizes the theism of the Philosophers and calls them *muḥaqiqūn*, exponents of the Truth. Like them, he credits reason and experience as our keys to understanding nature and divinity and the nexus between them. But beyond the Philosophers' intentions, he respects their rigor and the relative coherence of their arguments.

Maimonides knows of Epicureans (1.105b; 2.29a, 72b; 3.31b); he wrestles with Galen over key philosophical issues and concurs with him on others. Indeed, Galen's contentions, alongside those of the critics and commentators of Aristotle, are key sources for his knowledge of varied positions in philosophy, including the idea of *formatio mundi*, an alternative to *ex nihilo* creation often ascribed to Plato but dismissed by Maimonides as no better, in the end, than eternalism (2.28b–29b). He knows of Skeptics and, like Galen, dismisses them as Sophists for their inadequate seriousness about the veracity of senses (1.117b). He knows that Aristotle argued for the reality of change, against ancient thinkers who had denied it, in service to an agenda, as he sees it (1.57b). He relies on Aristotle's having proved (in the face of denial) "that nothing natural is a matter of chance" (2.48, 101b). He knows of varied views about the character of time. And he sees no reason not to mount philosophical arguments of his own, as he does, say, in behalf of natural causality (e.g., 3.24a; 2.73b; 3.55a) and human agency (1.14a; 3.34b–36a; Eight Chapters 8)—or the world's creation (cf. 2.46a).

If the *Guide* is "under no circumstances a philosophical book," Strauss writes, "as a corollary we have to add that the *Guide* cannot be called a theological work, for Maimonides does not know theology as a discipline distinct from metaphysics. Nor is it a book of religion, for he expressly excludes religious, together with ethical topics from the subject matter of his work" (46). But the passage Strauss cites to back up that claim (III 8 *ad fin.*) is one of Maimonides' frequent apologies for a digression, an aside about the dignity of biblical language, not an attempt to demarcate the scope of the *Guide*, let alone to exclude ethics or religion.[17] Yet even here, as in many of the work's seeming digressions, the stinger is in the subtext. For Maimonides, unlike many another Jewish writer, thinks that languages, including Hebrew, are conventional, not natural or eternal (2.71b). The thought he presses, as if in passing, relates to the twin sisters of diction and ethos. He sharpens his point when he contrasts the *learned tongue* Isaiah calls God's gift to Israel (50:4) with the rude "ditties and yarns" ambient in other cultures (3.14a) and the tales of jinn and ghouls that haunt folk fantasy (3.65a). Hebrew, in his view, reflects and empowers a turning away from sensate culture and toward ideas. It does not create a nation of philosophers, but like the repertoire of beliefs and practices that Israelites are urged to share, it orients one toward the spiritual.

Maimonides does call metaphysics theology. But so did Aristotle by naming as theology the highest reaches of the inquiry into being as such.[18] So when Maimonides identifies *Maʿaseh Merkavah* with metaphysics and calls it divine science (1.3b), quite the usual name for metaphysics in his time, he sets theology at the heart of the *Guide*.[19] The word "metaphysics" itself was not yet coined in Aristotle's time. That term first labeled what followed the *Physics* when Aristotle's canon was edited long after his death. In time it came to name the inquiry more general than Physics, conceived as the study of nature. But although Aristotle lacked the word metaphysics, he did formalize the subject, like many others. He called it First Philosophy as well as theology, and it was he who defined its subject as "being *qua* being."[20] Metaphysics, on this account, seeks to know what it means to say that a thing exists. Ontology, a quest to inventory the varieties of being, was the broad plain from which theology rose like Kilimanjaro. For we cannot assume (or deny) that only bodies exist without reaching beyond physics. In that sense, even the foundations of physics become integral to metaphysics, as they must, if physics seeks to know its own limits. Once we raise the question 'Is the natural world all there is?' we face questions about the reality of, say, purposes, values, judgments, thoughts, theories, relations, and minds, of course, but also even facts. At its highest peaks, metaphysics is about ultimates, what the Greeks called *archai* (Arabic, *mabādiʾ*):[21] It seeks an understanding of ultimate reality, ultimate causes, ultimate value, ultimate truth.

Maimonides knows that Rāzī wrote a book titled *Theology* meant to advance his own philosophical theology. The Rambam hates the work (3.18a), but not because he thinks its subject matter beyond reach in the *Guide*. He thinks Rāzī was wrong and wrongheaded, not least for holding that evils outweigh goods in this world,[22] one thesis in philosophical theology that Maimonides will argue against in the *Guide* (3.19b). But there's far more metaphysics than that in the *Guide*. Indeed, Hegel will write that the *Guide* contains *echte Metaphysik*.[23] Consider its account of Moses' theophany at the burning bush, where God calls Himself *I am* and charges him to tell Israel's elders that His name is *I AM THAT I AM*. There is no more metaphysical sentence than that in the Torah[24]—and no more metaphysical reading of it than Maimonides proposed (I 63).

It's metaphysics again when Maimonides urges that all God's acts are good, "For He produces only being, and all being is good" (3.17a). Likewise when he targets the Philosophers' denial of God's knowledge of particulars, deploying their conceptualism against their view that God knows only universals and reminding them that by their own account, universals must be notional—a metaphysical thesis that Maimonides himself endorses: "Only individuals and groups of individuals exist outside the mind" (3.38a).

No question of theology is more fraught than the problem of evil, and Maimonides turns to metaphysics to address it, as we've seen, in his spirited reading of the Book of Job. Treating evil, natural and moral, as privation, he traces lack to matter and takes the Philosophers to task for inadequately exploiting their own account of matter in explaining sin, suffering, and lack. Matter's hunger for ever new forms, he argues, grounds morbidity and mortality—yet also underwrites the stability of nature in the constant dance of forms (II 29, III 10–12, 22–23). Matter here, as we've noted, is the "otherness" without which only God would exist. Had the Philosophers consistently applied their own metaphysics, he suggests, they might have seen more clearly how to address the problem of evil and not fallen afoul of the difficulties they faced regarding divine knowledge and providence (III 16, 22).

Metaphysics, as Maimonides saw, needs to plant its feet firmly in physics, and physics in the *Guide* means cosmology. That is why he so readily concedes the Aristotelian command of terrestrial physics (2.54a), little knowing the full impact of what Philoponus, prophetically, had seen: that celestial physics is not so safely sundered from terrestrial physics. For here, too, even on earth, there is theology—or, as Aristotle told his squeamish students, quoting Heraclitus, here, too, there are gods (*On the Parts of Animals* I 5, 645a8–25).

The *Guide*, in fact, has much to say about physics in Aristotle's broad sense, as the study of nature—not just because metaphysics strikes root in physics (1.38b, 67ab, 98b) but because it is a central aim of the work to show how naturalism is compatible with radical monotheism. Maimonides had worked hard in his juridical works to isolate and discredit the superstitious survivals of pagan beliefs and practices too often disguised and secreted in the heart of presumed monotheistic piety. A parallel goal in the *Guide*, beyond exposing the pagan roots of superstitious beliefs and practices, is to protect naturalism from the wishfulness of kalām occasionalism. Natural causality and the arts and sciences it undergirds, he holds, are not only compatible with theism but critical to it. (For what would creation mean if God did not impart powers, dispositions, and capacities to the objects of His creation?) Here again, in upholding the efficacy of natural causes—organic, inorganic, or deliberative—the *Guide* sets a tent post where natural science, theology, metaphysics, morals, and religion meet: Not only is it uncalled for to sacrifice science, human agency, and animal or natural activity (along with the scientific arts like medicine, architecture, mechanics, and engineering) on the altar of an overweening piety, but it is destructive of piety itself.

Maimonides trusts Aristotle's idea of bodies as composites of matter and form. He accepts Aristotle's four terrestrial elements. All minerals, plants, and animals, including humans, are compounded of these elements, but all get their qualities from their forms. Forms, unlike bodies, do not change (2.25ab). They (including the distinctive human form, the rational soul) are eternal, imparted (and informed) by the Active Intellect that mediates between God and nature. No material thing is everlasting. Bodies, as composites, can lose the form that makes them what they are. So they can, and in time will, be destroyed—not annihilated but denatured by the contrary qualities of other natural things. Even the four elements are transformed into their opposites in nature's course. But the ongoing cycles of change explain not only death and destruction but also the stability of the cosmos. For in nature's ongoing cycles, the destruction of one thing is the rise of another. No one body can last forever, but those living beings blessed with procreative powers do endure in their species.

The art of medicine practiced and taught by Maimonides and the science behind it are undergirded by an Aristotelian frame. Maimonides prizes such science, poles apart from kalām occasionalism, where things have no essential natures but only "accidents," imposed at God's arbitrary pleasure. Where occasionalists sacrificed nature to God's omnipotence, the *Guide* aims to conciliate theism with the naturalism that the sciences and their allied arts beget, rest on, teach, and underwrite. So it is untrue that the *Guide* neglects physics. It does concede to the Philosophers the lion's share of nature that lies at hand, but it still has much to say even about terrestrial physics—not least when affirming natural causality, rejecting kalām atomism and the void, or adopting Aristotelian geodesy and teleology and the psychology built on Peripatetic footings by Fārābī and Avicenna. Maimonides does read the mathematical models of Ptolemaic astronomy "instrumentally" (2.53b–54a). But he knows that astronomy has advanced since Aristotle's day (2.13b), and he holds the door open, as Averroes and other "moderns" do, hoping for better theories to explain the apparent "retrograde" motions of the planets (2.53a–54b).

What, then, of ethics? Given the prominence of the mitzvot in Judaism, it is as bizarre to say that the *Guide* excludes ethical concerns as to pretend that it avoids religious matters. The work advances clear criteria for distinguishing a God-given law from a humanly devised legal system (II 40). And in the interest of seeing the Torah, like nature, as an expression of God's grace and wisdom, it surveys the full range of the mitzvot, affirming (as against a traditionalist penchant for legal positivism) that every biblical law has reasons and serves a valid purpose (3.57ab). These reasons and purposes Maimonides outlines in broad terms (III 25–26, 35–50), judging it a fool's errand to try to specify reasons for the detailed modalities of every precept (3.58b), since any law is underdetermined by the purposes that justify it.

The *Guide* is not a poor man's Code. Its treatment of the mitzvot does not just recap the work of the *MT*. Here the focus is biblical, not rabbinic, and the interest is more philosophical than juridical. Among the questions addressed: What is the relation, in Halakhah, between legal continuity and legal change (3.91ab)? Or between general rules and special cases (III 34)? How are values like humaneness and household economy—or reverence and convenience—intertwined and balanced in biblical ritual (3.58ab)? How does the Torah accommodate or adapt pagan traditions, and where and why does it draw the line and abominate them (3.77b)?

Maimonides' exploration of such questions may seem mere fustian to Strauss. Did they bore him? He suggests as much when he speaks of "long stretches of silence" in the *Guide*, "i.e., of insignificant talk" (53–54). Clearly, some passages in the work do not fit Strauss' matrix. But the explanation he offers is that much of the word count is cant or camouflage. Yet Maimonides hates verbal padding, as he remarks often enough, and we find no word or sentence in the *Guide* that proves insignificant or insincere. Still, as Henri Bergson said when it fell to his lot to teach Lucretius, one does not fully, richly understand a philosopher distant from oneself without entering his world.

Moral judgments and arguments run far too thick in the *Guide* to be listed here. Readers won't miss them as they read the work. The notion that it excludes ethical discussions is simply untrue. If ethics is a guide to life, Maimonides sees the Torah as the ideal such guide, as he says clearly (1.13b). Nor is he at all unclear about what he takes to be the Torah's moral message: Our goal as human beings is to realize what is most distinctively human in ourselves, our reason, the root of our affinity to God. Reason gains its highest goal, knowledge of God, in good part through mastery of the natural sciences. For we discover God's grace and wisdom in the bounty and intricate design of nature. But only a pure soul can win the intimate presence with God that is our ultimate felicity, anchors us in God's providence, and opens the way to immortality. Hence the centrality of morals. The Torah's laws guide us toward perfection of the human and humane moral virtues. But the flowering of intellect, underwritten by moral advance, redounds to the further growth of those virtues, as Maimonides argues forcefully as the *Guide* reaches its climax (III 51–54). Far from eschewing ethics, the work embeds a comprehensive scheme of moral and intellectual virtue ethics congruent with the Torah's moral message as Maimonides sees it and closely akin to the moral teachings of the philosophers of the great tradition.

The *Guide* is replete with ethical thoughts and inferences, and it bears its own explorations of moral theory. Indeed, the work presumes and advances an implicit metaphysic of morals. Ethics, in Arabic (*akhlāq*), as in Greek philosophy, regards character, and most of the Torah's mitzvot, Maimonides argues, seek to enhance the character of those who observe them (3.133b). He advances that theme broadly (III 27, 33, 35, 38) and gives numerous examples of how the Torah's precepts, as he understands them, seek to further its moral aim of aiding in the progress toward human perfection of those who study its precepts and pursue its practices. Circumcision, for instance, as Maimonides interprets it, is meant, in good part, to blunt sexual appetites as well as cement the bond of Israelites to one another (3.117b–18a). In the laws of ritual slaughter, to single out another example, Maimonides sees a paradigm case of the Torah's project of refining human character (3.58ab). He finds a like intent in the mandate to release the mother bird and in the ban against slaughtering a beast and her young the same day (3.112a).

With deep intensity, Maimonides voices his revulsion at the ancient cult of child sacrifice, the pinnacle of the paganism that the Torah seeks to efface (3.100a; *SM* Negative 7). Moral and spiritual abominations fuse in such perversions of piety, confounding holiness with violence in lurid counterparts to the fusion of mercy and grace with the love of God and His creation salient in the Torah.

The biblical sin offering, again, is understood in moral, not magical, terms: "The whole point . . . is to impress upon the conscience of every wrongdoer that he must reflect on and be ever mindful of his sin"—to correct a moral failing and not let it deepen (3.106a).[25] It's worth expanding on that thought here. For in the twentieth century it took the hermeneutic genius and learned patience of a Jacob Milgrom to unriddle the symbolism of the sacrificial cult rendered canonical in Leviticus and to see and show that here was no propitiatory performance but a morally purgative symbolic ritual. The moral and spiritual significance of the sacrificial ritual's terms are eclipsed for many a modern reader by the baleful glow of its blood-drenched practices—and for ritualist literalists by the false assumption that the meaning of a ritual is locked within its practice. Lack of a poetic sensibility underlies both of these exegetical blind alleys. True to his axiom that it takes a poetic mind to fathom the Torah's use of symbols, Maimonides saw the Torah's sacrificial cult as mother's milk to ancient Israel, a people attuned to the symbolic language that was the ancient repertoire of piety. For the people whose needs the ancient cult addressed, the idiom of sacrifice was the very language of worship. Its poetry bore meaning. But at the same time the tenor of the symbols deployed in the Torah's highly regulated recension of those modalities could be efficacious in weaning the people away from the all-too-familiar propitiatory and magical nisus of pagan piety—just as the idiom of ancient pagan myth was familiar enough for its elements to be adopted, parodied, and semiotically "refuted" in Genesis, guiding its recipients to radically new ideas alien to the pantheon it sought to displace. No medieval literalist or ritualistic behaviorist (and no hermeneutical reductionist today) could adequately grasp the Torah's message and discern how Leviticus was meant as a vehicle of moral self-transformation (*teshuvah*), or how Genesis might be a lasting beacon of spiritual enlightenment and growth. For want of poetic sensibilities, both Genesis and Leviticus would remain opaque to the point of unintelligibility. And it was here that Maimonides *was* an enlightener, even at the risk of being branded a mere historicist in his presentation of what the Torah itself presents as God's commands.[26]

Of the Torah's morally freighted demand that a day worker be paid promptly and in full, he wrote, "It is a matter of compassion that a worker (or even a beast!) is not to be deprived of some of the fruits of his labors, as the Torah requires." Inheritance law, too, he argues, is "a moral matter"—lest anyone be scanted his due (3.94b). He reads Psalms 19:8 not blandly, as saying just that the Law of the Lord is perfect, "restoring the soul," but as arguing that the Torah shares its perfection by guiding human beings toward a perfection of their own (2.84b; Eight Chapters 4).[27]

Moral and spiritual concerns unite in the command to emulate God's holiness (Leviticus 19:2). The Sages read the imperative to walk in God's ways (Deuteronomy 10:12, 28:9; cf. 4:4) as calling us to model our actions on God's grace and mercy (cf. *SM* Positive 8; *MT* Ethical Laws 1.6). Maimonides broadens the thought (III 54). Reading these prescriptions in the light of Plato's call to become as like to God as humanly possible—through justice and piety (*Theaetetus* 176b)—he argues that we emulate God's perfection by honing the moral virtues, which, in turn, help us strengthen our intellectual affinity to God. Maimonides' prooftext for reading *imitatio Dei* in intellectual as well as moral terms (2.79a; 3.61a, 124b, 134b) is no less than the imperative to love God with all our heart, and soul, and might (Deuteronomy 6:5). For *heart* in the Torah means the mind (1.46a; cf. 57b, 73b; 2.83b). The life of moral virtue is both a necessary condition and (as Plato too urges) a practical expression of spiritual fulfillment (3.130b, 135a).

Maimonides touches on the metaphysic of morals near the outset of the *Guide* when he argues that only rational subjects are given moral precepts (1.14a; cf. 3.33b).[28] He holds onto that thought when he argues near the end of the work that personal providence reaches only human beings by virtue of our unique form (3.36a). If it is not a metaphysical thesis that it is through reason that we come under the wings of providence and win immortality (III 18), it's hard to say just what would count as one. But the idea is fraught with moral consequences. One such consequence is Maimonides' moral realism again, evident in many places in the *Guide*, but not least in the fierce intellectual honesty that fires his (epistemic) scorn for kalām attempts to build a world around one's theological desiderata rather than trust in sound argument (1.95ab).

The *Guide* pursues the metaphysic of morals when Maimonides calls it outrageous to hold that an innocent babe is born deformed "by God's wisdom." Such views are branded in the *Guide* as an ugly consequence of misguided efforts to save face for God. Likewise when Maimonides bucks the Sages' authority and denounces their doctrine of the sufferings of love—that God afflicts innocents so as to enhance their eternal reward. He calls that doctrine unbiblical and untrue, since it impugns God's justice (3.34a–36a). Maimonides' moral realism is at work again when he affirms that God would never simply build it into human nature to live as He commands (3.71b). For that would subvert the gift of reason and the freedom it underwrites. Indeed, in his view, such preprogramming would obviate the very purpose of revelation, which for Maimonides is to inform us of the means by which to seek human perfection by our own free choice and effort so as to return the rational soul to its divine Source.

The Torah itself is not shy of philosophy. Its text is rich with philosophical import, although its idiom is not that of a philosophical treatise (2.33b).[29] The religion of Moses and Abraham, Maimonides holds, is in harmony with philosophy and the sciences that shelter under philosophy's wings: "Ours is a learned and enlightened religion," he writes (2.24ab)—ancient, perhaps, but alive and open to the world. So he has no fear or cause for fear of understanding. Philosophy, as he sees it, reaches well beyond the metaphysical canon of *falsafa*. Its repertoire includes what he calls the real sciences, and he singles out its Aristotelian exponents not for want of an awareness of other philosophical practitioners but because he thinks best of the school who honor themselves by embracing the name of Philosophy. These are not the views of an obscurantist.

Maimonides has a richer understanding of the Torah than many a contemporary of his own age, or ours, and a more generous appreciation of the inspiration of the biblical writers. Their poesy, as he reads it, articulates a perennial philosophy that will prove, when unfolded, to have much in common with the best philosophy and science accessible to any learned, thoughtful, and insightful thinker. Biblical philosophy is not, of course, uniformly congruent with the Greek traditions. But it is not threatened by philosophical reasoning or by the findings that scientific inquiries have spawned and continue to spawn. Indeed, the Torah's differences from the thoughts bequeathed by the ancient Greeks and taken up by their acolytes among Maimonides' contemporaries are not weaknesses in his eyes but among its strengths.

TEN

Breadcrumbs

The *Guide*, Strauss holds, bears a message meant to be unseen by most readers. The Torah, too, he says, is an esoteric text for Maimonides—for it does work on more than one level: "The *Guide*, then, is devoted to the esoteric explanation of an esoteric doctrine. Consequently it is a book with seven seals. How can we unseal it?" (55; cf. 60). The key, I'd say, must lie in the needs of the reader for whom Maimonides wrote the work. But Strauss has his own ideas of such readers and their needs. The *Guide*, he writes, presents itself as a defense of "the Jewish creed" against "the opinions of '*the* philosophers'"[1]—but it is, in fact, an intentionally failed polemic meant to reveal, by the pallor of its arguments, that the precepts of Judaism are rationally indefensible. The work, dressed up as an apologia (as the wise are meant to see), is sub rosa a declaration of the intellectual bankruptcy of Judaism.[2]

Maimonides was too smart, Strauss assumes, to hold the views he purports to defend. That makes him, in effect, a Grand Inquisitor. Naive readers of the *Guide* are dupes, led to think that Maimonides has vindicated their religion even as he signals just the opposite to those tuned to the right wavelength: He did not really believe in creation; his frequent affirmations of human agency are a sham, betrayed by his acknowledgment of God as the ultimate cause; he did not believe in immortality any more than resurrection; he did not believe in prophecy—or even in the God of Abraham. For he seems sympathetic to the

Patriarch's presumptive adversaries, the "Sabian" star worshippers, cast as archetypal pagans. He may well have held with "Avicenna's esoteric teaching, viz., the identification of God with the heavenly bodies" (126).

Yet Maimonides ridicules "Sabian" doctrines as "ravings," sick and mad; and the practices of star worship shoring up those doctrines he calls detestable abominations, revolting and bizarre (III 29–30). Like paranoiac certitudes, Strauss' thesis is irrefutable: Counterevidence, as Herbert Davidson put it, "merely demonstrates how deep the plot ran"—leaving one to ask why Maimonides devoted years of his life to writing the *MT* and his Mishnah commentary if he did not sincerely credit the Torah's project.[3]

The ready, if reductive, answer is political: Maimonides' protestations are window dressing; the Torah's laws and the fabric they weave sustain the social order. Why, then, *these* laws? Surely the line of least resistance was to embrace Islam. Maimonides repeatedly called the Torah's laws the best (3.60a; 33, 73ab, 91a, 104a, 115b). Was that, too, window dressing? The claim of the Torah's excellence is tied to the idea of its divine authorship. But Maimonides does not argue from authority, as a Grand Inquisitor might do. He finds the evidence of the Torah's divine origin in its perfection as a body of law (II 39–40, 3.68b), its excellence readily discernible to human reason in Israel and other nations (Deuteronomy 4:6–8). Some biblical warnings and inducements, yes, are meant to strike fear in the hearts of would-be miscreants or to counter pagan promises or threats. But these are not the core of the Torah's wisdom.

Strauss found it paradoxical, if the *Guide* is not philosophy, that it focuses on *Ma'aseh Bereshit* and *Ma'aseh Merkavah*, identified with Physics and Metaphysics, "the most exalted topics of philosophy." Here Strauss finds the first of the many contradictions Maimonides left behind, breadcrumbs marking the path to the true message: The *Guide* "does not intend to treat physics and metaphysics" but to "show that the teaching of these philosophic disciplines . . . is identical with the secret teaching of the Bible" (45–46). Yet the substance of that hidden teaching is, in fact, sheer (and cynical) politics, the politics of the noble lie. Modeling his piece on the esotericism he sees in Maimonides, Strauss leaves his own verdict unstated, merely suggesting a resonance with Spinoza's most disaffected view: that the Law aims only for obedience—quite a contrast to Maimonides' affirmations of the Torah's wisdom and justice and his calling it "the guide of every generation from first to last" (1.13b).

"Contradictions," Strauss writes, "are the axis of the *Guide*" (74). The key to its mysteries is "the rule that of two contradictory statements in the *Guide* or in any other work of Maimonides that statement which occurs least frequently, or even which occurs only once was considered by him to be true" (74). Strauss' evidence: In the *Treatise on Resurrection*, Maimonides finds resurrection "contradicted by many scriptural passages" but "asserted only in two verses of the Book of Daniel" (73). So did Maimonides take resurrection to be the Torah's secret central teaching? What, then, of his noting, in that treatise, that *the LORD is one* (Deuteronomy 6:4) "is not repeated in the Torah" (73)? Was God's unity the Torah's secret message? And are Maimonides' frequent and vehement rejections of star worship and astrology mere decoys to distract attention from a secret paganism? What, then, becomes of the supposed emptiness of negative theology? Is the secret message paganism, or is it atheism? As Strauss admits, Maimonides made his point about repetition to stress that repetition does not make a claim truer—for he had been criticized for not dwelling on resurrection. He cited *the LORD is one* as a reductio ad absurdum against that critique, not to signal discontent with monotheism—nor to claim that God's oneness was the Torah's secret message.

Strauss muffles his deflationary conclusions by entering the lists to urge, despite traditional Jewish affirmations that practice matters most in Judaism, that Maimonides in fact favored knowledge. But there's no need here to reenact the pageants of medieval jousting between active and contemplative lives or Christian contests between faith and works. Maimonides, like the Sages[4] and like Aristotle, saw a complementarity between the life of action and the life of the mind. That's part of his point in painting Abraham and Moses as paragons of the highest kind of life: Both men were leaders and teachers, and both retained their focus on God even while fully engaged in an active life (3.126b–127a). For everything they did as leaders, or just in making a living and caring for their families, was in God's service.

The Sages did set study above the life of the commandments. Their aim in addressing and resolving this topic was simply to stress how learning anchors and informs the life of the mitzvot. Maimonides, for his part, saw the life of moral virtue as paving the way to the fulfillment of the mind's spiritual quest. But the intellectual virtues in turn promote and inform the moral virtues.[5] Are we to see a conflict here where Maimonides, like the Sages, saw complementarity? Just as Baḥyā showed the life of merely mechanical obedience to the ritual laws to be empty without adequate understanding of the intentions and purposes served by those laws, Maimonides saw that reason itself is lost without the guidance of a higher love. Is law to do its work without foundation? Strauss saw only a lack of foundation: Prophets, as he reads Maimonides, may descend from the heights to govern. But if they offer guidance, it is by "parables." Their mission is to the populace. But their inspiration, at its peak, reaches only emptiness. The Law, then, as Strauss reads the *Guide*, is for the masses; philosophy, for the inevitably disappointed wise. The two discourses are best left unmixed. For when they meet, unless in genial fictions, only anarchy can result.

The chasm Strauss sees between thought and action belies all that Maimonides and the biblical and rabbinic traditions behind him sought to achieve.[6] But before becoming anxious over the slide from negative theology, say, to atheism and then nihilism—or paganism—we need to recall that what Strauss wrote was just a lecture, a paper, a chapter, not a treasure map to higher truths. It does reflect how the world looked to many in the mid-1930s and again in the mid-1950s. But it betrays a pessimism about piety that Maimonides did not share, although he, too, had seen dark days—and it projects a cynicism belied by Maimonides' more penetrating gaze.

An esoteric text—biblical, rabbinic, or Maimonidean—does work on multiple levels. But Strauss' reading of the *Guide* blocks the light from every plane but one, presumed to be rock bottom. Maimonides' Torah shines far more brightly; its precepts, in fact, far more open and inviting than Strauss fancied. And so, for that matter, does the *Guide*. Strauss rightly reads it as a work not meant to be just scanned, whipped through, or rifled as a reference (as the *MT* might be in search of sound halakhic guidance). The *Guide* is meant to be read in the way that Wolfson describes traditional Jews studying the Torah or the Talmud. The work does emulate orality, as Daniel Davies notes.[7] The reason is its implicitly dialectical nature: It opens up debates that the Sages characteristically entrusted to aggadic midrash and their debates with one another. In this, it parallels the work of the *MT*, which, "far from terminating the halakhic discussions, actually served as a new starting point for them." Does that lively method make the *Guide*, any more than Rabbi's compiling the Mishnah, "a conscious transgression of an unambiguous prohibition" (48)?

Maimonides did offer his *MT* as a work of reference. It can obviate lifetimes spent conning over halakhic minutiae. The Rambam knew the Talmud intimately and never thought he had wasted his time studying it and marshaling its rulings. But he also believed that the Law is to be lived by, not made an object of ritual fascination, or a surrogate fetish of adoration. Study for its own sake, to Maimonides, reached its highest goal in the study of nature, including human nature—alongside Halakhah. For the hand and the handwriting of God are visible in both domains: in creation and in revelation. But what we must not forget is that despite the dialectics of the rabbinic palimpsest, or indeed in response to them, Maimonides did not see Halakhah as a maze to wander in endlessly with no practical or spiritual result.

In the *Guide*, as in halakhic or scientific study, the goal was not the trap of fascination: Yes, this work too must be studied closely, as nature warrants study, and as the Torah does, or the works of Aristotle, or the discourse of the Rabbis. But the aim was not interminable inquiry. Aristotle, the philosopher Maimonides most deeply respects, did say that philosophy begins in wonder. But as Kenneth Seeskin reminds us, wonder (*thaumadzein*) for Aristotle "is another name for puzzlement (*aporein*)"—a counterpart to the perplexity Maimonides wrote the *Guide* to address. And puzzlement, as Aristotle wrote, prompts one to recognize one's own ignorance, as Socrates goaded his interlocutors to do. So wonder leads on to philosophy (*Metaphysics* α 982b12–20; cf. Plato, *Theaetetus* 155d).[8] And philosophy leads on to understanding. For like Aristotle, Maimonides does not believe philosophy has succeeded if it ends in wonder—or leaves one in greater doubt than one began with, tempted to fob off the great questions of metaphysics with polite or political responses.

Meaningful questions, for Maimonides, have meaningful answers. Granted, ever new questions arise—as they do in any real science. But unless some big questions have answers, the life of the mind dies sterile (see I 34, 39a), and the new questions wither and curl into circularity. For in any real science—be it cosmological, biological, mathematical, astronomical, or theological—new questions could not be asked if earlier ones had not been, with some degree of adequacy, answered or reframed. The ground would be too unstable, the terms too ill defined, as, say, the notions of force, energy, momentum, and the like were ill defined in pre-Newtonian physics.

The *Guide* does not just open up inquiries. It makes assumptions, frames arguments, and draws conclusions, some of them sound, some admittedly conjectural (1.101a; 2.50a), and some, as we now know, sapped by insufficient knowledge in medieval times of, say, astronomy and biology, both key sciences for Maimonides. He knew that astronomy had advanced since Aristotle and that it needed to advance much further—although he could hardly guess just how far it would need to move from Ptolemy to Galileo and Copernicus, Newton, Einstein, and a quantum cosmos. Likewise in biology: Maimonides knew that living beings breed true, but like others before Darwin and DNA, he did not know the profound significance of individual variation in a species. He knew that hair color and skin color are not essential traits (1.101b). For they do not affect one's humanity (as he held that character can; 1.18a). But he did not know (nor did Darwin) that even such traits as hair and skin color are significant functionally and adaptively in a given environment. Had he known such things, he'd have seen wisdom and grace even in the variation within species (which he allows for) and not just in species constancy. And had he known even the little we now know about astronomy, he might have seen the placement of the stars not just in terms of God's free choice—and recognized the need to shift another fact of nature from the column of God's will into that of His wisdom, as he did with the anatomy of muscles, tendons, and veins (2.44a; 3.69a).

Seeking the hidden message of the *Guide*, Strauss builds on what he calls Maimonides' "contempt" for poems and stories, dismissed as "frivolous." So he finds it unlikely that the "stories" embedded in the *Guide* can be accepted "at face value." They must be meant "to instill either some true opinion or some good moral habit into the minds of his readers." Strauss expands the category of "stories" to include Maimonides' thumbnail history of kalām, his "story of the two books" he had begun on biblical and rabbinic language, the story of the sophisticated man's critique of Eden's loss, and even the letter dedicatory of the *Guide*. All these are fictions, fabrications meant at once to hint and cover up the secret message, "to hide the truth rather than to reach it" (65–66).

The key to the mysteries of the *Guide*, for Strauss and his many followers and imitators, lies in the contradictions knowingly strewn within its pages to guide the astute through the weeds and tares to the work's hidden political thesis. Maimonides lists seven causes of real or apparent contradictions or inconsistencies seen in a work (1.10ab):[9]

1. An author has assembled conflicting views from disparate sources.
2. He has changed his mind but has not updated his text.
3. Figurative language has been taken literally. The contradictions disappear when the imagery is resolved.
4. Qualifications, exceptions, or shifts of reference were left unstated.
5. Pedagogical oversimplifications remain to be explained.
6. A lengthy train of argument conceals a contradiction.
7. Conflicting premises were used—some, perhaps, introduced for the sake of the argument but suppressed.

(1) Maimonides notes frequent instances of the first issue in the rabbinic canon, marked by the Sages' searching for the authors of seemingly disparate views. Modern Bible critics apply similar tests to Scripture, often seeing discontinuities far less jarring than contradictions.

(2) Maimonides himself changed his mind occasionally. But he did update his text, as his holograph of *CM* reveals.

(3) Resolving biblical imagery in the interest of coherence and credibility is critical to the project of the *Guide*: We add credibility to coherence here. For, as Saadiah held, if Scripture is true, it must be consistent with the rest of what we know, whether from logic, from another biblical text, from the sciences, or from sound tradition.[10] Maimonides put it pithily in his *Treatise on Resurrection*: "What we find impossible if taken literally, we must interpret."[11] The demand for maximal coherence is the hallmark of the sciences and plays no mean role in philosophy. It underlies Maimonides' project of eliciting a biblical theology. His vehemence against sacrificing nature to one's theological desiderata reechoes in an equally powerful rejection of the sacrifice of moral knowledge to perceived theological imperatives, as in the theistic subjectivism of the Ashʿarites—or the rabbinic doctrine of the sufferings of love.

Maimonides himself employs biblical imagery—as when he speaks of God's greater "wrath" against those who assign attributes to God than even against idolaters (1.44a). He sets the would-be worshipper who adores not God but a projective figment of his own imagination even "farther" from God than the idolater who expects access to the Highest through a spirit-emissary resident in his carved or cast icon. We know that God is not subject to passions and that the language of distance, near or far, does not help much, since God has no spatial location. We need to resolve images of space and passion and resist the heady appeal to the imagination of all such picture-thinking if we're to catch the thrust of Maimonides' talk of divine wrath, distance, or approach. But that does not keep the Rambam from using such imagery when he thinks it hits home—any more than it inhibits the Sages.

(4) Overgeneralization is a common weakness of rhetoric. But missed contextual cues may prompt misunderstanding, suggesting contradictions where there are none. Philosophers today, as in the past, often seize upon a salient case to herald some pet thesis but expand the presumed paradigm to generality and overlook key countercases.

(5) Reliance on imagination is critical here. Ideally, explanations will be perspicuous conceptually. But metaphors can mislead if taken literally. Poets know that a metaphor may be most apt and artful when it reveals its own artifice, allowing art to whisper and make known its presence. Awareness of that fact is critical in reading Scripture not just for its beauty but for its truth.

(6) Latent contradictions can beset the best of philosophers, who have spent a lifetime seeking coherence, hoping to resolve perceived disparities in experience or in their own accounts of its thrust or meaning.

(7) Arguments are readily suspected of contradiction if one misses the fact that a premise was introduced for argument's sake. Maimonides does use such premises, but he hardly conceals his moves. He presents eternalism as a key premise of the Philosophers' theism. He prefers creation. But his *demonstratio Dei* in the *Guide* is disjunctive: Either the world began and needs a Creator, since it cannot have made itself, or it is eternal and so must have an incorporeal cause to sustain forever the orderly motion that Aristotelians postulate that we observe. The full argument works only if both disjuncts are valid: If the posit of an

> eternal cosmos is permitted, the Philosophers' argument works, Maimonides holds. It may leave miracles and special prophecy in the cold. But that is still a far cry from kalām ad hockery. The Mutakallimūn had grasped theology from the wrong end, trying first to prove the world created and arguing from there that it must have had a Creator. Better to establish God first as a necessary being, as Avicenna did, and then address the question of creation.

Maimonides' main focus in his troubleshooter's list is the scriptural canon. Hence the centrality of poetics in the *Guide*, well beyond its review of biblical anthropomorphisms—as, for example, when the Rambam shows that some Prophets' talk of cataclysm is part of their idiom in describing civil upheaval and military defeat, not a portent of apocalypse (II 29). Similarly, when he turns to Ezekiel's vision (III 1–7), the aim is to decode its symbolism for the light it may shed on God's interface with nature: What prophets see in their dreams or visions are symbols of truths known to reason but splashed vividly across the imagination. Such visions, sleeping or waking, have meaning only once their symbols are unriddled—although, as Maimonides is at pains to stress (3.54a), what a prophet sees is real for him; what he hears is true and certain; what is projected symbolically for him bespeaks truths not to be doubted and commands not to be shirked. There's no Jungian prodding of the white-hot coals of the subsoul here seeking to stir up some recumbent incubus. For what distinguishes a true prophet from a false is the source of a true prophet's inspiration, in God Himself.

There's a ready example of the sort of contradiction the *Guide* aims to help readers resolve in the opening lines of the work's first chapter: The Torah avoids describing God and forbids graphic representations of divinity. Yet it tells us that we humans are made in God's image. Does God, then, have a visage, although we cannot safely see it and may not cast or carve it? The text in Genesis helps by teaching that both male and female human beings are created in God's image (1:27). Since we humans are sexually dimorphic, 'image' here cannot be taken literally. The figure, Maimonides argues, points to the rational soul. As Rabbi Simeon said, God, like the soul, sees but is unseen (B. Berakhot 10a). So even in its opening chapter, the Torah prompts us to look beyond the senses. The "contradiction" was a goad. The Torah's "contradiction" between affirming and rejecting notions of a divine image is pedagogical, leading us toward discovery of our true link to God.

Maimonides returns to questions of incorporeality when he considers (I 54) what Moses was given to see when God told him *thou canst not see My face* (Exodus 33:20)—and, pointedly, when he himself confronts the question at the heart of the Account of the Chariot, as to just what it was that Ezekiel saw in the vision. What was it that he saw, and what did it portend? What was projected in Ezekiel's imagination by the vision of which he seems to say that he saw God (III 5)? For openers, we might learn that what is most uniquely our own is also not to be seen.

There is a clockwork in the *Guide*, but its wheels, springs, and armatures are under wraps. Likewise with a subtler point: Genesis keeps silent about God's purposes. But it does report that God saw that His work was good (1:4)—very good once completed (1:31). Again, Maimonides sees the selvages of a contradiction that he believes may prove instructive: Neither creationists nor eternalists, he argues, have any business seeking an overall purpose in creation (III 13). Eternalists cannot do so (despite Averroes' rather unconvincing gestures in that direction). For only what is made can have a purpose—that for which it was made. But creationists, too, Maimonides urges, should avoid assigning a single purpose to creation: In seeing that His work was good, God saw that it met His purpose (3.25a). But we risk a crude reduction of divine perfection to a fanciful projection if we presume to plumb God's ends and capture them in some pious adage like "God made all things for man's sake, and man that he might worship God."

God, Maimonides cautions, does not need our worship, and the notion that all things exist for our sake alone is both arrogant (3.26b) and ignorant. We know that rain falls where no one lives and there are no crops to water (Job 38:26). Maimonides, like a Neoplatonist and unlike a Stoic, sees all things as made for their own sakes, a humbler thought than the anthropocentric alternative (3.18b)—and better confirmed by experience. There are purposes in organs and in organisms (3.22b–23a). But both scientific study and a fitting grasp of God's universal grace (Psalms 145:9) reject reduction of God's purposes to our selfish interests.

If we do hope to press beyond local purposes and toward a cosmic plan, Maimonides is happy to affirm the principle of plenitude: "Only ignorance of nature," he says, "would make one say such things [as that 'apes were created to make people laugh']—failing to see that God's whole purpose was to give being to all that can be in the world we know" (3.55b). God, he writes, made all things for His glory. But to the Rambam, as we've seen, this means that God made all things for their own sakes (3.24b). God saw, of course, that all that He had made was good. For He created only being, and all being is good (3.17a). Evil is lack, reflecting the deficiencies inherent in the creation of finite beings. But God was free to create beings of all sorts and generous in doing so. To say that God saw that creation met His purpose, then, is to affirm that He made all things in keeping with His will and wisdom—which, in God, are one (3.26ab). God gives being to all sorts of things. Creation is rich and intricately devised, and all things attest to the Creator's wisdom and grace by their profusion and the variety of their effectual and elegant design. God, unlike a human artisan, has no wants or needs but spins His creativity in nature as He deems best. So here again a seeming contradiction (the appositeness or inappositeness of thoughts of an overarching cosmic purpose) leads on to deeper truths about divinity.

Straussians target items 5 and 7 in the Rambam's list, the two sources of seeming contradictions that he confesses might be found in the *Guide*. Many an author might get lost in his own argument, and even good philosophers can oversimplify. Maimonides admits that he has done the latter. We see a fine example when he calls silence the prayer of the wise (1.73ab). For the prayer made in a moment of epiphany is not the deadly silence of frustrated love but the pregnant silence of encounter.[12] And David, of course, did not keep his every prayer to himself. Indeed, as Maimonides knows well, the wise have much to say, and do, and teach.

For Strauss, item 7 is chief among the *Guide*'s seven seals, not least for its bearing on creation and eternity. Maimonides does countenance the use of rejected premises for the sake of an argument—here, to make room for the Philosophers' eternalism, the motive spring of the Aristotelian case for the incorporeality of the divine. The Philosophers' arguments for theism are valid, he argues (II 1–2). But if they are to be sound as well, all their premises must be true, and one key premise, the world's eternity, is contested, although Maimonides grants it for the sake of the argument. Still, far from suppressing or disguising that premise—critical, in his view, in making the Philosophers' Unmoved Mover infinite, eternal, and incorporeal—he prominently posits its stipulation, his honesty rewarded with lasting suspicions that his own sustained case for creation is disingenuous (1.9a). The secret teaching of the *Guide*, then, would be eternalism? But Maimonides lays out the Philosophers' brief plainly and finds their arguments valid but not sound, since the world's eternity was granted only for the sake of the argument. He agrees with Ibn Ṭufayl that the Aristotelian eternalists are theists but argues, dialectically, that there are good grounds for deeming creation the less problematic hypothesis.

The subtlety here lies in the fact that Maimonides' case for theism was dialectical.[13] Dialectic, as Aristotle explained, although less rigorous than apodeictic proof, is also indispensable—whether for training, for raising issues, or for allowing common discourse among those committed to disparate views (*Topics* I 1). In some situations, dialectic is more powerful than demonstration: If an interlocutor refuses, say, to accept the law banning contradiction, one can hardly refute him without begging the question. But one can, Aristotle explains, reduce him to silence—not a refutation, but in some ways no less effective.

Maimonides' case for theism was dialectical because it rests on a disjunction: eternity or its denial, a necessary division. But the world's eternity, as Maimonides is at pains to show, is not an undeniable truth, as some took it to be. It is but a "common notion," common at least among the Philosophers. Aristotle, Maimonides holds, knew well that eternity was not demonstrable (II 15). That is why the Stagirite labored to muster a case for it. But his arguments (and those of his formidable successors) are not probative. Given the eternity of time and the dependence of time on motion, we do get an eternal cosmos, ever in motion; and such motion, Maimonides agrees, requires the infinite causal power of an incorporeal Mover. But if time began at the creation, as astute creationists affirm, Aristotle's keystone crumbles and his Prime Mover retreats, even without rejection of the premise that the spheres cannot move themselves.

As for the creationist wing of the argument, here, too, there's room for dispute. That the world began does not logically entail that it had a cause, let alone a Creator. Maimonides is careful to distinguish the claim that the world had an origin from the stronger claim that it was brought to be, although he does think creation the best explanation. Logic does not require a cause. The world might have just begun for no reason. There's no internal contradiction in that. Hence, in part, the importance of causality for Maimonides; hence, too, the kalām search for a determinant and the Aristotelian premise that the natural order cannot have sprung up by mere chance (II 20).

Causality, as Ghazālī had shown in his critique of the Philosophers, does not amount to logical necessity. Maimonides knows that truth well. He relies on it in motivating his idea of natural necessity as distinguished from the logical necessities so prized by the Philosophers. The need for causal explanations is an assumption made credible by the dependence on it of so much of our general knowledge, practice, and experience—as is the assumption that a cause must be adequate to and determinative of its effect. Maimonides shares these assumptions with Aristotelian eternalists, his unseen interlocutors. But the key premises are hardly undeniable.

Following up on Joel Kraemer's noting Maimonides' reliance on dialectical reasoning, Seeskin points to the stress, in item 7, on the issue of the problematic premise. Are we to assume that the world began or that it did not? Maimonides, Seeskin reasons, tests the reader's readiness to engage in some serious thinking: "To someone who thinks that religious matters are simple and straightforward, the suggestion that plausible arguments can be made on either side of an issue and that neither side can be demonstrated may be profoundly disturbing."[14] Seeskin alludes here to Kant's antinomies, the first of which was the impasse between creation and eternity.

Maimonides candidly admits that he has no knock-down, drag-out proof of creation (1.96a). He concedes that his argument for theism is not apodeictic. But he does think he's made a better dialectical case for creation than Aristotelians have against it, despite their confident (but also dialectical) arguments for eternalism that so many found impressive. Following Alexander of Aphrodisias' advice, he chooses what he finds the least problematic option: Creation, he argues, offers a better explanation, say, for the placement of the stars (1.93a; 2.44a) than the Philosophers' projected necessity, which does little to explain the seeming randomness in the stars' placement. That thought, Maimonides reasons, makes creation more credible than eternalism, more probable cosmologically. And the fact that creation preserves God's freedom renders it preferable theologically. The Philosophers' essentialism traps them in a logicist determinism that in the end demands that whatever can exist must exist. So God, and man, too, it seems, must do as they do, and empiricism, in the end, retains no place in science: The future is not open but closed.

Maimonides calls the rotation of the spheres "the strongest" argument for God's existence (1.93a *ad fin.*). He finds the approach attractive, since the Philosophers' postulate of the world's eternity makes the cause of that rotation incorporeal. For he assumes, with the Philosophers, that no physical force could sustain an unending effect. Indeed, it cannot, at least not on the impetus theory of force and motion, now long discredited by the work of Galileo and Newton. The case to be made for God's incorporeality on the Philosophers' eternalist assumptions is especially precious to Maimonides, since incorporeality is the gateway to divine transcendence.

The best creationist argument for theism, for Maimonides, is the placement of the stars. For (Aristotelian) science seemed unable to reduce their scattered locations to system. The Rambam might have pled a simpler and less vulnerable case. (Nowadays we have pretty good naturalistic explanations for much that we know about the placement of the stars, and astronomers do not rule out the play of randomness in the modern versions of the nebular hypothesis.) Maimonides might better have focused his appeal on "the rotation of the spheres." Ghazālī, after all, had argued that the rotation might have had the opposite sense from the one we know. Or had he had access to the kind of knowledge we now believe we have, he might have appealed to some other asymmetry in nature, like the apparent prevalence of matter over antimatter or the prominence of L- versus D-amino acids in living beings. Using a homelier example, he made his challenge dialectically: Are we to say that God could not have made "a fly's wing any longer or a grub's foot any shorter than it is"? (2.49a). Any contingency in the natural order argues that the world exhibits determinations beyond the sheer requirements of logic and disarms the Philosophers' project of calling on the essences of things to reduce causal to essential necessities and thus to necessities of logic. Contingency renders empiricism unescapable in the natural sciences, and for Maimonides, it reveals a realm of ordained determinations that welcomes the distinction of natural from logical necessities and lets us glimpse the play of divine creativity, allowing us to see facets of the laws of nature that are better understood in terms of will than wisdom.

Once Maimonides has shown that eternity is not demonstrated, he's free to make a full-throated appeal in behalf of creation, and that is what we find him doing when he turns to the tradition and adds the weight of Moses and Abraham to the scale. Tradition would help not at all were creation proved untenable. But if the refutations proposed by eternalists from Parmenides to

Aristotle, to Proclus and Fārābī have proved nothing, the account of Genesis remains standing.

What, then, of breadcrumbs in the *Guide*? Davidson caps his study of the *Guide* with this appraisal:

> I have not been able to identify a single contradiction in the *Guide* which fits the specification for deliberate contradictions of the seventh type. . . . The threads out of which Maimonides wove his arguments for creation derive from the Islamic thinker Ghazālī, and he conceded that the arguments fall short of being apodictic demonstrations. They nevertheless constitute the most original set of proofs for creation in medieval Jewish philosophy. What odd cast of mind would lead someone to design a new set of arguments and present it to those whom he was trying to enlighten if by doing so he was inducing them to embrace a position opposed to the one he himself held?[15]

Generalizing on Kraemer's recognition of the reliance of the *Guide* on dialectical arguments, Davies has shown how key "contradictions" purportedly left behind in the work to signal a secret contrarian message dissolve when its arguments are read as dialectical—as Maimonides avows they must be. Beyond the issue of creation, Davies finds that this is so also regarding God's freedom, perfection and unity, knowledge and providence, perfection and transcendence. Summing up his own reading, Seeskin writes near the close of his study of the *Guide*,

> Against Strauss I want to argue that the *Guide* does not contain *a* true teaching that is hidden from the reader but a patchwork of doctrines, conjectures, and observations dealing with speculative matters. It is esoteric because it is difficult to achieve certainty in a field where all we have are brief glimpses of the truth; but there are no booby traps, and the *Guide* is not a book with seven seals. . . . Maimonides' method for keeping the uninspired majority away from unsettling results is very simple: the book itself, which is to say a long, daunting, slow-moving exposition that presupposes a high degree of technical training and makes no concessions to popular taste. He claims that even a beginner ought to derive some benefit from reading his book. . . . But he also claims that a person who finds nothing of value in it should think of

> it as if it had never been written. As one who has taught the *Guide* for many years, I can say with assurance that many students have taken this advice to heart.
>
> In short, normal esotericism is enough to ensure that untrained readers will have no access to Maimonides' views on obscure matters. . . . In truth it is difficult even for an advanced student to work through the *Guide* without a profound sense of humility. Thus there is no need to think that Maimonides violated the talmudic injunction. . . . In fact, Maimonides accepts much more of the philosophy and science of the day in the *MT* than he does in the *Guide*. We must therefore ask what purpose would be served by adopting an esotericism as deep as the one Strauss proposes.
>
> In my view, not only is no purpose served, but the literary integrity of the book is seriously compromised. It was, after all, Strauss who called attention to the fact that the *Guide* is not a treatise but a letter written to a student. While the text indicates that Joseph is a man of good character and intelligence, there is nothing to indicate that he is a budding genius. On the contrary, he has come to Maimonides because he is perplexed. What sort of book would put him on the right track? We can imagine a demanding one that would require close attention to every word and twist of argument. But if the book were more than demanding, if the truth were buried so deep that it is hard to see what philosophic contribution Maimonides has made, then the book would not relieve Joseph's perplexity or anyone else's.[16]

As the scholarship on the *Guide* has grown, the Straussian approach has faded, as Sarah Stroumsa reports. So Alfred Ivry, acknowledging his debt to both Strauss and Pines, can suggest that the tide has gone out. He finds himself in "essential agreement" with a Straussian reading but recognizes that "Strauss's hermeneutical excesses" bred "a cottage industry" of interpretive literature but also provoked "a backlash"—and that "Strauss's attempt to keep Maimonides' teachings secret . . . affected the otherwise magnificent translation of Shlomo Pines." All this by way of explaining why Ivry will not devote his book on the *Guide* to following in Strauss' footsteps *or* seeking to erase them—and why he must part company with Pines' readings of "crucial terms and sentences." For, as he says, "times have changed, and the need to rescue the *Guide* from obfuscation and misunderstanding is great."[17]

Whether the *Guide* is indeed a patchwork or a more carefully woven but still intricate tapestry will depend, in the end, on the eyes and insights of the reader. As in a quilt or a tapestry, much depends on stitches that don't show on the surface—linking the components of *Maʿaseh Bereshit* and *Maʿaseh Merkavah* as Maimonides understands them. But it does seem safe to say that any reticence in the work reflects not a defensive posture but a genuine concern for the unready reader. It is for this reason that Maimonides avoids directly stating the problems the *Guide* will address, relying instead on topic headings, as the Sages urge in Ḥagigah. For a topic is not a thesis or even a question. Maimonides knows that those who have struggled with the problems he will address do not need to hear their own questions read back to them. The rubrics that signpost the *Guide* point to familiar topoi that he believes the Torah, sensitively read, not only raises but can help resolve—aided, at times, by the Midrash, critically filtered and creatively deployed. Readers who have agonized over the problem of evil, or wondered what the Torah can mean by its talk of angels, or troubled themselves as to how revelation is possible, or pondered over the meaning of life—or how providence might work, or whether divine omniscience leaves room for free will—will be alive to the issues broached in the *Guide* and ready to hear any insight Maimonides may have to offer or elicit from the sacred text or the fountain of tradition. Others, as Seeskin suggests, may well find only a desert of words.

Naive readers, as Maimonides observes, may hardly flinch at the most startling of the claims they think they see in Scripture (1.5b). Some assume that nothing rational could come from God. For some, only the pointless and bizarre can count as divine (3.68ab). Many, by dint of habit or bad experience, presume philosophy has no relevance to their core concerns, perhaps halakhic or simply worldly, or some mix of the two. They may be right: The problems confronted in the *Guide* may well concern them but fail to interest them. They will bypass the issues Maimonides grapples with and miss the sparks of enlightenment he strikes in his reading of the inspired texts and the best reflections of the Sages. Impatient readers may well think the *Guide* has set itself some simple, sheerly exegetical or apologetic task, if not the covert debunking Strauss darkly conjures. They'll move on before grasping the full import of the text or feeling the full impact of its argument. Most modern readers are unused to the idea that a serious writer need not lay all his cards on the table, and a hasty reader might make a similar mistake, not watching closely enough as Maimonides weaves, and so miss the argument, hardly realizing that this, too, was part of the intent, to keep the unready from getting in over their heads.

Yet the kind of winnowing that works best at the task Maimonides intended is self-selection: The ill suited and ill prepared can exclude themselves—a gentler and more effective screen than posting "keep out" signs around the threshing floor. Willful but hasty readers soon lose the thread of the argument, and the *Guide* does become a labyrinth for them, leaving some unable even to name the subject of major sections. This much seems sound in the thesis that the *Guide* is an esoteric work. But it is not a mystery wrapped in an enigma. It is, in fact, more than forthright in stating many of its central and most controversial claims and patiently explicit in laying out its arguments for them.

Conclusion

THE *GUIDE* TODAY

Aristotle's spheres have crashed to the ground, and astronomy has undergone (and undertaken) far more extensive reframing than any contemporary of Maimonides anticipated. Galenic medicine is no longer the clinical standby. It is displaced by expansive and expanding knowledge of health and disease, surgery, pharmaco-chemistry, and biochemistry. We now know that fire, water, earth, and air are not elements; we can identify well over a hundred elements and have the technology to fashion more, although the additions to the periodic table, given the mass of their nuclei, are highly unstable. All of today's atoms prove to have parts, and their parts too have parts. The smallest components into which we can divide matter have many properties not conceived simply or at all in terms of mass and extension. Matter and energy are now known to be interchangeable—much as Aristotle's elements once were—and new concepts of both matter and energy have replaced their ancestral counterparts.

Electromagnetic induction and nuclear radiation are familiar concepts now, and we know a fair amount about the valences underlying chemical reactions. Physics today speaks of fields and orbitals. Newton's laws of motion, gravitation, and inertia have displaced the old notions of impetus, "heaviness," and "lightness." Newton's laws, in turn, are now understood to be special cases of the broader principles charted in Einstein's Theory of Relativity—and those, in turn, may well be subsumed under broader, seemingly paradoxical but exigent, demands stemming from quantum physics. We have a burgeoning knowledge of evolution and genetics, brain science and computer science. Cybernetics has become a servant if, at times, feared as a challenger. We know now that it is not nonsense to posit a void or to conceive of a cosmos of infinite extent. New geometries make the Euclidean system, too, a special case, much as Einstein's work bracketed Newtonian physics—and often for the same reason. For relativity demands a revision of the presumption that space must hew to a strictly rectilinear Cartesian grid.

Maimonides and many another scriptural monotheist would have given his eye teeth to know what we know from the red shift in the spectra of distant stars: that there is strong evidence of an initial singularity, confirming claims that the cosmos did indeed begin—a thesis Maimonides thought eluded proof. But scientistically inclined ideologues still abound. Today they typically ignore that evidence for the cosmic origins and invest in cynical talk of neo-Darwinism, trusting evolution to obviate talk of God in much the same self-assured spirit that Maimonides saw among dilettantes with a smattering of astronomy who were sure that philosophy had proved the world eternal (2.33b).

Maimonides was ready to grant that Aristotelians could prove God's existence on their terms, since their posit of the eternal motion of the spheres seemed to require an incorporeal Prime Mover. For he agreed with the Aristotelians that all bodies must be finite and assumed, as they did, that only finite force or power could be expected from a finite body. But that reasoning rested on the now discredited impetus theory of motion. Modern ideas of inertia allow and indeed require a body in motion to remain in motion unless and until something brings it to a halt. And of course, no one before Sir Arthur Eddington had any inkling of fusion, which can derive not infinite but near inexhaustible stores of energy from minute masses of matter.

Emanation, the flow of ideas from an incorporeal divinity, proves strikingly more viable than the once apparent rigor of the Aristotelian Prime Mover idea, with its dependence on archaic mechanical accounts of energy and matter. A new physics has brought us new concepts of mass and wholly new conceptions of the once obscure idea of energy. But the challenge to scriptural monotheists today comes not from confident assertions that the cosmos is eternal but from the idea of "causal closure," which bars entry into the universe of any cause not allowed for in today's (or tomorrow's) physics.

Physics has narrowed its conceptions of causation and explanation, first to mechanism of the pushmi-pullyu variety of the sort prominent in the nineteenth century and then to the mathematical correlations dominant today in field theory and other key areas. But theism still has much to say about nature's dynamism. Matter, one might say today, is far from inert in the old sense of the term. The matter known to today's cosmology is still active like Maimonides' needy matter. But what it now pursues is not some new (Aristotelian) form, complementary to the form it now has, but ever new configurations and possibilities, groping by way of processes that can only with the help of hindsight be called quests.

A paradigm case is the "cooking" of new elements in the stars. But alongside that, we find processes familiar to Maimonides (2.85a), the forming of new compounds. With the help of the fossil record and confirmation from the DNA of ancient and still living species, we can trace the ancient rise of new life-forms evolving on our commodious planet. Stability, procreation, evolution, intelligence, and creativity are among the goals marked by emergence in its varied phases. Mechanism—even when embellished with fields of an electromagnetic, gravitational, or other character—is still the privileged paradigm in notions of causal closure. But mechanism is ill equipped to chart the parameters of emergence.

The idea of causal closure, today's candidate to replace yesterday's "laws" of the (separate) conservation of matter and of energy, stands now where the finitude of force (impetus) available from (or in, or to) a finite body once stood. The exponents of causal closure brand as mere magic any theist's appeals to nonphysical sources of creative energy, just as their counterparts, in dealing with the relations of body and mind, treat any notion that the mind can direct the body or be affected by it (say, in perception) as a superstition that treats the body as a machine haunted by an inexplicable ghost. But the self-assurance that reductive naturalists press in the name of causal closure smacks of the same sort of overconfidence (or dogmatic appeal to authority) that Maimonides faced from those of his contemporaries who voiced their certitude that the world, despite the old biblical tale, was eternal.

Theist cosmologists today cannot help noting that Jaegwon Kim's assertion that every phenomenon has either a natural cause or no cause at all "is not an argument for atheism; it is the premise of atheism."[1] In other words, those who reject theism in the name of their own rather narrow brand of naturalism have begged the question and dismissed all thoughts of God's presence, action, and impact in nature by an appeal to the authority of their own rather reductionist account of nature's workings.

As a result, we might well take a hint from Maimonides' cosmology. For, as the Rambam writes, inspired by Aristotle as well as by the Torah, there are at least four kinds of causation at work in nature, not just one. Where mechanical causes fail or fall short as modes of explanation, we may still do well to look to the intellectual, specifically, and to the realms of value and design that reflect another sort of energies. For information, as any designer knows, is a powerful partner to energies of the more familiar sort. The laws of nature still reveal evidence of wisdom in the workings of the cosmos. And the conatus of things, their drive for persistence and expression, reveals an insistent searching for perfection.

Such groping is observable in all things, in keeping with their natures and the potentials that those natures open to them. Its protean thrust, the pursuit of value and quest for purpose that are so prominent in nature reveal causal energies rather different from those that physics traditionally studies although not alien to some of the dimensions of causality that technology often handles. And the source of those energies may well be boundless in power and in creativity.

Due recognition of emergence reflects the rebirth of teleology—itself an emergent concept. For purposes themselves, inextricable in biology, are emergent and increasingly autonomous as they rise. The value dimension, long taken for granted (and thus readily ignored) in the reductionism that attaches like a lamprey to naturalistic thinking, points unerringly but insistently toward God. The openness of value ideas to thoughts of divinity may help explain why notions of elegance, purpose, and ingenuity have tended to be banished from scientific discourse. Values, the claim goes, are subjective and therefore have no standing in nature and deserve no place in science.

Should the sciences open themselves to the recognition that life and thought are more than the biochemical or electrochemical events on which their emergence depends and that compounds in their lively interchanges are more than the elements that compose them, we might well see a rebirth of metaphysics and theology in the discourses of cosmology at large and in biology and brain science in particular. In that rebirth, a revised Aristotelian/Spinozistic teleology and a new Maimonidean theism could join hands—although new forms of cynical and dismissive reductionism would no doubt rise to meet each new theistic synthesis. For denial in such a case is more a reflection of the moods and attitudes of the deniers than of the science on the ground, or in the heavens.

Maimonides, unlike Empedocles or Epicurus, did not think in terms of natural selection. But the rationalism that underlies his theism precludes attributing nature or anything in nature to mere chance (II 20, 3.31b, 40ab). For chance, after all, is not an explanation, and appeals to chance amount to a refusal of explanation. Or if the word chance stands in as a surrogate for randomness, as it so often does, then we must recognize, as Maimonides does, much in Aristotle's spirit, that chance, in that sense, is indeed "but a superfluity of natural causes" (2.101b). That fact helps explain why randomness at one level of complexity (or of emergence) is so rich a source of order at another.

The world, Maimonides believes, has changed since its creation: We cannot assume, he argues, that the settled order familiar now represents nature as it was *in statu nascendi*. Nor can we project back to the beginning, he argues, rules even as basic as the need for matter to ground potentiality, the posit that Aristotelians long pled to vindicate their scientific/religious postulate of the eternity of the cosmos. As a student of nature, Maimonides seeks natural explanations of natural phenomena. As a philosopher, he holds that every train of causal explanation portends a first cause (2.101a, cf. 2.7a, 46a–47b). But material and mechanical causality, as he teaches and as he learned from Aristotle, are not the only varieties of causation. Here is a truth known to every poet, painter, inventor, architect, or designer. So Maimonides, at home in the reticulated complexities of the law and of the human body, is not slow to remind us.

Aficionados of science today might profit, for that reason, from Maimonides' teaching, as he profited from that of Aristotle (and Galen), in recognizing that efficient causes are not the only sort: "Every effect," he argues, "has four causes: matter, form, end, and agent (or maker *fāʿil*)." God is not just the world's Maker or efficient cause but also its Final and Formal Cause. These lines of causal dependence, no less than the familiar, mechanistic kind, point back to an ultimate (1.89ab). That makes God the Prime Mover, not to the exclusion of the proximate causes studied in the sciences, but as the ultimate Source of the energies and directionalities that animate all things and toward which they (often blindly) reach, grapple, or aspire. God, on this account, would be the Author of the ideas implicit in the design of things and the Goal of the diverse goods that each individual and each type pursues—and, through its efforts and its project, defines.

For Aristotle, as for Maimonides, the Prime Mover moves all things as the goal they seek, each in its own way, each expressing its own nature—all, in their diverse or disparate ways, pursuing the perfection fully found only in God. If we think of the pattern or design of things as their forms in an Aristotelian sense and of the energies that animate all beings as the conatus underlying their capacities to act, we can see what Maimonides means in calling God the formal and efficient cause of all things—and, in that sense, their Maker but also their final cause, the goal motivating their activity and energizing it, indirectly, through the natures all things are given or empowered to develop. We can see here, too, what it means to say that in God the ultimate final, efficient, and formal causes of all that is are one: As the highest good and ultimate font of wisdom and truth, God is rightly called the Creator, not (as in the occasionalist kalām) to the exclusion of the natures He imparts, but by their means and for their sake.

Some philosophers have pronounced teleology dead. Many believe that Darwin killed it. But as you study *The Origin of Species*, note how often the word good appears. The word is far more frequent here than in Genesis. It is critical to the theory of evolution by natural selection that the form and function of every organ and life process in a living being serves a purpose (or once did) for that organism or its kind. The theory of evolution aims to explain how that came about. It would be unwise in the extreme for any theorist to let reductionism get so out of hand as to purge the explanandum—in this case, the fact of adaptation or the higher-order fact of adaptability. Darwin was never so foolish as to erase the very phenomenon he set out to explain: how it is that organs, organ systems, and life processes serve the species in which they are found.

Teleology is evolution's meat. Scientists often find the word teleology embarrassing, since it seems to point toward God as a highest good and Source of all the rest. So scientism and other secularist ideologies work hard to make the word unfashionable and suppress it. But as the famous evolutionary biologist J. B. S. Haldane put it, "Teleology is like a mistress to a biologist: he cannot live without her but he's unwilling to be seen with her in public."[2] Darwin's son

Francis put it squarely: "One of the greatest services rendered by my father to the study of Natural History is the revival of Teleology. The evolutionist studies the purpose or meaning of organs with the zeal of the older Teleologist, but with far wider and more coherent purpose."[3]

Maimonides, we've noted, rejects the notion of a single overarching purpose in all things (III 13). Such a purpose is typically imagined to boil down to serving humankind so that we, in turn, may serve God. For Maimonides, as for the Neoplatonists before him and Spinoza long after, all things exist for their own sakes. It's here that Maimonides sees God's glory. So teleology in Maimonides, as in Aristotle and in Darwin, is, in the first instance, local. God's glory shines in His empowering creatures to seek their own perfection, and that of their kind, insofar as in them lies. Each species and individual can be seen to pursue that goal in the way best suited to it and by the means available to it. Notably, in the human case, that means the flourishing of each unique individual. And that flourishing, in the human case, given the inevitably social nature of our species, means the flourishing of the human race as well. Here we see an ember of the lasting wisdom to be found in Maimonides' *Guide*.

Notes

Introduction

1. Maimonides wrote that he completed his Mishnah commentary in Egypt in 1168 at age thirty. The birth year of 1135, still seen in some sources, based on testimony of the Rambam's grandson, is now seen to be superseded by Maimonides' own testimony.

2. Halbertal, *Maimonides*, 92–94.

3. Kraemer, *Maimonides*, 170; and see *MT* Introduction.

4. Halbertal, *Maimonides*, 95–96; Kellner, *Maimonides' Confrontation*, 79 *n*.

5. See Stroumsa, *Andalus and Sefarad*, 150. The title Maimonides gives the opening book of *MT*, Laws of the Foundations of the Torah, a new usage in Hebrew, reflects the focus on fundamentals prized in Islamic jurisprudence, where legal foundations, as distinguished from black-letter law, are traditionally called *Uṣūl al-Fiqh*. See Stroumsa, *Maimonides in His World*, 70. Maimonides' Hebrew calque on that expression affirms his assumption, shared with Baḥyā Ibn Pāqūdah, that the Torah's practical (and ritual) prescriptions rest on intellectual foundations.

6. In the Aristotelian psychology pursued by Maimonides, there are three facets to the human soul, the broad term for what distinguishes living from nonliving beings. Given their diverse functions and foci, these are sometimes called three souls. In a human being, all three are distinctively human. But the facet governing growth and reproduction is called vegetative, since its general functions are those we have in common with plants—although what sustains a plant is not the same as

what we humans need. The facet governing pursuit and avoidance is called the animal soul, although, again, human motility and irritability are distinctively human and only generically akin to the corresponding functions in nonhuman animals. The facet concerned with thought, practical or theoretical, is called the rational soul, reason, intellect, or simply the mind. The rational soul is the one most distinctively human. Here Maimonides finds our real link with God.

7. See Twersky, *Introduction*, 527.

8. The Rambam's explicit rejection of legal positivism and refutation of the notion that any of the mitzvot are arbitrary and thus pointless (III 25) parallels Philo's reading of the Torah's subtext. To Philo, too, the Torah's laws "are meant to inculcate" specific "intellectual and moral virtues," which are, indeed, their "underlying meaning." Mere external observance is the body of the laws, but their moral and intellectual sense is their soul: "There is no indication that some laws were considered by him as being arbitrary commands by God." Harry Wolfson, *Philo*, 2.223, citing Philo's *On the Migration of Abraham* 16.93.

9. Halbertal, *Maimonides*, 164.

10. Maimonides, *Iggrot*, Shailat, 401.

11. Maimonides, *Iggrot*, Shailat, 256. Hence the Rambam's intention, voiced in the introduction to *SM*, to bypass mere disputes.

12. Maimonides, *Iggrot*, Shailat, 440–41. Before Rabbi's endeavor—that is, the work of Judah the Patriarch—Maimonides holds, Halakhah was not really oral, but individual scholars collected their notes as to the rulings they had heard or inferred; there was no commonly promulgated body of law (*MT*, Introduction).

13. Baḥyā, *Hovot ha-Levavot* (Duties of the Heart), introduction. No one could see that distinction more clearly than Jews who survived the Almohad persecution in Spain and knew what it meant to pay lip service and go through the motions of a piety not accepted in their heads or hearts.

14. See Twersky, *Introduction*, 473.

15. See Maimonides, *SM*, Introduction, tr. Chavel, 2.362; Maimonides, *MT*, Introduction; and Twersky, *Introduction*, 354. Chanan Ariel tracks a handful of divergences in the *MT* from the usages of mishnaic Hebrew mainly, it seems, for clarity's sake (Ariel, "Deviations").

16. Cf. Plutarch, *On Isis and Osiris* 2, 352a, LCL 5.8–9.

17. According to Leibowitz, "To use a modern concept taken from the field of cybernetics, we can depict the relation between the practical commandments and religious faith—in other words, between *halakhah* and philosophy—as feedback mechanism. The *halakhah*, which is an instrument for educating man toward faith, is then reconceived—by means of this faith—not as a means, but as the purpose itself" (*Faith*, 24).

18. The reason Maimonides himself gives is that he did so for the sake of brevity

(*MT*, Introduction). But that explanation itself seems apocopated: The *Yad* clearly aims to sidestep interminable talmudic debates.

19. See Halbertal, *Maimonides*, chap. 4.

20. Dienstag, "Relationship of Maimonides." 42–43. In a letter, Maimonides tells of a visitor demanding to know his rabbinic source for a ruling regarding homicide recorded in *MT*. He was sure he had seen the point of law somewhere but, to his chagrin, could not pinpoint it in two attempts. He found it soon after the man left and sent after him to show him the fugitive text in B. Yevamot. See Halbertal, *Maimonides*, 57–58; and Sarachek, *Faith and Reason*, 34.

21. Assaying differences in Maimonides' handling of key biblical passages in the first fifty chapters of the *Guide* as compared with his treatment of the same texts in later chapters, Hannah Kasher has argued that one can detect two layers in its composition (Kasher, "Is There an Early Stratum?"). Y. Tzvi Langermann argues that in collating the ideas that he would marshal in the *Guide*, Maimonides used the same method as he used in his medical work, compiling a dossier of *fuṣūl* and collating his thoughts on key passages and issues, much as Fārābī had in philosophy and as Rāzī had done in medicine. The Rambam's use of the term *fuṣūl* in the title of the Eight Chapters on ethics that he prefaced to his commentary on M. Avot and his retention of the term for the chapters of the *Guide* support Langermann's thesis. See Langermann's "*Fuṣūl Mūsā*," 325–44.

Chapter 1: Setting the Scene

1. See Goodman, "Greek Impact on Arabic Literature" and "Translation of Greek Materials into Arabic."

2. Starr, *Lost Enlightenment*, 71, 136.

3. See Dong Xiuyuan, "The Presence of Buddhist Thought in Kalām Literature."

4. See Goodman, *Islamic Humanism*, 161–211.

5. Galen, *That the Best Physician Is Also a Philosopher*; Lieber, "Galen: Physician as Philosopher; Maimonides: Philosopher as Physician."

6. See Klibansky, *Continuity of the Platonic Tradition*, 15.

7. Al-Khwarizmī, the inventor of algebra, introduced Hindu numerals into Arabic and explained the use of the numeral zero in the astronomical tables he prepared for the ʿAbbāsid caliph al-Manṣūr in 813. The word "algorithm," based on his name, originally referred to a number system using decimals. Early Greeks did not use a zero and tended to resist the idea that nothing could be something, a bias reflected in Maimonides sharing his Aristotelian predecessors' denial of the reality of the void.

8. See Margoliouth, "Discussion."

9. See Fārābī, *Fī Taḥṣīl al-Saʿādah* § 53, tr. Mahdi, 43.

10. See Sarachek, *Faith and Reason*.

11. Ibn Khaldūn, *Muqaddimah*, tr. Rosenthal.

12. See Stroumsa, *Sefarad and Andalusia*, 28–29.

13. See Lewis, *Islam*, 1.123–34; and Wasserstein, "Family Story."

14. The fetwa is translated (from the 1977 Spanish rendering of Maria Viguera) by Campanini in *Al-Ghazali and the Divine*; cf. O'Callaghan, *History of Muslim Spain*, 210.

15. Ibn Bājjah is the exception that proves the rule. He served in several Almoravid courts and even became a wazīr. But he also served time in an Almoravid prison and in the end seems to have been assassinated by poisoning, a hazard of court life. See Stroumsa, *Andalus and Sefarad*. Understandably, then, he applied to himself and other philosophers al-Fārābī's image of the philosopher or the nonconforming thinker as a weed, an image that Ibn Ṭufayl would paint in rather more hopeful colorations; see *Guide* 2.79b *n*.

16. The burning was authorized by the Almoravid Qāḍī of Cordoba, angered by Ghazālī's criticisms of the *ʿulemāʾ*, who were salaried authorities under the regime. According to the logician Ibn Ṭumlūs, the jurists denounced Ghazālī's writings for potentially shaking the faith of Muslims. See Stroumsa, *Maimonides in His World*, 69.

17. See Stroumsa, *Andalus and Sefarad*, 69–70.

18. See Le Tourneau, *Almohad Movement*, 38–39.

19. Herbert Davidson, *Moses Maimonides*, 10.

20. Ibn Da'ud, *Sefer ha-Kabbalah*, Cohen, Hebrew, 65–66, English, 87–88.

21. For the rigid and controlling hierarchies of Almohad sociopolitical, religious, and educational organization and their rejection of the Islamic tradition of distinct legal schools, see Stroumsa, *Andalus and Sefarad*, 128–34.

22. Like other puritanical movements, the Almohads condemned music, art, and poetry. Maimonides, strikingly, opens the *Guide* by noting his disciple's poetic skill. He treats music as calming (2.80a) and sees lovely objects and pleasant surroundings as fitting in the recreation of the soul (Eight Chapters 5). Poetic sensitivity is critical in reading scripture; see *Guide* 1.2a, 4a–5b, 7ab, 34b, 39a, 2.57b, 59b–62b, 100a, 3.73b, 96b–97a, 126b, 129a. For Maimonides' own verses at the opening and close of the *Guide*, see Zori, "Comments," 767–69; and Kozodoy, "Prefatory Verse," esp. 260 and 266–67, noting Maimonides' use of verses of his own to open *CM* and to open and close the *MT* and the *Guide*. The verses used in the *Guide* are, in fact, attested and preserved in Maimonides' own hand.

23. Stroumsa is skeptical of Marrākushī's account of the caliph's commissioning Averroes' commentaries on Aristotle at Ibn Ṭufayl's instance (*Andalus and Sefarad*, 135–42). But Marrākushī reports the story directly from a disciple of Averroes, who had it from the master himself. The report vividly exposes the double-edged life of the Abū Yaʿqūb Yūsuf as an Almohad ruler and an amateur of philosophy. The same

doubleness recurs in Averroes and Ibn Ṭufayl. Maimonides, too, writes on more than one level, but in part, at least, as we'll see, for a different reason. Still, as Stroumsa stresses, "attempts to present the Almohad regime as a philosophical state in the making are nothing short of fantastic"—as are images of a fideist Maimonides erected on the foundations of his Thirteen Articles of Belief (146–47).

24. Ben-Zaken, *Reading* Ḥayy Ibn-Yaqẓān, 46; Attar, *Vital Roots*; Russell, *"Arabick" Interest*; Goodman, "Molyneux, Mysticism, Empiricism."

25. See Bennison, *Almoravid and Almohad Empires*, 171–76; Fierro, "Legal Policies," 226–48; and Fierro, *Almohad Revolution*.

26. Varied explanations are given for the Almohads' abolition of the protected status of *dhimmī*s, precarious and prejudicial as it was. The most plausible, Stroumsa finds, is Maribel Fierro's: The Almohads wished to expand to all their domains the sanctity of the Hijāz in Arabia, "where no non-Muslims are allowed." See *Maimonides in His World*, 56. Clearly, this radical departure from the usual (but hardly universal) norms of an Islamic imperium starkly reveals the totalizing demand of Almohad theology. It is of a piece with other norms of Muslim *takfīrī*s, those who even today damn as unbelievers all who fail to conform to a projected Islamic ideal. A priori doubts have been raised by some about the reality of the Almohads' fatal demand: "The accumulated evidence of the diverse sources, however, leaves no doubt that the rule was applied in all Almohad lands, and in particular in al-Andalus itself" (Stroumsa, *Maimonides in His World*, 56).

27. Marrākushī, ed. Dozy, 223; Kraemer, *Maimonides*, 92.

28. Marrākushī, ed. Dozy, 223–24.

29. See Stroumsa, *Maimonides in His World*, 130–33.

30. Maimonides, *On Asthma* 13.49, Bos, 1.109; tr. after Bos.

31. Maimonides, *On Asthma* 13.19–32, Bos, 1.90–98.

32. Maimonides, *On Asthma* 13.6, Bos, 1.84; tr. after Bos.

33. Kraemer lays out the evidence convincingly (*Maimonides*, 101–21).

34. Maimon's letter is translated in Simmons, "Letter of Consolation."

35. Maimonides, *Iggeret ha-Shemad* §2, Shailat, 1.43; Stitskin, "Letter of Maimonides," 51.

36. Herbert Davidson, *Moses Maimonides*, 10–27, 501–9; cf. Friedländer's introduction to Maimonides' *Guide* in his translation, xxxiii–xl. The *Iggeret* bears Maimonides' name in every complete manuscript.

37. B. Rosh ha-Shanah 19a, Taʿanit 18a, Meʿilah 17a.

38. Maimonides, *Iggeret ha-Shemad*, Shailat, 1.53–54; translation here is mine.

39. See Halbertal, *Maimonides*, 79; and for the argument of the *Iggeret*, see the nuanced discussion on pp. 28–33.

40. Ibn ʿAqnīn, *Commentary on the Song of Songs*, ed. Halkin, 430.

41. According to Langermann, "Maimonides' use of Quranic phrasing is well

documented" ("Al-Ghazālī's Purported 'Influence'"; cf. S. Harvey, "Al-Ghazali and Maimonides"). We hear such echoes at I 54, 65b; I 72, 102b, I 76, 125b, II 29, 59b–60a, 61b; II 30, 69b; III 3, 6b. The echoes cluster when the *Guide* speaks of natural disasters (I 5, 16b; 31, 35a; III 12, 19a). Langermann finds Qur'ān 2:16, 2:185, and 16:36 echoed when the Letter to Yemen speaks of "deliverance from error," a familiar Islamic phrase given currency by its use by Ghazālī as the title of his spiritual autobiography. The use of such phrases, like talk today of good Samaritans, or using one's talents, or not hiding one's light under a bushel, by itself proves nothing but only reflects the milieu in which the Rambam lived. Judaeo-Arabic regularly calls God *Allāh* and the Torah *Sharīʿa*. The Qur'ānic echoes in Maimonides' early work on logic are more telling.

42. In *Moses Maimonides*, Herbert Davidson impugns the authority of Ibn al-Qifṭī and Ibn Abī ʿUṣaybiʿa.

43. Kraemer, *Maimonides*, 127.

44. It is not known just where they walked. The city was filled with churches, and the Temple Mount was exceedingly difficult of access for Jews and Muslims. See Kraemer, *Maimonides*, 135–38.

45. See *Guide* III 29; 2.18a, 28a. For Maimonides, Moses and Abraham are paradigms of Jewish belief (2.29b, 51a); but Abraham, he argues, was not Moses' equal as a prophet: He taught by precept and example but did not frame a law (II 39). Still he was the natural theologian par excellence. At *Guide* 1.22b, citing Isaiah 51:1, Maimonides couples Sarah with Abraham as a founding figure—not so Moses' wife Zipporah.

46. Baron, *Social and Religious History*, 3.105–6; Kraemer, *Maimonides*, 154.

47. See Goitein, *Mediterranean Society*, 6 vols.; and Hoffman and Cole, *Sacred Trash*.

Chapter 2: Learning

1. See Gandz, "Date of the Composition."

2. Kraemer, *Maimonides*, 63.

3. Kraemer, 59.

4. Kraemer, 64; Halbertal, *Maimonides*, 19–20, 76.

5. Maimonides recalls great thinkers of the past—Judah the Patriarch, al-Fāsī, Ibn Migash, and Aristotle—with nostalgia and lost pride. See Shailat, *Introductions*, 125–26. Menachem Kellner systematically treats Maimonides' demurral from the presumption of decline with the passing generations of halakhic decisors in *Maimonides on the "Decline of the Generations."*

6. Alive to the challenge of historical and cultural change, Maimonides speaks of Israel's spiritual infancy on first receiving the Torah; cf. his references to progress in astronomy. He regularly distinguishes modern investigators (*muta'akhirūn*) from

the ancients; see *Guide* 1.94b, 120b, 121b, 2.13b, 19b, 30b, 31a, 41a, 46ab, 52a, 3.34b, 35b, 112b, 133a.

7. Maimonides' taking exception to rabbinic dicta is not unprecedented. The Sages often countered one another vigorously. And Saadiah, we note, at Esther 1:11, demurs at the Sages' midrashic notion (B. Megillah 12b) that when Ahasuerus wished Vashti to appear at his feast in her crown, she was to wear nothing more (cf. Herodotus, *History* 1.8). She was, in fact, to be royally attired, "for one does not wear a crown without donning the attire" (Saadiah, *Book of Conviviality*, Wechsler, 160). But, as Arthur David remarks, Maimonides is notably independent minded: "Rarely, if ever, did a Rabbinic authority dispute previous Geonic opinions." But to Maimonides, the status of the Geonim "did not confer any superior significance to their decisions. . . . He did not hesitate to overrule the great Isaac Alfasi, whom he revered." Maimonides, in fact, counted some thirty points on which he had done so—just as he (not unlike al-Rāzī) named some forty errors in Galen (Maimonides, *Commentary to Mishnah* Aboth, tr. David, 147–48 *n.* 70).

8. Naḥmanides (ad Gen. 46.1) faults Maimonides for overstating Onkelos' skirting of anthropomorphisms. Citing Maimonides' statement that Onkelos "made it his aim to purge corporealism, substituting fitting glosses for any biblical description suggesting God's embodiment" (1.30a), Naḥmanides catalogs passages that disappoint that expectation: Genesis 46:3–4, Exodus 19:20, Deuteronomy 31:3, 31:18, and the many biblical references to God's speech and to His hearing and seeing. He discounts Maimonides' explanations, which located some of these cases in the context of a prophetic dream or vision or his thought that Onkelos must have taken, say, *the finger of God* that etched the commandments on stone at Sinai to be a created object (see Exodus 31:18, 32:16, glossed at I 66) and explaining some of the anthropomorphisms that Onkelos let stand by reference to the idea of transcendence so that poetically, God cannot *look on evil* (Habakkuk 1:13, cited at 1.16a). Clearly, Onkelos was not perfectly consistent. But some of his tolerance reflects a respect for the biblical idiom that Maimonides shares; see II 48. Naḥmanides is not just nitpicking, however. He sees kabbalistic mysteries behind the anthropomorphisms he stets. For the topos and the literature it spawns, see Naḥmanides, *Perush ha-Torah*, ed. Chavel, 2.236–42; tr. 2.243–53. See the discussion and an entrée to the literature in Kellner, *Maimonides' Confrontation*, 177 *n.* 78.

9. See *CM* ed. Kafiḥ, 1.37 and 6.2.738.

10. There's more truth than meets the eye here: "Maimonides' knowledge of astronomy progressed over the years. . . . Before he studied astronomy seriously, he said that the moon was visible in the east before sunrise and in the west after sunset on the same day. Later, in his *Commentary on the Mishnah*, he declared that whoever believed such a thing . . . has no more awareness of the celestial sphere than *an ox or an ass* (1 Samuel 12:3)." Kraemer, *Maimonides*, 67. The aspersion was self-deprecating,

Kraemer notes—at least for those who noticed the discrepancy. Herbert Davidson disputes Joel Kraemer's point; see *Moses Maimonides*, 145–46.

11. Herbert Davidson denies Maimonides' authorship of the work, largely on a priori grounds (*Moses Maimonides*, 313–22). For the evidence of its authenticity, see Stroumsa, *Maimonides in His World*, 126–28; M. Z. Cohen, "Logic to Interpretation."

12. Pines, in his introduction to the *Guide* (lix), names Averroes as one of the philosophers praised in Maimonides' letter of 1199 to Ibn Tibbon. But the addition of that name seems to be a later interpolation, made, perhaps, by one of Averroes' many Jewish admirers. See Doron Forte's impressive analysis of the manuscript tradition of the oft-quoted letter, "Back to the Sources," 47–90.

13. Maimonides, *Treatise on Logic* §8, Efros, English, 49; see 1.96a–97a, 2.32a–33a, 51a. It was customary in works of Islamic theology to refer to logical reasoning as *qiyās*, analogy, given the relevance of arguments from analogy in drawing inferences from legal precedent, since Muslim theologians were often jurists first and foremost—and, besides, the word for logic, *manṭiq*, smacked of *falsafa*.

14. For the "poetic syllogism," see Kemal, *Poetics*; and Goodman, *Avicenna*, 220–22.

15. See Stroumsa, *Andalus and Sefarad*, 90–94.

16. Fārābī, *K. Fī Taḥṣīl al-Saʿādah* (Hyderabad, 1345 AH), in Sezgin's collection *Islamic Philosophy*, 16.8–9; tr. Mahdi §§ 10–12, 18–19.

17. For the course of study approved and pursued by Maimonides and others who aspired to higher understanding, see Stroumsa, *Andalus and Sefarad*, 90–94.

18. See *Kobetz* 2.25 (cited on 3.62b). *MT* Laws concerning Alien Worship 2.2–3 finds the study of pagan worship halakhically forbidden, given Deuteronomy 12:30. But the grounds Maimonides states are telling: Persons ignorant of the rules of reasoning might be drawn to doubt the truth of biblical monotheism and wonder if there is not some truth behind pagan devotions. Such wondering involves no overt act, so it is not punished, but the straying mind frays its link to God. Yehudah Parnes dissolved Maimonides' seeming inconsistency in studying what he deemed forbidden texts by explaining that the ban did not apply to study needed to ground juridical rulings. Lawrence Kaplan and David Berger pressed the point, arguing that even the initial prohibition must be hemmed in lest it seem to ban studying any text that might shake one's faith—even, say, the Book of Job, or elegies for the rabbinic martyrs of the Roman imperium, or the many Jewish martyrs of the Crusades. The issue turns on how one parses 'study.' In *SM*, Maimonides articulates the norm clearly: Banned is not mere examination of pagan doctrines but their pursuit. Maimonides' "primary intention," the authors argue, "is not to foreclose inquiry into critical areas of religious discourse but to regulate an enterprise that he regarded as not merely permissible, but essential, obligatory, and standing at the very apex of

the Torah itself." (Kaplan and Berger, "Freedom of Inquiry," 37–50, responding to Parnes, "Torah U-Madda," 68–71; cf. Gevaryahu, "Maimonides as a Historian"). To eschew idolatry, the Sages taught, in a way encompasses all the commandments. But one can hardly observe that mitzvah unless one knows what idolatry is—or observe it intelligently if one does not understand why it has had so long and powerful a hold on human minds.

19. Stroumsa, *Maimonides in His World*, 103–4.

20. Maimonides views the history of Christian and Muslim dominance with the same theocentric lens: These two religions, only pave the way for the Messiah. They are, in a Jewish sense, a *praepartio evangelica*, teaching the world to accept monotheism. See *MT* Laws of Kings and Wars 11.4; cf. 3.62b. Muslims may dismiss the Torah, and Christians may read it allegorically as a prefiguration of their own faith. But with the coming of the Messiah, all will see the light. The *MT* passage cited here was censored and deleted from the *Yad* by medieval Christians, but it survives in precious manuscripts and is preserved in good modern editions; see Stroumsa, *Maimonides in His World*, 108–9.

21. See Ira Robinson, "Evolution of Divine Worship," 266–76.

22. See Plato, *Republic* VII 527d–530e.

23. The words *falsafa* for philosophy and *falāsifa* for philosophers stand out in Arabic: They burst the triliteral consonantal frame typical in words originating in Semitic languages, and they show no visible connection to thoughts of the love of wisdom that can be cited in languages with tight semantical links to Greek.

24. Nowhere, Harry Wolfson found, did Maimonides use his analytic powers more incisively than in drawing up the twenty-five propositions from which to derive, "in compact and pithy form," Aristotle's main doctrines, "supplemented by some from Avicenna" (*Crescas' Critique*, 1). With the added posit of the world's eternity, Maimonides held (II Introduction), the Philosophers could demonstrate God's existence, unity, and incorporeality.

25. See Schwarz, "Who Were Maimonides' Mutakallimūn?"

26. Al-Ashʿarī, *K. Maqālāt al-Islāmiyyīn*.

27. Fakhry pays tribute to Maimonides' "comprehensive account," valued by Albertus Magnus and Thomas Aquinas, in *Islamic Occasionalism*, 25–26.

28. See Harry Wolfson, *Philosophy of the Kalām*, 46, 112–42.

29. See Plotinus, *Enneads* 3.4.3, 4.1.11, 4.8.8, 5.1.10, 6.2.22; cf. Baḥyā and Ibn Ezra.

Chapter 3: Cairo

1. Halbertal, *Maimonides*, 18.

2. As Bernard Lewis showed, this would have been Amalric I, not Richard the Lionheart. See Bernard Lewis, "Maimonides, Lionheart, and Saladin."

3. See Kraemer, *Maimonides*, 190, 269–73.

4. Kraemer, *Maimonides*, 241–42; and see Halbertal, *Maimonides*, 47–56.

5. The letter's Arabic original is edited by Shailat in Maimonides, *Igrot* 1.82–112, with Ibn Tibbon's Hebrew translation, 1.113–68; ed. Kafiḥ, 15–60, with modern Hebrew tr.; English tr., by Kraemer in Lerner's *Maimonides' Empire of Light*, 99–132; and by Abraham Halkin in Hartman and Halkin, *Crisis and Leadership*, 91–131.

6. See Azzam, *Saladin*, 141; Kraemer, Maimonides, 193.

7. For the sect's tally of assassinated leaders, see Lewis, *Assassins*.

8. See Gibb, *Life of Saladin*, 19. For the Nizārīs' attempts on Saladin's life and the sect's split from Ismāʿīlī Shīʿism, see Hodgson, *Order of Assassins*, 188–89.

9. Brockelmann, *History*, 229.

10. Brockelmann, 230–31; Hitti, *History of the Arabs*, 439; Kraemer, *Maimonides*, 205–6.

11. ʿImād al-Dīn, cited by Kraemer, *Maimonides*, 210.

12. Hitti, *History of the Arabs*, 427.

13. Reduced and more equitable taxes, Plato had argued, enhance state revenues. Miskawayh, a philosopher/wazīr (932–1030), had applied the approach successfully.

14. Kraemer, *Maimonides*, 198–99.

15. Gibb, *Life of Saladin*, 46–48.

16. Brockelmann, *History*, 231.

17. Kraemer, *Maimonides*, 162, citing Maimonides, *CM* Kellim 17.16.

18. Marco Polo, *Travels*, 1.107.

19. Kraemer, *Maimonides*, 159, draws on Goitein's work with the record preserved in the Cairo Geniza.

20. Gibb, *Life of Saladin*, 50.

21. The story of David's letter is beautifully detailed in Kraemer, *Maimonides*, 249–51.

22. Kraemer, *Maimonides*, 251.

23. Marco Polo, *Travels*, tr. Yule, 1.107–8; cf. Kraemer, *Maimonides*, 252. The "fish oil" was whale oil. The stitched vessels, up to two hundred tons burden, Yule reports, were still used until steamships made them uncompetitive on the open seas (1.83–84).

24. Maimonides' letter to Japhet ben Elijah, quoted in Kraemer, *Maimonides*, 255.

25. Hertz, ed. and tr., *Sayings of the Fathers*, 30. Rabbi Hertz here cites Shemayah's dictum: "Love work, hate being an overlord, and don't be beholden to authority" (M. Avot 1.10).

26. *MT* Gifts to the Poor 10.18, quoting B. Pesaḥim 113a; cf. Laws of Torah Study 1.9; *CM* at M. Avot 4.5.

27. Rabban Gamliel's son was quoted as saying, "All my life I grew up among the Sages and found nothing better for anyone than silence. Action, not learning, is

what matters. Much talk leads only to sin" (M. Avot 1.17). Maimonides comments, "Concision is the mark of a sage; verbosity, that of a fool, as it says, *many words mark the voice of a fool* (Ecclesiastes 5:2)." *CM* at Avot 1:17. The previous verse in Ecclesiastes underscores the point: *God is in heaven, and thou art on earth. Therefore let thy words be few* (5:1).

28. See *MT* Laws concerning Torah Study 3.10, Gifts for the Poor 10.18, Acquisition 12.17, Sanhedrin 23.5.

29. Twersky, *Introduction*, 5.

30. Ibn Abī Usaybiʿa, *ʿUyūn al-Anbāʾ fī Ṭabaqāt al-Aṭibbāʾ*, 582; and see *On Asthma*, Bos, xxvii *n.* 19; Kraemer, *Maimonides*, 215.

31. See Kraemer's reading of Maimonides' letter to an inquirer who was seeking private instruction on the *Guide* (*Maimonidean Studies* 1.97).

32. See Bos, "Maimonides' Medical Works," 249–50.

33. Maimonides, *On Poisons*.

34. Kraemer, *Maimonides*, 193, 199.

35. Maimonides, *On Coitus*, Bos's introduction, ix.

36. Moses was denied entry to the promised land (Numbers 20:9–13, 24; Deuteronomy 32:51), Maimonides holds, for letting things slip to the point that he could succumb to anger, falling away from the character Israel gave him as a paragon of virtue, and addressing the people with less than the dignity they deserved (Eight Chapters 4).

37. Maimonides, *Medical Aphorisms* 25.1, 59.

38. See the discussion in Kellner, *Maimonides' Confrontation*, 159–78.

39. See Rāzī, *Shukūk ʿalā Jālīnūs*.

40. Maimonides, *Medical Aphorisms* 25.64. See *Guide* 2.21b *n.* 86.

41. Cf. *MT* Laws of Tefillin and Mezuzot, 5.4; Laws concerning Alien Worship 11.

42. Maimonides, "Letter on Astrology," Marx, 349–50.

43. *MT* Laws regarding Pagan Worship 11.16; cf. *SM* Negative 34–38.

44. Cf. Bos, "Maimonides' Medical Works," 257–61. The Sages allow incantations for victims of snakebite or a scorpion sting, but only, Maimonides insists, to allay the victim's terror (*MT* Laws regarding Pagan Worship, 11.11). Marc Shapiro catalogs the many rabbinic rulings sidelined as superstitious in the *MT* or given naturalistic explanations (*Studies*, 96–150). Characteristically, Maimonides takes the practice of changing the name of a person who is dangerously ill (B. Rosh ha-Shanah 16b) not as a device to deceive the angel of death but as an act of penitence, "as if to say, I am a different person" (Laws of Repentance 2.4).

45. See Leviticus 19:16; Deuteronomy 5:30, 8:1, 16:20, 30:6, 30:16–20; *MT* Shabbat 11.4, Yom ha-Kippurim 2.9, 3.2; Laws regarding Murder and Preservation of Life 1.14, 1.16.

46. *MT* Laws concerning Theft and Lost Property 1.1; *CM* Vows 4.4; see 3.131a.

47. Lieber, "Medical Works," 13–24.

48. Maimonides, *Commentary on Hippocrates'* Aphorisms 1.28, tr. after Bos, 1.54–55.

49. *MT* Laws regarding Forbidden Foods 17:29–30.

50. For the moral and spiritual dimensions of health in Maimonides' view, see Goodman, "Bahyā and Maimonides," 78–84.

51. *MT* Neighbors 10.3–4. See M. Bava Batra 2.8–9, Tosefta, ed. Saul Lieberman, 1.10; Maimonides, *On Asthma*, last chap.; and Rosner, "Moses Maimonides," 574.

52. *MT* Laws regarding Murder and Preservation of Life 11:4–5.

Chapter 4: A New Life

1. Exodus Rabbah 31.3.

2. Twersky, *Introduction*, 5.

3. See Friedman, "Social Realities," 180–85.

4. Kraemer, *Maimonides*, 255.

5. See Ibn al-Qifṭī, *Taʾrikh al-Ḥukamāʾ*, Lippert, 317–19.

6. See Gibb, *Life of Saladin*, 20.

7. Stroumsa, *Andalus and Sefarad*, 94–101, 145–46.

8. See Stroumsa, *Maimonides in His World*, 117.

9. *CM* at Avot 1.17, tr. David, 20–21; cf. 3.14a.

10. Ibn Sanaʾ al-Mulk and Maimonides apparently did business together too, for there is a record that both of them had lent money to the same man. Kraemer, *Maimonides*, 206–7.

11. Kraemer, *Maimonides*, 471.

12. Halbertal, *Maimonides*, 69.

13. "For the saintly no tombstone is set on their graves. Their deeds are their memorial" (*MT* Laws of Mourning 4.4).

Chapter 5: Believing

1. For the text of the Thirteen Articles of Belief, see *Maimonides' Commentary on the Mishnah: Tractate Sanhedrin*, tr. Rosner, 134–88, or Blumenthal, *Commentary of R. Hoter ben Shelomo*. Kellner reprints Blumenthal's rendering in *Dogma*, 10–17. For a reading not unlike mine, see Hyman, "Maimonides' Thirteen Principles"; cf. Kellner, *Dogma*, 36–43.

2. Alexander Marx counted over ninety Hebrew versifications of the Thirteen Articles (Kozodoy, "Prefatory Verse," 257–58). For the checkered history of the articles in Judaism, see Shapiro, *Limits of Orthodox Theology*.

3. See Urbach, *The Sages*, 1.29, 354. Thus the wicked son of the Passover Hagaddah, pictured as "belying the central principle" (*kafar ba-ʿikkar*). He denies not the exis-

tence but the providence of God: His scoffing at the Paschal celebration exposes his refusal to see the hand of God in history.

4. Kellner, *Dogma*, 5.

5. See Kellner, 21–24.

6. In *MT* Laws regarding Pagan Worship, Maimonides writes that heretics of Jewish origin (*minim*) should not be treated as Jews or accepted as penitents; they have no portion in the World to Come. But in Laws of Repentance, he writes that such sectarians are debarred from the World to Come only if they die unrepentant. There is no inconsistency here, he urges in a responsum: The first ruling was social; such recusants should be treated as the heretics they are. The second regards their relationship to God: If they truly repent, God's forgiveness cannot be excluded.

7. See *MT* Laws of Kings and Wars 8.11 and the key discussions in Kellner, *Maimonides' Confrontation with Mysticism*, 241–50 and Kellner and Gillis, *Maimonides the Universalist*, 33 *n.* 72. Notice the powerful difference Maimonides presumes between belief and knowledge when he (like Rāzī) ascribes much interhuman bloodshed and warfare to differences in belief, which he hopes and expects will dissolve when human beings are united in the knowledge of God, III 11, 3.17b.

8. M. Sanhedrin 10.1; cf. *MT* Laws of Kings and Wars 8.11.

9. See *MT* Laws of Repentance 3.5; cf. Maimonides' letter to Hasdai ha-Levi in *Kovetz* 2.23d–24a. For Maimonides' universalism, see Kellner, *Maimonides' Confrontation*, 15, 229–33.

10. Strauss calls Maimonides' Platonizing account of prophecy "the most developed form of medieval prophetology as such" (*Philosophy and Law*, 56).

11. Building on B. Bava Metzia 32b, Maimonides sees priority in helping one's enemy: The mitzvah aims to improve one's character (and the communal ethos; III 51, Eight Chapters 4).

12. See Goodman, *Holy One of Israel*, 13–18, 43, 115.

13. R. Abbahu of Caesaria speaks to the problem Maimonides faces and obliquely anticipates his solution: "In the future many will say with astonishment: Where does So-and-so abide, who has never studied the Torah or the Mishnah? He actually abides with his ancestors and converses with them! God replies to them: Why are you astonished? It is perfectly just that it should be so, because during their lifetime they obeyed Me" (*Aggadat Bereshit*, ed. Buber, 163, tr. after Marmorstein, *Studies*, 171–72).

14. See Kellner, *Dogma*, 54.

15. Leibowitz, *Faith*, 21, 26, 40, 50–52.

16. Summing up the Rambam's view, Leibowitz writes, "Maimonides' philosophy is belief in God . . . in God *alone* and not in anything 'other . . .'—in anything added to Him by the human imagination . . . which he raises to the rank of God. . . . God's unity is not an arithmetical oneness, but an essential one. . . . There is no thing

which has any resemblance to God" (*Faith*, 21). God's oneness, Leibowitz writes, "is qualitative and not quantitative . . . in no way similar to anything whose qualities or attributes are conceived by human consciousness. . . . He is the transcendent God, the God who is beyond anything which exists in human awareness. . . . This belief is an extremely hard task imposed on man, whose consciousness naturally tends to relate only to things . . . which he can perceive with his senses or imagine to himself. If this is how a man relates to his God, it follows that he is worshiping himself" (41).

17. I. A. Richards wrote, "It would seem that the original and primary function of metaphor and kindred images is to express some idea not adequately expressible otherwise. . . . The problem of expressing in speech immaterial mental concepts was solved by borrowing language which originally expressed simple physical actions and material objects" (*Philosophy of Rhetoric*, 76). In the *MT*, Maimonides cites the references to God's hands, feet, finger, eyes, and ears at Genesis 38:7; Exodus 9:3, 24:10, 31:18; and Numbers 11:1, treating all as accommodations of the commonality (Laws of the Foundations of the Torah 1.9). But at 1.31a, he praises Onkelos for treating the feet in Exodus 24:10 as belonging to the throne of God's Glory. At 1.21b and 31b, he takes biblical references to God's feet to intend His agency. The more nuanced approach shows the advance of his thinking about biblical anthropomorphisms beyond the stage seen in the *MT*.

18. See also Letter to Yemen, in Hartman and Halkin, *Crisis and Leadership*, 103.

19. In the *MT* Introduction, under the heading "Rabbinic Commandments," Maimonides explains that the Sages do institute new laws, as, for example, by ordaining the celebrations of Purim and Hanukkah, relying on the authority imparted by Deuteronomy 17:11. These do not amount to additions proscribed by the law (13:11). For the new authority does not pretend to act by God's command but simply implements (and, indeed, elaborates) what the Torah ordains (e.g., thanking God for His grace)—or, in the case of *eruvim* (the notional boundaries that allow one to carry things on Shabbat beyond what would otherwise be ritually permissible) or handwashing before meals, to render keeping the law workable and dignified. The elaborations, in effect, do not count as radical or substantive changes.

20. Maimonides denies providence "in the sense of a service provided for man by God," since such notions treat God merely instrumentally (Leibowitz, *Faith*, 29). That reading does not exclude the oversight and judgment affirmed here. But it does call for a far-from-anthropomorphic reading of accountability; cf. Maimonides' treatment of Moses' failing and of the hardening of Pharaoh's heart (Eight Chapters 4, 8).

21. Israel's subjugation in exile is clearly uppermost in Rabbi Samuel's mind and in the Rambam's, but he universalizes the point given the premise that the transformation hoped for and expected in the Messianic Age is moral, socioeconomic, and political although not apocalyptic in the familiar lurid sense.

22. For the virtuous circle of the Messianic Age, see Goodman, *On Justice*, 156–94.

23. Maimonides' particularism here harks back to Halevi's sly condemnation of the *Falāsifa* as exponents of a universal way of thought that seeks, somehow, to stand aloof from the world's struggle. Their pure quest for beatitude seems, in the end, empty-handed and empty-headed before the bloody conflict among nations and the sects that ride or rule their peoples; see *Kuzari* 1.2–3.

24. Cf. Plato, *Republic* 621c.

25. Maimonides seems in part to target Saadiah here, who falls victim to his efforts to include every rabbinic doctrine or biblical image he can; see *ED* VII, Kafiḥ, 218–36; Rosenblatt, esp. 276–88, and the variant text, 430–35.

26. Cf. Philo, *De Specialibus Legibus* 2.47.259.

27. Jacobs, *Law, Reason, and Morality*, 151.

28. Seeskin, *Searching for a Distant God*, 149–50; Seeskin rightly goes on to relate Maimonides' point to the shift in outlook that Job affirms after his epiphany (3.48b–49a).

29. Seeskin, *Searching for a Distant God*, 154–55.

30. See the Rambam's treatment of trial at *Guide* III 24.

31. See Saadiah, *ED* Introductory Treatise 3.

32. See Gellman, "Love of God," 219. Stoics see moral maturity in the realization that the life of virtue is its own reward; see Cicero, *De Finibus* 3.5–7.

33. Gellman, "Love of God," 219.

34. Gellman, 220–21; cf. Spinoza: *Ethics* 4 Propositions 63–73.

35. Gellman, "Love of God," 221.

36. Gellman, 222. Gellman goes on to show how the philosophic union of piety with science proposed in Maimonides' Mishnah commentary and in the *MT* but consummated in the *Guide* fosters the sense of agency and freedom critical in the service of God out of love.

37. See Seeskin's thoughtful disquisition on "Popular Religion and a Personal God" in *Searching for a Distant God*, chap. 7; and see Goodman, *Holy One of Israel*, 23.

38. Kraemer, *Maimonides*, 412. For the faded glory of the Baghdad academy, see Stroumsa, *Maimonides in His World*, 168.

39. Stroumsa, *Maimonides in His World*, 166.

40. Kraemer, *Maimonides*, 412.

41. See Kraemer, 412–13; and Rustow, "Ibn al-Dastūr."

42. *Letters* 7, Baneth, 85–90.

43. Stroumsa, *Maimonides in His World*, 166–72. Abraham Harkavy established the authenticity and sequence of the three works in the late nineteenth century. See his "Fragment einer Apologie," 125–28, 181–88.

44. Averroes in the West, facing comparable pressures, likewise attempted to draw a line of demarcation between religion and philosophy in his *Faṣl al-Maqāl* (ca. 1190).

45. Stroumsa, *Maimonides in His World*, 177, citing Hartman and Halkin, *Crisis and Leadership*, 246–48, 263.

46. Kraemer, *Maimonides*, 204.

47. Kraemer, 418.

48. Of what Maimonides entrusts to a letter, Leibowitz writes, "He generally abstains, to the best of his ability, from saying anything which is not, in his opinion, true—but at the same time, he does not find it fair to say the *whole* truth, if he thinks that the recipient of the letter is incapable of understanding it" (*Faith*, 21, 40, 50–19). Burke first used 'economy' in our present sense in *Letters on a Regicide Peace* (1796), calling it "a sort of temperance, by which a man speaks truth with measure that he may speak it the longer." Newman cited the counsel of Jesus against casting pearls before swine (Matthew 7:6).

49. Taking 'Sabian' here as a generic term for pagans (just as Maimonides uses it), one can say that Averroes was right: Immortality for the ancient Greeks meant divinity and was thus a pagan notion. Plato, who held the rational soul to be divine, was keen to bite that bullet. But few later thinkers, least of all among modern theologians in the West, have grappled with the pagan implications of calling human souls deathless. In Maimonides' case, as in that of his philosophical role models among scriptural monotheists—men like Avicenna, Ibn Bājjah, and Ibn Ṭufayl—personal immortality required careful navigation of the terrain between monopsychism and some variety of *ḥulūlī* immanentism dangerously near a type of pantheism. For Maimonides' cautious disclaimers here, see *Guide* 1.121b and note.

50. *Tahāfut al-Tahāfut*, tr. after Van Den Bergh, 1.359–60. According to Aristotle, "Not every problem or thesis should be scrutinized, but only those that might puzzle someone in need of an argument, and not punishment or perception. For those who wonder whether one should honor the gods and love one's parents need punishment, and those who wonder whether snow is white need perception" (*Topics* 1.11, 105a2–7).

51. Kraemer, *Maimonides*, 418. Aristotle sets the tone Averroes takes here, when he writes,

> Our forefathers in the most distant ages passed down to us, their progeny, a tradition in the form of a myth, that these (celestial) substances are gods and that all nature is embraced by the divine. The rest of the tradition was added in mythical form with a view to persuasion of the multitude, and to its legal and practical expedience: These gods, they say, have human or animal form. . . . We must regard this as an inspired pronouncement, and reflect that, while probably each art and

science has many times developed as far as possible and then perished, these beliefs are preserved to the present like relics. It is only so far, then, that the beliefs of our ancestors and earliest forerunners make sense to us. (*Metaphysics* Λ 12.8, 1074b1–14)

52. Jewish traditionalism is called orthodoxy somewhat misleadingly. For its exponents may play fast and loose with matters of creed but set ritual practice at the pinnacle of concern. The resulting ethos can foster a distaste for Maimonidean inquiries into the roots and warrants of the mitzvot that outruns the worry that observance may be dropped by those who feel able to achieve the presumptive ends of the laws without their halakhic means. One unwholesome result: an outright anti-intellectualism prompted by fears lest curiosity stray beyond the prescribed parameters of Halakhic study. Indeed, the centrality of the mitzvot can and does lead to the theurgic (and magical) notions found in Hasidic thinking, where ritual performances are conceived as cosmic levers, with each mitzvah fulfilled contributing to the denouement in the cosmic drama.

53. Aviv Rosenblatt, in a personal communication, suggests that Rabad sought at least as much to defend rabbinical authority as to combat the sway of reason, science, and logic. That thought clearly has merit. But what is sad, borderline tragic, is that Rabad, unlike Maimonides, saw a conflict between reason and tradition, one that Maimonides had the power and grace to surmount.

54. Abraham ben David (Rabad), *Hasagot*, at *MT* Laws of the Sanctification of the New Month 7.7. Saadiah's astronomical studies complemented his halakhic learning in settling a controversy on the Hebrew calendar. Solomon Maimon records Rabad's dismissal in his *Autobiography*, 131.

55. See Kellner, *Dogma*, 241 *n.* 220.

56. See also *CM* Sanhedrin 10; *MT* Laws of the Foundations of the Torah 1.7–8, 11; *Guide* 1.12a *n.*

57. Baron, *Social and Religious History*, 8.40–41. Those Jewish mystics whose corporealist leanings are betrayed in a sometimes guilty fascination with the *Shiʿur Komah* typically fanned hopes of bodily resurrection with fantasies, rejected by Maimonides, of the torments of the damned. Their Albigensian contemporaries denied both hell and physical resurrection (Sarachek, *Faith and Reason*, 4, 80).

58. See Shapiro, *Studies*, 93; and Solomon Maimon, *Autobiography*, 130–31.

59. See Bos, "Maimonides' Medical Works," 259; Maimonides, *Medical Aphorisms*, ed. and tr. Bos, 22.35–70; and Bos's introduction, xx–xxii.

60. Halbertal, *Maimonides*, 19.

61. Halbertal, 9–10.

62. Kraemer, *Maimonides*, 66.

63. Kraemer, 67.

64. Sabra, "Andalusian Revolt," 133–53.

65. Averroes abandoned epicycles and eccentrics in his long commentary on Aristotle's *Metaphysics* (Λ 8, 1073b):

> That an eccentric sphere or an epicyclic sphere exists is unnatural. The epicycle is simply impossible. For a rotating body must revolve about the center of the universe and no other point. What revolves *makes* the center what it is. If there were rotation about some other point, there would have to be another center and another earth, all of which physics has shown to be impossible. Likewise, it seems, were the eccentric Ptolemy posits to exist: If there were multiple centers of rotation, heavy bodies would not fall to earth. The center would not be the midpoint but extended and divisible. But all this is unsound. If there were eccentrics, moreover, some heavenly bodies would be otiose, having no more function than to fill the space, as is supposedly the case in animals' bodies. But no observation of the planetary motions requires positing an eccentric or epicyclic sphere. (*Tafsīr mā Baʿḍa al-Ṭabīʿa*, ed. Bouyges, 3.1661–62)

66. Resianne Fontaine sees Ibn Daʾud as a key figure among those that Maimonides admired in affirming his intellectual kinship with the thinkers of al-Andalus (Fontaine, "Was Maimonides an Epigone?").

Chapter 6: Defining the Issues

1. Maimonides frequently admonishes his reader to give careful consideration to the points made in each chapter of the *Guide*, even where his exposition may stray from the immediate topic addressed. His word for consideration here is *iʿtibār*, which connotes close philosophical scrutiny. See Warren Zev Harvey, "Averroes and Maimonides," 75–83 (Hebrew).

2. Kellner translates the passage in "Maimonides' Commentary on Mishnah Ḥagigah II 1."

3. As Strauss points out, Maimonides, like the Mutakallimūn, does not believe that prophets *perform* miracles—not that he denies human agency as kalām occasionalists did but because he rejects the notion that God interferes in the settled order of nature once His timeless will has ordained its pattern. See *Philosophy and Law*, 96.

4. Cf. Strauss, 47.

5. Parmenides, frag. 8, from Simplicius, *In Phys.* 78, 5 and 145; see Kirk, Raven, and Schofield, *Presocratic Philosophers*, 273.

6. Cf. Strauss, *Philosophy and Law*, 45; and Seeskin, *Searching for a Distant God*, 66–87.

7. For the embarrassment of the Geonim, see Lorberbaum, "Anthropomorphisms."

8. See Freudenthal, "Maimonides on the Scope of Metaphysics."

9. Marmorstein tracks the post-Pauline rejection of the Law and the Rabbis' response in *Studies*, 179–224. Against the argument that the Patriarchs kept no such rituals, the Sages posit that the Patriarchs knew and kept them all; against the charge that the mitzvot (beyond the Decalogue) were empty, they cite texts affirming God's welcome of them; against the charge that observance was tedious, they cite the joy inherent in sincere observance: "One who loves the mitzvot never has enough of them" (Deuteronomy Rabbah 2.18).

10. See *Ḥayy Ibn Yaqẓān*, tr. Goodman, 151–55.

11. Kraemer, *Maimonides*, 370, notes the "intimate and conversational" style of the *Guide*. Maimonides, he notes, calls it a *maqālah*, not a *risālah*, underscoring its turn toward spoken language.

Chapter 7: Problematics

1. The idea of continuous creation peeks out in the Hebrew prayer book when God is hailed as *meḥadesh bi-ṭuvo bi-khol yom tamid Maʿaseh Bereshit*, "in His goodness, each day ever renewing the act of creation—as it is said, *To Him who maketh great lights. For His love is everlasting* (Psalms 136:7)." The liturgist celebrates the constancy of God's love playfully, taking the present participle to suggest that God creates the cosmos ever anew. Maimonides himself can sign onto the trope by way of his thesis that God sustains the world inasmuch as He is the ultimate Source of all the forms that give His creatures their constancy. See I 69.

2. See Stern, *Matter and Form*, 148–59, 280–86; and Alper, "Avicenna's Argument."

3. Lorberbaum, "Anthropomorphisms," 317.

4. Rosenzweig, *Star of Redemption*, tr. Hallo, 23.

5. See Harry Wolfson, *Studies*, 2.269; and Davies, *Method and Metaphysics*, 55.

6. Armstrong, *Architecture*, 116; cf. Goodman, *Holy One*, chap. 6, "What Is Positive in Negative Theology?"

7. In using the term *dhāt*, Maimonides means not "essence" but Godself, His unique Identity or Ipseity.

8. For metaphor and other figurative usages in Arabic literature, see Abu Deeb, *Al-Jurjānī's Theory*, 178–79. Jurjānī (1009–1078 or 1081) developed his classic theory of imagery in *Asrār al-Balāgha* (Inside Rhetoric) and *Dalāʾil al-Iʿjaz* (The Signs of Inimitable Style).

9. Maimonides had cited the same words from the Sages (*MT* Laws of the Foundations of the Torah 1.8–9), anent some of the Torah's most striking anthropomorphisms. The *Guide* returns to address the issue more circumstantially rather than simply sweep all the cases into the category of accommodation of vulgar sensibilities.

10. Some of the Sages, tellingly, identified Jacob's ladder with Mount Sinai (Genesis Rabbah 68.12). That midrashic equation is especially revealing, given the role this ladder plays in Maimonides' ontic/axiological hierarchy and the light his reading of it casts on his conception of the Torah's perfection and the universality of its wisdom. Cf. Klein-Braslavy's exploration of Jacob's dream in *Maimonides as Biblical Interpreter*, 89–123.

11. As Strauss writes, for Maimonides, "Scripture and tradition prove that as God's activity is perfect as such, so too is the Law given by Him. This Law—the Law as a whole and every single commandment—necessarily has a basis, a rational purpose. Divine Law distinguishes itself from human laws in that it serves the highest purpose, the proper perfection of man. The proper perfection of man is knowledge, the knowledge of God. The purpose of the Law is thus identical to the purpose of philosophy" (*Philosophy and Law*, 69). For Maimonides' ideas about happiness in the broader medieval context, see Goodman, "Happiness."

12. Cf. Faur, *Homo Mysticus*, 94.

13. Pines seems to absorb the Positivists' dichotomy of fact and value—as if the notion of a moral fact were oxymoronic. The objector was betrayed by the assumption that the biblical Adam and Eve were created without reason or moral discernment. Yet they are portrayed as paradigms of humanity. The Sages assume they had such discernment, and Maimonides argues that it would make no sense to speak of their being given a moral charge unless they already were seen as moral agents (1.14a; cf. Maimonides' response to Galen, 2.21b *n.*). See Goodman, "Is Maimonides a Moral Relativist?"

14. Jospe reads the Book of Job itself as a kind of biblical *Guide to the Perplexed*. See his *Jewish Philosophy*, 2.96–106.

15. The link of Anaximander's thought to that of Maimonides is al-Fārābī, who writes,

> Once things exist it is their wont to persist. But since these (terrestrial) beings are of matter and form, and forms here are contrary to one another, and matter is no more apt to one form than to its opposite, any of these bodies makes a claim by virtue of its form and another by virtue of its matter: By its form it is entitled to remain as it is, but by its matter it is entitled to be different and to have the opposite form. Since it cannot be both at once, it must take now one form and now the other. So it exists and persists for a time in one form and then perishes, and its opposite is what exists. This goes on constantly. For neither alternative is more fitting and deserves more to last than the other. So each must have its share of existence and duration. (*K. Mabādi' Ārā'* 1.9.1, ed. Walzer, 145–47)

Anaximander (ca. 610–ca. 546) saw nature's stability in terms of just such a balance. It was he who made the first Greek world map, the first Greek star map, and the first gnomon (to allow measurement of the hours of the day and their seasonal variance). He explained the earth's stability not by resting it on some imagined plinth or platform but by placing it at the center of the cosmos: There was nowhere for a geocentric earth to fall. His ideal of cosmic justice made a like case for cosmic stability in qualitative terms.

16. Goodman, "Saadiah Gaon's Interpretive Technique."

17. For Aristotle's proto-emanation views, see *Metaphysics* Λ; and Sedley, *Creationism and Its Critics*, chap. 6.

18. See Aristotle, *De Anima* III 5; *Eudemian Ethics* VII 14, 1248a18–29; and *Posterior Analytics* II 19.

19. Alexander struck a telling blow against materialism in his refutation of the Stoic notion that the *pneuma* permeating and enlivening the world was a physical reality filling the same space as other bodies. The work is edited and translated in Todd, *Alexander of Aphrodisias*.

20. A portable clepsydra, or water clock, was built by the physician Herophilus (ca. 335–255 BCE) for taking the pulse rate of patients, as reported by Galen in *De Pulsuum Differentiis*. Galen himself considered quite a variety of features in the pulse, but in Galen's wake, pulse *rate* seems not to have been deemed medically important until Nicholas of Cusa (1401–1464) proposed gauging it by the weight of the water passing through a water clock in the course of one hundred heartbeats.

21. Kabbalists found a natural metaphor, beyond the flow of light and water, in the biblical image of God's sharing His spirit. Facing near rebellion by the exhausted Israelites and pleading to God that he cannot carry His people alone, like a nurse in his bosom, Moses is told by God to gather seventy elders: God will reserve—or extend (*atzalti*)—some of the spirit that has inspired Moses and lay it upon them (Numbers 11). The experiment with shared prophecy is not as successful as Jethro's advice to Moses that he must share his judicial burdens (Exodus 18). The elders do prophesy, but the gift does not last and seems to have no actionable or intelligible content. The crisis passes, and Moses shows his humility by soothing Joshua's alarm that two men, Eldad and Medad, have kept up their ecstatic raving. Moses wishes that all God's people were prophets. But that was not to be. Mosaic prophecy was unique. Jewish mystics make *atzelut* a treasured emblem of spiritual communion and ultimately a landing in the pleroma.

22. See Plotinus, *Enneads* 2.4; and Dillon, "Solomon Ibn Gabirol's Doctrine." Cf. Aristotle, *Physics* 187a, 192a.

23. See Aristotle, *Metaphysics* A 6, 988a13.

24. See Goodman, "Matter and Form."

25. Kellner and Gillis, *Maimonides the Universalist*.

26. See Hyman, "From What Is One and Simple."

27. Novak, *Athens and Jerusalem*, 143.

28. See Urbach, *The Sages*, chap. 11.

29. Proclus, *Ten Problems*, tr. Opsomer and Steel. The work is cited in Ibn al-Nadīm's *Fihrist*; key passages summarized by Yaḥyā, show it was known in Arabic, for Yaḥyā did not read Greek. Pines discussed Yaḥyā's text in 1955, *Works*, 5.177–210. The work is included in Yaḥyā b. ʿAdī, *Philosophical Treatises*, ed. Khalīfāt. And see Proclus' *Commentary on Plato's* Timaeus, tr. Morrow and Dillon, 306–8.

30. Proclus, *Ten Problems* 5, tr. Opsomer and Steel, 74.

31. Proclus, *Ten Problems* 7, tr. Opsomer and Steel, 75–76.

32. Proclus, *Ten Problems* 33, tr. Opsomer and Steel, 94–95.

33. According to Van der Heide, "Maimonides consistently rejects the idea that there is any positive element in suffering" ("Maimonides and Naḥmanides," 307).

Part III: Esoterics

1. See Cicero, *De Finibus* 5.5, LCL 402–3.

2. Aristotle, *On the Parts of Animals* I 5.

3. Lucian, *Auctio Vitarum* 26.

4. Maimonides, *ʿAl Gezerat ha-Kokhavim* (On the Stars' Decree, 1194), ed. Shailat, in *Igrot* 2.478–91. Lerner translates the Hebrew original in *Maimonides' Empire of Light*, 178–87. The Provençal rabbis who wrote asking about astrology included Rabad, the astringent critic of the *MT*; see Kraemer, *Maimonides*, 426–27, 432. Marc Shapiro writes,

> R. Joseph Kafiḥ's commentary on the *MT* cites many examples of sages who misinterpreted Maimonides because they were unaware of his philosophical views. One particularly surprising example of this appears in Feinstein, *Igerot Mosheh*, Yoreh Deʿah, 2.239. Although R. Moses Feinstein was the greatest *posek* (decisor) of his time, he seems to have had no knowledge of Maimonidean philosophy. He was therefore able to state that Maimonides believed in the protective power of holy names and the names of angels, as used in amulets. For Maimonides' rejection of this, see his commentary on Mishnah Sotah 7.4 and *Guide* I 61–62. (*Limits of Orthodox Theology*, 157 *n.*)

Chapter 8: The Esoteric Style

1. Aristotle, *Poetics*, tr. with commentary, Margoliouth.

2. See Goodman, *God of Abraham*, 312, *n.* 30.

3. Margoliouth, "Introduction: On the Esoteric Style," *Poetics*, 46.

4. Harry Wolfson, *Crescas' Critique*, 25–28.

5. Wolfson, 25–28.

6. Wolfson, 26.

7. Novak, personal communication.

8. Harry Wolfson, *Crescas' Critique*, 28.

Chapter 9: Not Philosophy?

1. Strauss, *Persecution*, 24–25.

2. The limits of medieval Muslim monarchs' power show up vividly in Ghazālī's *Naṣīḥat al-Mulūk* and that of his patron, Niẓām al-Mulk. The devices meant to prop up an "oriental despot's" sway sharply betray the limits of his power.

3. See Naimark, *Stalin's Genocides*; Jisheng, *Tombstone*; and Jisheng, *World Turned Upside Down*.

4. See Urban, "Persecution," 153–79.

5. See Rabbi Shapira's *Esh Kodesh* (Sacred Fire) and Daniel Reiser's critical edition, *Derashot mi-shnot ha-Zaʿam*, Sermons from the Years of Rage. See the studies included in Seeman, Reiser, and Mayse, eds., *Hasidism, Suffering, and Renewal*.

6. See Cone, *Artists under Vichy*; and *French Modernisms*.

7. See Taylor, "Some Incoherencies."

8. Strauss, *Persecution*, 19. Further citations to that work are made here parenthetically. Errol Harris mounts a trenchant and devastating critique of Strauss's parallel treatment of Spinoza in *The Substance of Spinoza* (chap. 9) in arguing that the *Tractatus Theologico-Politicus* was written with "double intent." Harris argues that Strauss "goes beyond, and frequently misrepresents, the evidence" (125).

9. Strauss, *Philosophy and Law*, 58.

10. A case in point, beyond Pines's positivistic misreading of I 2, is his reading into the *Guide* of Kant's thesis that knowledge must always have a sensory base; see 1.4a and our note there as to the "highly polished" bodies Maimonides speaks of.

11. Strauss, *Philosophy and Law*, 82.

12. Strauss, 82.

13. If we must cite Maimonides' predecessors, we should not omit his favorite among the Muslim philosophers: For Maimonides, as for Fārābī (and Plato before them), belief was the practical surrogate for knowledge. For that reason, Fārābī anchored his politics in metaphysics (not vice versa). And he linked the sway of metaphysics to the beliefs of the populace. Hence the title of his key work: *On the Principles underlying the Beliefs of the People of the Virtuous State*. Nor can we overlook the urgency of Fārābī's vigorous and rigorous defense of the open future in the face of Ashʿarite theological determinism in his commentary on Aristotle's *De Interpretatione* 9. There he calls the suspension of human free agency "repugnant to all religions and very, very dangerous for people to believe." Not everyone will be able to follow the logic of Fārābī's argument. But everyone will need to have confidence in the beliefs that the argument undergirds.

14. Stroumsa, *Maimonides in His World*, 177. Stroumsa underscores her point in

Andalus and Sefarad: "Leo Strauss argued that medieval philosophers such as al-Fārābī and Maimonides, living in a hostile society, took recourse to an esoteric way of writing that would be apparent to their fellow philosophers without arousing the suspicion of the political authorities, the religious orthodoxy, or the uninitiated. Contrary to Strauss' analysis, however, persecution does not seem to have been primarily the problem of the Andalusian Aristotelian philosophers. It was mainly those suspected of *bāṭinī* [Ismāʿīlī] inclinations who were targeted by the authorities" (95).

15. In the same way, we capitalize "Sages" when the reference is to the ancient rabbinic authorities and Mutakallimūn when the reference is to the occasionalists that for Maimonides typify what he finds most problematic in kalām.

16. See *Guide* 1.6a, 23a, 73a, 86b, 89a, 92b, 94b, 96a, 106b, 2.19a, 33a, 40a, 3.22a, 62b, 63a.

17. Among the many passages treating religion in the *Guide* are 1.22b, 43b, 86b, 96a, 124b, 2.28a, 29b, 65ab, 73b, 3.35a, 62b, and 66b. Maimonides' apology for the digression, which he says was called for by his argument, does not say that religious and moral topics per se are irrelevant in the *Guide* but that the particular ethical and religious excursion just completed drew his discourse beyond the topic of III 8, which more strictly concerned the rightful rule of matter by form—and thus of the body by the soul. It was that broader topic that elicited his moral reflections.

18. For the names and scope of metaphysics in Aristotle, see Reale, *Concept of First Philosophy*.

19. Scholars today often call mutakallimūn dialectical theologians—or just theologians. Maimonides does not call them that. Like Fārābī, he sees them as dialectical thinkers—their occasionalism at once the root and the fruit of their suppositious method.

20. Cf. *MT* Hagigah 2.1.

21. Conventionally, *archai* are called "first principles." But that phrasing may be deceptive. For in English, "principles" typically means rules, and principles are usually thought to be abstract. We capture the sense better if we understand *archai* as ultimates. So when Fārābī explains that metaphysics regards ultimates, he orients us to ultimate realities, yes, but also scans a wider horizon: ultimate causes, ultimate truths, ultimate values. We can see here *why* Fārābī was called the Second Teacher, after Aristotle.

22. Saadiah, too, held that view and used it to argue for eternal punishments, since mere worldly requitals would not suffice to punish, say, multiple murderers (Saadiah, *ED* 9.1, Rosenblatt, 325–26). He seems also to expect eternal rewards for the righteous not just as recompense for consummate sufferings but also because he holds, with the Sages, that the preponderance of one's deeds merits eternal requital (*ED* 5.2, citing B. Kiddushin 38b, Rosenblatt, 210–12). Maimonides avoids naming

Saadiah when rejecting the excess of evils over goods in this life. He lets Rāzī serve as the whipping boy.

23. As Joel remarks, Hegel, in his *Lectures on the History of Philosophy*, found "real metaphysics" in Maimonides (Joel, "*Über Maimonides*," 18; see Hasselhoff, "Rediscovery of Maimonidean Influence," 467).

24. See Goodman, *Holy One*, 45–46, 205–7. Rabad's demonic reading of what Moses saw at the burning bush presents a telling contrast to the Maimonidean view. See Kellner, *Maimonides' Confrontation*, 270 *n*.

25. Biblical ritual is a riposte to pagan axiology just as biblical narratives are to pagan mythology. Milgrom's *Anchor Bible Leviticus* and his *Leviticus: A Book of Ritual and Ethics* bring to bear the resources of today's biblical scholarship to reveal the moral themes at the heart of the semiotics of the Torah's sacrificial cult, substantiating in detail what Maimonides saw intuitively.

26. What would become of the Torah's sacrificial cult when the Temple was restored in the Messianic Age, when knowledge filled the earth and the sacrificial institution had fulfilled its transitional function, Maimonides wisely left to the divinely chosen ruler of that age.

27. Cf. Plato, *Laws* III 688.

28. The thought had its alternative in the Ashʿarite view that implied rejection of the idea familiar to modern philosophers in the dictum that 'ought' implies 'can.'

29. See Goodman, *Judaism*, 1.

Chapter 10: Breadcrumbs

1. Strauss, *Persecution*, 42–43 (italics are Strauss's).

2. It is sometimes said that all serious works are somewhat autobiographical. If so, we can ponder the words of one serious student of Strauss's who never became a Straussian: that Strauss wanted to be a believer but could not. Is Strauss projecting his personal struggle onto his subject? His own esoteric gestures suggest it.

3. Herbert Davidson, *Moses Maimonides*, 400; cf. 393–402.

4. See B. Giṭṭin 60a and Urbach, *The Sages*, 1.603–20.

5. Scholars who find a conflict in Maimonides' thought between moral and intellectual virtue are arguing, in effect, over which is better, the flower or the fruit. Kellner offers a subtler account of Maimonides' synthetic view in *Maimonides on Human Perfection*. See also Warren Zev Harvey, Alfred Ivry, David Shatz, and Lawrence Kaplan in their contributions to *The Thought of Moses Maimonides*, ed. Robinson, Kaplan, and Bauer. And see Goodman, *Holy One*, 10–18; and Goodman, *Judaism*, 90–101.

6. Cf. Goodman, *God of Abraham*, chap. 5.

7. Davies, *Method and Metaphysics*, 13–15.

8. Seeskin, *Searching for a Distant God*, 12.

9. Maimonides voices great concern about contradictions in his halakhic writings (*Responsa* § 217, pp. 382–83). Kraemer, *Maimonides* (170) details his care and that of his descendants to ensure that the fair copy of the Mishnah commentary was consistent with *MT.*

10. See Goodman, "Saadiah Gaon's Interpretive Technique."

11. Maimonides, *On Resurrection*, in *Kobetz*, ed. Shailat, 2.10b.

12. Kabbalists reading Maimonides' treatment of prayer, Elliot Wolfson writes, would not have seen a desire to supplant traditional prayer with silent meditation: "The religious need for conventional prayer persists, but its ultimate purpose is to lead one beyond speech-acts to gestures of unsaying," fixing the mind on the divine, the sole fitting way to connect with God's unity ("Beneath the Wings," 235).

13. For the reliance of the *Guide* on dialectical reasoning, see Kraemer, "Maimonides' Use of (Aristotelian) Dialectic," 115, citing Maimonides' *Treatise on Logic* 8, Efros, 47–49. And see Davies, of course, in *Method and Metaphysics.*

14. Seeskin, *Searching for a Distant God*, 180.

15. Herbert Davidson, *Moses Maimonides*, 399. Davidson surveyed the full repertoire of pertinent arguments in the literature accessible to Maimonides in *Proofs for Eternity.*

16. Seeskin, *Searching for a Distant God*, 181, 187.

17. Ivry, *Maimonides'* Guide . . . *A Philosophical Guide*, 66.

Conclusion

1. See Steane, *Science and Humanity*, 186. Steane's reflections here are inspired in part by Peter van Inwagen.

2. See Goodman, *Creation and Evolution*, 144.

3. Francis Darwin, introduction to Charles Darwin's *Autobiography.*

Bibliography

Abraham ben David (Rabad). *Hasagot* (Glosses on the *MT*), JTS MSS 38477, and Adler 1179.

Abu Deeb, Kemal. *Al-Jurjānī's Theory of Poetic Imagery* (Warminster: Aris, 1979) 178–79.

Alper, Ömer Mahir. "Avicenna's Argument for the Existence of God: Was He Influenced by the Mutakallimūn," in *Science and Philosophy in Medieval Islam*, ed. Jon McGinnis and David C. Reisman (Leiden: Brill, 2004) 129–41.

Annas, Julia. *An Introduction to Plato's* Republic (Oxford: OUP, 2004).

Ariel, Chanan. "Deviations from Mishnaic Hebrew Syntax in Mishneh Torah Due to the Influence of Arabic: Subordination or Intentional Usage?," in *Studies in Mishnaic Hebrew and Related Fields*, ed. Elitzur A. Bar-Asher Siegal and Aaron J. Koller (New Haven: Yale Program in Jewish Studies, 2014) 1–36.

Armstrong, A. H. *The Architecture of the Intelligible Universe in the Philosophy of Plotinus* (Amsterdam: Hakkert, 1967).

al-Ashʿarī. *K. Maqālāt al-Islāmiyyīn wa-Ikhtilāf al-Muṣallīn*, ed. Hellmut Ritter (Wiesbaden: Steiner, 1963).

Attar, Samar. *The Vital Roots of European Enlightenment: Ibn-Tufayl's Influence on Modern Western Thought* (Boulder: Lexington Books, 2007)

Averroes (Ibn Rushd). *Commentary on the Republic*, tr. E. I. J. Rosenthal (Cambridge: CUP, 1966); tr. Ralph Lerner (Ithaca: Cornell University Press, 1974).

———. *K. Faṣl al-Maqāl* (On Drawing a Line between Religion and Philosophy and Determining Their Relations), ed. George Hourani (Leiden: Brill, 1959); tr. by Hourani as "The Decisive Treatise" in *Averroes on the Harmony of Religion and Philosophy* (London: Luzac, 1976).

———. *Kashf ʿan Manāhij al-Adilla fī ʿAqāʾid al-Milla* (Exposition of the Modes of Argument on Religious Tenets), ed. Maḥmūd Qāsim, 2nd ed. (Cairo: Anglo-American Library, 1964); tr. Ibrahim Najjar as *Faith and Reason in Islam: Averroes' Exposition of Religious Arguments* (Oxford: Oneworld, 2001).

———. *Tafsīr mā Baʿda al-Ṭabīʿa* (Commentary on the Metaphysics), ed. Maurice Bouyges (Beirut: Imprimerie Catholique, 1952) 3 vols.

———. *Tahāfut al-Tahāfut* (Beirut: Catholic Press, 1930); tr. Simon Van Den Bergh as *The Incoherence of the Incoherence* (London: Luzac, 1969) 2 vols.

———. Talkhīs Ma Baʿda al-Tabiʿa (Short Commentary on the Metaphysics), ed. Uthman Amin (Cairo: Maktabat Muṣṭfā al-Bābī al-Halabī, 1958).

Avicenna (Abū ʿAlī Ibn Sīnā). *Danesh Nameh Alāʾī*, tr. Mohammad Achena and Henri Massé as *Le Livre de Science* (Paris: UNESCO, 1955–58).

———. *Fī ʾl-Nafs* of the *Najāt*, tr. Fazlur Rahman as *Avicenna's Psychology* (London: OUP, 1952; repr., Westport, CT: Hyperion, 1981).

———. *Ilāhiyyāt* of the *Shifāʾ*, ed. and tr. Michael E. Marmura as *The Metaphysics of the Healing* (Provo: BYU Press, 2005).

———. *K. al-Ishārāt wa-ʾl-Tanbīhāt*, ed. J. Forget (Leiden: Brill, 1892); tr. Amélie Goichon as *Livre des Directives et Remarques* (Paris: Vrin, 1951).

———. *K. al-Nafs* of the *Shifāʾ*, ed. Fazlur Rahman as *Avicenna's* De Anima (London: OUP, 1959).

———. *K. al-Samāʿ al-Ṭabīʿī*, ed. and tr. Jon McGinnis as *The Physics of the Healing* (Provo: BYU Press, 2010) 2 vols.

———. *On Prayer*, ed. F. Mehren in *Traités Mystiques d'Avicenne* (Leiden: Brill, 1894); tr. A. J. Arberry in *Avicenna on Theology* (London: Murray, 1951) 50–63.

———. *Réfutation de l'astrologie*, ed. and tr. Yaḥyā Michot (Beirut: Al-Burāq, 2006).

Azzam, A. R. *Saladin* (Harlow: Pearson, 2009).

Baḥyā Ibn Pāqūdah. *K. al-Hidāya ilā Farāʾiḍ al-Qulūb*, ed. A. S. Yahuda (Leiden: Brill, 1912); tr. Menahem Mansoor as *The Book of Direction to the Duties of the Heart* (London: Routledge and Kegan Paul, 1973).

Baneth, David. "Joseph Ibn Shimon: The Important Student of Maimonides and Joseph Ibn ʿAqnīn," *Otzar Yehudei Sefarad* 7 (1964) 11–20 (Hebrew).

———. "Maimonides Translating His Writings as Compared with His Translators," *Tarbiz* 23 (1952) 170–91.

Baron, Salo Wittmayer. *A Social and Religious History of the Jews* (New York: Columbia University Press and JPS, 1960) 18 vols.

Bennison, Amira K. *The Almoravid and Almohad Empires* (Edinburgh: Edinburgh University Press, 2016).

Ben-Zaken, Avner. *Reading* Ḥayy Ibn-Yaqẓān*: A Cross-Cultural History of Autodidacticism* (Baltimore: Johns Hopkins University Press, 2010).

Blumenthal, David. "Maimonides' Intellectual Mysticism and the Superiority of the Prophecy of Moses," in *Approaches to Judaism in Medieval Times*, ed. Blumenthal (Chico, CA: Scholars Press, 1984) 27–52.

Bos, Gerrit. "Maimonides' Medical Works and Their Contribution to His Medical Biography," *MS* 5 (Jersey City, NJ: Ktav, 2008) 243–66.

———. *Novel Medical and General Hebrew Terminology in the 13th Century*, JSS Supplement 27 (Oxford: OUP, 2011).

Brockelmann, Carl. *History of the Islamic Peoples*, tr. Joel Carmichael and Moshe Perlmann (New York: Capricorn, 1960; original German edition, 1939).

Campanini, Massimo. *Al-Ghazali and the Divine* (London: Routledge, 2019).

Cicero. *De Finibus*, LCL.

Cohen, Mordecai Z. "Logic to Interpretation: Maimonides' Use of al-Farabi's Model of Metaphor," *Zutot* 2 (2002) 104–13.

———. *Three Approaches to Biblical Metaphor: From Abraham Ibn Ezra and Maimonides to David Kimhi* (Leiden: Brill, 2003).

Cone, Michele C. *Artists under Vichy* (Princeton, NJ: PUP, 1992).

———. *French Modernisms: Perspectives on Art before, during, and after Vichy* (Cambridge: CUP, 2001).

D'Ancona, Cristina. "Platonic and Neoplatonic Terminology for Being in Arabic Translation," *SGA* 1 (2011) 23–45.

Darwin, Francis. Introduction to Charles Darwin's *Autobiography*, ed. Francis Darwin (New York: Dover, 1982).

Davidson, Herbert. *Alfarabi, Avicenna, and Averroes on the Intellect* (New York: OUP, 1992).

———. *Moses Maimonides: The Man and His Works* (New York: OUP, 2005).

———. *Proofs for Eternity, Creation, and the Existence of God in Medieval Islamic and Jewish Philosophy* (New York: OUP, 1987).

Davidson, Israel. *Saadiah's Polemic against Ḥiwi al-Balkhi: A Fragment Edited from a Genizah MS* (New York: JTS, 1915).

Davies, Daniel. *Method and Metaphysics in Maimonides'* Guide for the Perplexed (New York: OUP, 2011).

Diamond, James A., and Menachem Kellner. *Reinventing Maimonides in Contemporary Jewish Thought* (London: LL, 2019).

Dienstag, Jacob I. "The Relationship of Maimonides to His Predecessors: Sources and Possible Sources for the Mishneh Torah—an Alphabetical Survey," *JLA* 1 (1978) 42–60.

Dillon, John. "Female Principles in Platonism," in *The Golden Chain: Studies in the Development of Platonism and Christianity* (London: Routledge, 1991).

———. "The Ideas as Thoughts of God," *Études Platoniciennes* 8 (2011) 31–42.

———. *The Middle Platonists* (Ithaca: Cornell University Press, 1996).

———. "Signs and Tokens: Do the Gods of Neoplatonism Care?," in Julius Rocca, *Teleology in the Ancient World: Philosophical and Medical Approaches* (Cambridge: CUP, 2017) 92–103.

———. "Solomon Ibn Gabirol's Doctrine of Intelligible Matter," *Neoplatonism and Jewish Thought*, ed. L. E. Goodman (Albany: SUNY Press, 1992) 434–59.

Dong Xiuyuan. "The Presence of Buddhist Thought in Kalām Literature," *Philosophy East and West* 68 (2018) 944–73.

Eran, Amira. "Intuition and Inspiration: The Causes of Jewish Thinkers' Objection to Avicenna's Intellectual Prophecy," *JQR* 14 (2007) 39–71.

Fakhry, Majid. *Al-Fārābī: Founder of Islamic Neoplatonism* (Oxford: Oneworld, 2002).

———. *Islamic Occasionalism and Its Critique by Averroes and Aquinas* (London: Allen and Unwin, 1958).

al-Fārābī. "Against Philoponus," tr. Muhsin Mahdi, *JNES* 26 (1967) 233–60; repr. in *Islamic Philosophy and Theology*, ed. Ian Netton (London: Routledge, 2007) 1.160–94.

———. Commentary on *De Interpretatione*, ed. Wilhelm Kutsch and Stanley Marrow (Beirut: Catholic Press, 1960); tr. F. W. Zimmermann, in *Al-Fārābī's* Commentary and Short Treatise on Aristotle's *De Interpretatione* (London: OUP, 1981).

———. *Fī Taḥṣīl al-Saʿādah*, ed. Ali Bu Mulḥim (Beirut: Dar wa-Maktabat al-Hilāl, 1995); *K. Tanbīh ʿalā Sabīl al-Saʿādah*, ed. Jafar Al-Yassin (Tehran, 1371 AH); *K. al-Jamʿ*, ed. F. Dieterici (Leiden, 1890); (Hyderabad, 1345 AH) in *Islamic Philosophy*, ed. Fuat Sezgin (Frankfurt am Main: Goethe University, Institute for the History of Arabic Science, 1999); tr. Muhsin Mahdi in *Alfarabi's Philosophy of Plato and Aristotle* (Ithaca: Cornell University Press, 1962).

———. *Fuṣūl al-Madanī*, ed. and tr. D. M. Dunlop as *Aphorisms of the Statesman* (Cambridge: CUP, 1961).

———. *Fuṣūl Muntazaʿah*, ed. F. M. Najjar (Beirut: Dār al-Mashriq, 1971).

———. *K. al-Siyāsah al-Madaniyya*, ed. F. M. Najjar (Beirut: Catholic Press, 1964); tr. Charles Butterworth as *The Political Regime* in Al-Farabi: *The Political Writings*, vol. 2 (Ithaca: Cornell University Press, 2015).

———. *Kitāb al-Ḥurūf* (The Book of Letters), ed. Muhsin Mahdi (Beirut: Dār al-Mashriq, 1986).

———. *K. Mabādiʾ Ārāʾ Ahli ʾl-Madīnati ʾl-Fāḍila* (The Book on the Principles underlying the Beliefs of the People of the Virtuous State), ed. and tr. Richard Walzer as *Al-Farabi on the Perfect State* (Oxford: OUP, 1985).

———. *Maqālah fī ʾl-Jihah allati Yaṣūḥu ʿalayhā ʾl-Qawl fī Aḥkām al-Nujūm*, ed.

Muhsin Mahdi in *Nuṣūṣ Falsafiyya* (Cairo: al-Hay'a al-Maṣriyya al-ʿĀmali 'l-Kitāb, 1976) 69–74.

———. *Risāla fī 'l-ʿAql* (Essay on the Intellect), ed. Maurice Bouyges (Beirut: Imprimerie Catholique, 1938); repr. in Fuat Sezgin, ed., *Islamic Philosophy* (Frankfurt am Main: Goethe University, Institute for the History of Arabic Science, 1999) 9.23–94.

Faur, José. *Homo Mysticus: A Guide to Maimonides'* Guide for the Perplexed (Syracuse: Syracuse University Press, 1998).

Feinstein, Mosheh. *Igerot Mosheh*, Yoreh Deʿah, 2.239.

Fierro, Maribel. *The Almohad Revolution: Politics and Religion in the Islamic West during the Twelfth–Thirteenth Centuries* (New York: Routledge, 2016).

———. "The Legal Policies of the Almohad Caliphs and Ibn Rushd's *Bidāyat al-Mujtahid*," *Journal of Islamic Studies* 10 (1999) 226–48.

Fontaine, Resianne. "For the Dossier of Abraham Ibn Daud, Some Observations on an Anonymous Commentary on *Ha-Emunah Ha-Ramah*," *Zutot* 7 (2010) 35–40.

———. "Was Maimonides an Epigone?," *Studia Rosenthalia* 40 (2007–8) 9–26.

Forte, Doron. "Back to the Sources: Alternative Versions of Maimonides' Letter to Samuel Ibn Tibbon and Their Neglected Significance," *JSQ* 23 (2016) 47–90.

Freudenthal, Gad. "Maimonides on the Scope of Metaphysics Alias Maʿaseh Merkavah: The Evolution of His Views," in *Maimonides y su Epoca*, ed. Carlos del Valle Rodriguez, Santiago Garcia-Jalón, and Juan Pedro Monferrer (Madrid: Sociedad Estatal de Conmemoraciones Culturales, 2007) 221–30.

Friedman, Mordecai. "Social Realities in Egypt and Maimonides' Rulings on Family Law," in *Sobre la Vida y Obra de Maimonides*, ed. Jesus Peláez del Rosal (Cordoba: Ediciones el Almendro, 1991) 177–86.

Galen. *De Differentiis Pulsuum*, ed. K. G. Kühn in *Claudii Galeni Opera Omnia* (Leipzig: Cnobloch, 1824) 8.493–765.

———. *On Problematical Movements*, Arabic ed. and tr. Vivian Nutton and Gerrit Bos (Cambridge: CUP, 2011).

———. *That the Best Physician Is Also a Philosopher*, tr. P. Brain in *Mediese Tydskrif*, South Africa, 1977, ed. K. G. Kühn (Leipzig: Cnobloch, 1821–33; repr., Hildesheim: Olms, 1964) 1.53–63.

Gandz, Solomon. "Date of the Composition of Maimonides' Code," *PAAJR* 17 (1947/48) 1–7.

Gellman, Jerome (Yehudah). "The Love of God in Maimonides' Religious Philosophy," in *Sobre la Vida y Obra de Maimonides*, ed. Jesús Peláez del Rosal (Cordoba: Ediciones el Almendro, 1991) 219–27.

Gerson, Lloyd. *Aristotle and Other Platonists* (Ithaca: Cornell University Press, 2006).

Gersonides (Levi ben Gershom). *Commentary on Song of Songs*, tr. Menachem Kellner (New Haven: Yale University Press, 1998).

Gevaryahu, Haim I. "Maimonides as a Historian of Religion: His Concept of Paganism," in *Sobre la Vida y Obra de Maimonides*, ed. Jesús Peláez del Rosal (Cordoba: Ediciones el Almendro, 1991) 229–41.

al-Ghazālī. *Al-Maqṣad al-Asnā fī Sharḥ Maʿāni Asmāʾ al-Ḥusna* (The Ultimate Goal in Explication of God's Most Beautiful Names), ed. F. A. Shehadi (Beirut: Dār al-Mashriq, 1971).

———. *Al-Munqidh min al-Ḍalāl*, ed. with French tr., Farid Jabre (Beirut: UNESCO, 1959); tr. William Montgomery Watt as *Deliverance from Error*, in *The Faith and Practice of al-Ghazālī* (London: Allen and Unwin, 1953).

———. *Faḍāʾiḥ al-Bāṭiniyya* (The Infamies of the Esoterics), ed. ʿAbd al-Raḥmān Badawī (Cairo: Dār al-Qawmiyya, 1964).

———. *Iḥyāʾ ʿUlūm al-Dīn* (Cairo: Muʾassasat al-Ḥalabī, 1968); Book 35, *al-Tawḥīd wa ʾl-Tawakkul*, tr. David Burrell as *Faith in Divine Unity and Trust in Divine Providence* (Louisville: Fons Vitae, 2001); Book 36, tr. Eric Ormsby as *Love, Longing, Intimacy, and Contentment* (Cambridge: Islamic Texts Society, 2013).

———. *Maqāṣid al-Falāsifa*, ed. Sulayman Dunya (Cairo: Dār al-Maʿārif, 1961).

———. *Mishkāt al-Anwār*, ed. and tr. David Buchanan as *The Niche of Lights* (Provo: BYU Press, 1998).

———. *Naṣīḥat al-Mulūk*, tr. F. R. C. Bagley as *The Book of Counsel for Kings* (London: OUP, 1964).

———. *Tahāfut al-Falāsifa*, ed. and tr. Michael E. Marmura as *The Incoherence of the Philosophers* (Provo: BYU Press, 2000).

Gibb, H. A. R. *The Life of Saladin* (Oxford: OUP, 1973).

Goitein, S. D. "A Letter of Historical Importance from Seleucia (Selefke), Cilicia, Dated 21 July 1137," *Tarbiz* 27(1958) 528–35 (Hebrew).

———. *A Mediterranean Society: The Jewish Communities of the Arab World as Portrayed in the Documents of the Cairo Geniza* (Berkeley: UC Press, 1967–93) 6 vols.

Goldstein, Bernard R. "Saving the Phenomena: The Background to Ptolemy's Planetary Theory," *Journal for the History of Astronomy* 28 (1997) 1–12.

Goldziher, Ignác, and Bernard Lewis. *Introduction to Islamic Theology and Law*. Modern Classics in Near Eastern Studies (Princeton, NJ: PUP, 1981).

Goodman, Lenn E. *Avicenna* (Ithaca: Cornell University Press, 2006).

———. "Baḥyā and Maimonides on the Worth of Medicine," in *Maimonides and His Heritage*, ed. Idit Dobbs-Weinstein, Lenn Goodman, and J. A. Grady (Albany: SUNY Press, 2009).

———. *Creation and Evolution* (New York: Routledge, 2010).

———. *God of Abraham* (New York: OUP, 1996).

———. "The Greek Impact on Arabic Literature," in *Cambridge History of Arabic Literature: Arabic Literature to the End of the Umayyad Period* (Cambridge: CUP, 1983) 460–82.

———. "Happiness: Jewish, Christian, and Muslim Perspectives," in *Cambridge History of Medieval Philosophy*, ed. Robert Pasnau (Cambridge: CUP, 2014) 1.457–71.

———. *The Holy One of Israel* (New York: OUP, 2019).

———. "Individuality," *Judaic Sources and Western Thought: Jerusalem's Enduring Presence*, ed. Jonathan Jacobs (Oxford: OUP, 2011) 238–61.

———. *Islamic Humanism* (New York: OUP, 2003).

———. "Is Maimonides a Moral Relativist?," in *Jewish Religious and Philosophical Ethics*, ed. Curtis Hutt, Halla Kim, and Berel Dov Lerner (London: Routledge, 2018) 87–106.

———. *Judaism: A Contemporary Philosophical Investigation* (New York: Routledge, 2017).

———. "Matter and Form as Attributes of God in Maimonides' Philosophy," in *A Straight Path: Studies in Honor of Arthur Hyman*, ed. Jeremiah Hackett et al. (Washington, DC: Catholic University of America Press, 1987) 86–97.

———. "Molyneux, Mysticism, Empiricism, and Independent Thinking," in *Molyneux' Question and the History of Philosophy*, ed. Brian Glenney (London: Routledge, 2020) 49–62.

———. *On Justice* (Oxford: LL, 2008).

———. "Saadiah Gaon on the Human Condition," *JQR* n.s. 67 (1976) 23–29.

———. "Saadiah Gaon's Interpretive Technique in Translating the Book of Job," in *Translation of Scripture*, ed. D. M. Goldenberg, *JQR* supplement (1990) 47–76.

———. "The Translation of Greek Materials into Arabic," in *Religion, Learning and Science in the ʿAbbasid Period*, ed. M. J. L. Young, J. D. Latham, and R. B. Serjeant (Cambridge: CUP, 1990) 477–97.

Gutas, Dimitri. *Avicenna and the Aristotelian Tradition* (Leiden: Brill, 1988).

Halbertal, Moshe. *Maimonides: Life and Thought* (Princeton, NJ: PUP, 2014; first Hebrew edition, 2009).

Harkavy, Abraham. "Fragment einer Apologie des Maimonidischen *Maʾamar Tehiyyat ha-Metim*," *Zeitschrift für Hebräische Bibliographie* 1 (1897) 125–28, 181–88.

Harris, Errol. *The Substance of Spinoza* (Atlantic Highlands, NJ: Humanities Press, 1995).

Hartman, David. *Maimonides: Torah and Philosophic Quest* (Philadelphia: JPS, 1976).

Hartman, David, and Abraham S. Halkin. *Crisis and Leadership: Epistles of Maimonides* (Philadelphia: JPS, 1985).

Harvey, Steven. "Al-Ghazali and Maimonides and Their Books of Knowledge," in *Be'erot Yitzhak: Studies in Memory of Isadore Twersky*, ed. Jay Harris (Cambridge: HUP, 2005) 97–117.

———. "Avicenna and Maimonides on Prayer and Intellectual Worship," in *Exchange and Transmission across Cultural Boundaries: Philosophy, Mysticism, and Science in the Mediterranean World* (in Memory of Shlomo Pines), ed. Haggai Ben-Shamai, Shaul Shaked, and Sarah Stroumsa (Jerusalem: Israel Academy of Sciences and Humanities, 2013) 82–105.

———. "A New Islamic Source of *The Guide of the Perplexed*," in *MS* 2, ed. Arthur Hyman (New York: Yeshiva University Press, 1991) 31–59.

Harvey, Warren Zev. "Averroes and Maimonides on the Obligation of Philosophical Contemplation (*iʿtibār*)," *Tarbiz* 58 (1989) 75–83 (Hebrew).

———. "Maimonides on Human Perfection, Awe, and Politics," in *The Thought of Moses Maimonides: Philosophical and Legal Studies*, ed. Ira Robinson, Lawrence Kaplan, and Julien Bauer (Lampeter, Wales: Edwin Mellen Press, 1990) 1–15.

———. "A Portrait of Spinoza as a Maimonidean," *JHP* 19 (1981) 151–72.

Hasse, Dag Nikolaus. "Averroes' Critique of Ptolemy and Its Reception by John of Jandun and Agostino Nifo," in *Averroes' Natural Philosophy and Its Reception in the Latin West*, ed. Paul J. J. M. Baker (Leuven: Leuven University Press, 2015) 69–88.

Hasselhoff, Görge. "The Rediscovery of Maimonidean Influence on Christianity in the Works of Moritz Steinschneider, Manuel Joel, Joseph Perles, and Jacob Guttmann," in *Moses Maimonides (1138–1204): His Religious, Scientific, and Philosophical Wirkungsgeschichte in Different Cultural Contexts*, ed. Görge K. Hasselhoff and Otfried Fraisse (Würzburg: Ergon, 2004) 449–78.

Hitti, Phillip K. *History of the Arabs from the Earliest Times to the Present* (London: Macmillan, 1956).

Hodgson, Marshall. *The Order of Assassins* ('s-Gravenhage: Mouton, 1955).

Hoffman, Adina, and Peter Cole. *Sacred Trash: The Lost and Found World of the Cairo Geniza* (New York: Schocken, 2011).

Hyman, Arthur. "From What Is One and Simple Only What Is One and Simple Can Come to Be," in *Neoplatonism and Jewish Thought*, ed. L. E. Goodman (Albany: SUNY Press, 1992) 111–35.

———. "Maimonides' Thirteen Principles," in *Jewish Medieval and Renaissance Studies*, ed. Alexander Altmann (Cambridge, MA: HUP, 1967) 119–44.

Ibn Abī ʿUṣaybiʿa. *ʿUyūn al-Anbāʾ fī Ṭabaqāt al-Aṭibbāʾ*, collaboratively edited (Leiden: Brill, Scholarly Editions, online); tr. Jan Van Geert Gelder (Oxford: OUP, 2020).

Ibn ʿAqnīn. *Commentary on the Song of Songs* (Perush Shir ha-Shirim), ed. Abraham S. Halkin (Jerusalem: Mikitzei Nirdamim, 1964).

Ibn Bājjah. *Fī Ittiṣāl al-ʿAql bi-ʾl-Insān* (On Contact of the Intellect with Man) and

Tadbīr al-Mutawaḥḥid (The Regimen of the Solitary), in *Opera Metaphysica*, ed. Majid Fakhry (Beirut: Dar an-Nahar, 1968).

Ibn Da'ud. *Emunah Ramah* (ca. 1168), ed. Norbert Samuelson and tr. as *The Exalted Faith* (Rutherford, NJ: Fairleigh Dickinson University Press, 1986).

———. *Sefer ha-Kabbalah*, ed. Gerson Cohen and tr. as *The Book of Tradition* (Philadelphia: JPS, 1967).

Ibn Khaldūn. *Muqaddimah*, tr. Franz Rosenthal with the subtitle *An Introduction to History* (New York: Pantheon, 1958) 3 vols.

Ibn al-Nadīm. *The Fihrist: A Tenth-Century Survey of Muslim Culture*, tr. Bayard Dodge (New York: Columbia University Press, 1970).

Ibn al-Qifṭī. *Ta'rikh al-Ḥukamā'* (History of Learned Men), ed. J. Lippert (Leipzig, 1903).

Ibn Ṭufayl, *Ḥayy Ibn Yaqẓān*, tr. with commentary, L. E. Goodman (Chicago: University of Chicago Press, 2009; first published in New York by Twayne, 1972).

Ivry, Alfred L. "The *Guide* and Maimonides' Philosophical Sources," in *The Cambridge Companion to Maimonides*, ed Kenneth Seeskin (Cambridge: CUP, 2005) 58–81.

———. *Maimonides'* Guide of the Perplexed*: A Philosophical Guide* (Chicago: University of Chicago Press, 2016).

Jacobs, Jonathan. *Law, Reason, and Morality in Medieval Jewish Philosophy: Saadiah Gaon, Baḥyā Ibn Pakuda, and Moses Maimonides* (Oxford: OUP, 2010).

Jisheng, Yang. *Tombstone: The Great Chinese Famine, 1958–1962*, tr. Stacy Mosher and Guo Jian (New York: Farrar, Straus and Giroux, 2013).

———. *The World Turned Upside Down: A History of the Chinese Cultural Revolution*, tr. Stacy Mosher and Guo Jian (New York: Farrar, Straus and Giroux, 2016).

Joel, Manuel. "*Über Maimonides und dessen Einfluss* auf die christliche Scholastik," in *Die Konstruktion des Jüdische in Vergangenheit und Gegenwart*, ed. Michael Konken, et al. (Paderborn: Schöningh, 2003).

Jospe, Raphael. *Jewish Philosophy: Foundations and Extensions* (Lanham, MD: University Press of America, 2008) 2.96–106.

Judah Halevi. *K. al-Radd wa 'l-Dalīl fī 'l-Dīn al-Dhalīl*, ed. David Baneth, completed by Haggai Ben-Shammai (Jerusalem: Magnes Press, 1977); tr. H. Hirschfeld (1905) as the *Kuzari* (New York: Schocken, 1964).

Kaplan, Lawrence, and David Berger. "Freedom of Inquiry in the Rambam—and Today," *Torah U-Madda Journal* 2 (1990) 37–50.

Kasher, Hannah. "Is There an Early Stratum in the *Guide of the Perplexed*?," *MS* 3, ed. Arthur Hyman (New York: Yeshiva University Press, 1995) 105–29.

Kellner, Menachem. *Dogma in Medieval Jewish Thought: From Maimonides to Abravanel* (Oxford: LL, 1986).

———. "Maimonides and Gersonides on Mosaic Prophecy," *Speculum* 42 (1977) 62–79.

———. "Maimonides' Commentary on Mishnah Ḥagigah II 1: Translation and Commentary," in *From Strength to Strength: Lectures from Shearith Israel*, ed. Marc D. Angel (New York: Sepher-Hermon Press, 1998) 101–11.

———. *Maimonides' Confrontation with Mysticism* (Oxford: LL, 2006).

———. *Maimonides on Human Perfection* (Atlanta: Scholars Press, 1990).

———. *Maimonides on the "Decline of the Generations" and the Nature of Rabbinic Authority* (Albany: SUNY Press, 1996).

Kellner, Menachem, and David Gillis. *Maimonides the Universalist: The Ethical Horizons of the Mishneh Torah* (LL, 2020).

Kemal, Abu Deeb. *Al-Jurjānī's Theory of Poetic Imagery* (Warminster: Aris, 1979).

Kemal, Salim. *The Poetics of Alfarabi and Avicenna* (Leiden: Brill, 1991).

Kirk, G. S., J. E. Raven, and Malcolm Schofield. *The Presocratic Philosophers: A Critical History with a Selection of Texts* (New York: CUP, 2019).

Klein-Braslavy, Sara. *Maimonides as Biblical Interpreter* (Boston: Academic Studies Press, 2011).

Klibansky, Raymond. *The Continuity of the Platonic Tradition during the Middle Ages* (London: Warburg Institute, 1981; first published, 1939).

Kozodoy, Maud. "Prefatory Verse and the Reception of the *Guide of the Perplexed*," *JQR* 106 (2016) 257–82.

Kraemer, Joel L. "Goitein and His Mediterranean Society," *Zmanim* 34 (1990) 6–17.

———. *Maimonides: The Life and World of One of Civilization's Greatest Minds* (New York: Doubleday, 2008).

———. "Maimonides' Use of (Aristotelian) Dialectic," in *Maimonides and the Sciences*, ed. Robert S. Cohen and Hillel Levine (Dordrecht: Kluwer, 2000) 111–30.

———. "Six Unpublished Maimonides Letters from the Cairo Geniza," *MS* 1 (1990) 61–94.

———. "Two Letters of Maimonides from the Cairo Geniza," in *Maimonidean Studies*, ed. Arthur Hyman (New York: Yeshiva University Press, 1990) 87–98.

Langermann, Tzvi. "Al-Ghazālī's Purported 'Influence' on Maimonides: A Dissenting Voice in Trending Scholarship," in *Interpreting Maimonides: Critical Essays*, ed. Charles Manekin and Daniel Davies (Cambridge: CUP, 2019) 26–45.

———. "The Epistle of Rabbi Samuel B. ʿAli Concerning Resurrection," *Qovetz ʿal Yad* 15 (2001) 39–94.

———. "*Fuṣūl Mūsā*, or On Maimonides' Method of Composition," in *MS* 5, ed. Arthur Hyman (New York: Yeshiva University Press, 2008) 325–44.

Leibowitz, Yeshaiahu. *The Faith of Maimonides*, tr. John Glucker (New York: Adama, 1987).

Lerner, Ralph. *Maimonides' Empire of Light* (Chicago: University of Chicago Press, 2000).

Le Tourneau, Roger. *The Almohad Movement in North Africa in the Twelfth and Thirteenth Centuries* (Princeton, NJ: PUP, 1969).

Levey, Martin. *Substitute Drugs in Early Arabic Medicine, with Special Reference to the Texts of Māsarjawaih, al-Rāzī, and Pythagoras* (Stuttgart: Wissenschaftliche Verlagsgesellschaft, 1971).

Lewis, Bernard. *The Assassins* (New York: Basic Books, 1968).

———. *Islam: From the Prophet Muhammad to the Capture of Constantinople* (New York: Harper and Row, 1974) 2 vols.

———. "Maimonides, Lionheart, and Saladin," *Eretz-Israel: Archeological, Historical and Geographical Studies* 7, L. A. Mayer Memorial Volume (1964) 70–75.

Lieber, Elinor. "Galen: Physician as Philosopher; Maimonides: Philosopher as Physician," *Bulletin of the History of Medicine* 53 (1979) 268–85.

———. "The Medical Works of Maimonides: A Reappraisal," in *Moses Maimonides: Physician, Scientist, and Philosopher*, ed. Fred Rosner and Samuel Kottek (Northvale, NJ: Aronson, 1993) 13–24.

Lim, Kevin. "God's Knowledge of Particulars: Avicenna, Maimonides, and Gersonides," *Journal of Islamic Philosophy* 5 (2009) 75–98.

Lobel, Diana. *Between Mysticism and Philosophy: Sufi Language and Religious Experience in Judah Halevi's* Kuzari (Albany: SUNY Press, 2000).

Lorberbaum, Yair. "Anthropomorphisms in Early Rabbinic Literature: Maimonides and Modern Scholarship," in his *Traditions of Maimonideanism* (Leiden: Brill, 2015) 313–51.

Lucian. *Auctio Vitarum*, tr. Paul Turner in *Satirical Sketches* (Baltimore: Penguin, 1968).

Maimon, Solomon. *Autobiography* (1792/93), tr. Paul Reitter (Princeton, NJ: PUP, 2019).

Maimonides. *Maqāla fī Sināʿat al-Manṭiq*, ed. Israel Efros and tr. as *Treatise on Logic* (New York: PAAJR, 1938).

———. *Kitāb al-Sirāj* (The Book of the Lamp, Commentary on the Mishnah), ed. with Hebrew tr. Y. Kafiḥ (Jerusalem: Mossad ha-Rav Kook, 1963).

———. *Maimonides Commentarius in Mischnam*, facsimile of Maimonides' holograph ms (Munksgaard: Ejnar, 1961).

———. *Maimonides' Commentary on the Mishnah: Tractate Sanhedrin*, tr. Fred Rosner (New York: Sepher-Hermon, 1981), containing the Thirteen Articles of Belief, 134–88; also translated by David Blumenthal, in his translation of *The Commentary of R. Hoter ben Shelomo to the Thirteen Principles of Maimonides* (Leiden: Brill, 1974), and reprinted in Menachem Kellner's *Dogma in Medieval Jewish Thought*, 10–17.

———. *Hakdamot ha-Rambam la-Mishnah* (texts of Maimonides' Introductions in *MC* to the six tractates of the Mishnah) (Maʿale Adumim: Maʿaliyot, 1995).

———. *The Commentary to Mishnah* Aboth, tr. Arthur David (New York: Bloch, 1968).

———. Eight Chapters (Maimonides' ethical introduction to his commentary on M. Avot in *CM*), tr. Joseph I. Gorfinkle as *The Eight Chapters of Maimonides on Ethics* (New York: Columbia University Press, 1912).

———. *Sefer ha-Mitzvot*, tr. Charles Chavel as *The Commandments* (London: Soncino, 1967) 2 vols.

———. *Mishneh Torah*, tr. by various hands (New Haven: Yale University Press, 1948–2004). All but volume one has appeared in the Yale Judaica Series, where Isadore Twersky's *Introduction* (1980) also appears. The Hebrew text, ed. Zvi H. Preisler (Jerusalem: Ketuvim, 1993) has all fourteen books in one volume.

———. *Dalālat al-Ḥā'irīn*, ed. S. Munk with French tr. as *Le Guide des Égarés* (Paris, 1856–66; repr., Osnabrück: Zeller, 1964); a new edition of Munk's text with brief biblical and rabbinic citations but without Munk's French translation and notes, ed. Issachar Joel (Jerusalem: Junovitch, 1929).

———. *Moreh Nevukhim*, modern Hebrew translations by Yosef Kafih (Jerusalem: Mosad Harav Kook, 1977); Michael Schwarz (Tel Aviv: Tel Aviv University Press, 2002).

———. *The Guide of the Perplexed*, tr. Michael Friedländer (London: Society of Hebrew Literature, 1881–85) 3 vols.; repr. in 1 vol. (New York: Hebrew Publishing Company, 1953). N.B., in the inexpensive Dover paperback reprint, Dr. Friedländer's notes were stripped out.

———. *The Guide of the Perplexed*, tr. Shlomo Pines (Chicago: University of Chicago Press, 1963).

———. *Igrot ha-Rambam* (Maimonides' Letters), ed. Isaac Shailat (Maʿaleh Adumim: Hotza'at Maʿaliyot le-Yad Yeshivat Birkat Moshe, 1987–88, 1995) 2 vols.; ed. D. H. Baneth (Jerusalem: Magnes Press, 1966); ed. Y. Kafiḥ (Jerusalem: Mossad ha-Rav Kook, Tashnad) 15–60, with modern Hebrew tr. *Iggeret ha-Shemad* is included in *Igrot*. Kraemer also translates selected letters in Lerner, *Maimonides' Empire of Light*; key letters tr. Abraham Halkin in Hartman and Halkin's *Crisis and Leadership*.

———. "Letter on Astrology," ed. Alexander Marx, *HUCA* 3 (1926) 311–58; also in Shailat, *Igrot ha-Rambam*, 2.474–77; tr. Ralph Lerner in *Maimonides' Empire of Light*, 179–87.

———. *Kovetz Teshuvot ha-Rambam ve-Iggerotav* (Responsa and Letters of Maimonides), ed. Isaac Shailat (Leipzig, 1859; repr., Jerusalem, 1967); *Teshuvot*, ed. and tr. Joshua Blau (Jerusalem: Mekize Nirdamim, 1975–86).

Medical Writings:

———. *Commentary on Hippocrates'* Aphorisms, ed. and tr. Gerrit Bos (Leiden: Brill, 2020).

———. *Medical Aphorisms*, ed. and tr. Gerrit Bos (Provo: BYU Press, 2004–17) 5 vols.

———. *On Asthma*, ed. and tr. Gerrit Bos (Provo: BYU Press, 2002).

———. *On Coitus*, ed. and tr. Gerrit Bos (Leiden: Brill, 2018).

———. *On Poisons and the Protection against Lethal Drugs*, ed. and tr. Gerrit Bos (Provo: BYU Press, 2009).

Mancha, José Luis. "Demonstrative Astronomy: Notes on Levi ben Geršom's Answer to *Guide* II.24," in *Studies in the History of Culture and Science: A Tribute to Gad Freudenthal*, ed. Resianne Fontaine (Leiden: Brill, 2011) 323–46.

Marco Polo. *The Travels*, tr. Henry Yule, 3rd ed. (London: Murray, 1903) 2 vols.

Margoliouth, D. S. *Commentary and Translation of Aristotle's* Poetics, tr. with commentary (London: Hodder and Stoughton, 1911).

———. "The Discussion between Abū Bishr Matta and Abū Saʿid al-Sirāfī on the Merits of Logic and Grammar," *JRAS* 37 (1905) 79–129.

Marmorstein, Arthur. *Studies in Jewish Theology*, ed. J. Rabinowitz and M. S. Lew (London: OUP, 1950).

Marrākushī. *al-Bayān al-Mughrib fī akhbār al-Maghrib*, ed. Reinhardt Dozy (Beirut, 1838; repr. Amsterdam: Oriental Press, 1968).

McGinnis, Jon. *Avicenna* (Oxford: OUP, 2010).

Merlan, Philip. *From Platonism to Neoplatonism*, 3rd ed. (The Hague: Nijhoff, 1960).

Midrash Aggadah, ed. Salomon Buber (Vienna: Avraham Fanṭo, 1894).

Midrash Tanḥuma, ed. Salomon Buber, tr. John T. Townsend (Jersey City, NJ: Ktav, 2003) 3 vols.

Milgrom, Jacob. *Anchor Bible Leviticus* (New Haven: Yale University Press, 2009) 2 vols.

———. *Leviticus: A Book of Ritual and Ethics* (Minneapolis: Fortress Press, 2004).

Mishnah, tr. Herbert Danby (Oxford: OUP, 1933); tr. Jacob Neusner (New Haven: Yale University Press, 1988); ed. Shaye Cohen, Robert Goldenberg, and Hayyim Lapin, tr. by various hands, *The Oxford Annotated Mishnah* (Oxford: OUP, 2022) 3 vols.

———. *Avot*, tr. Joseph Hertz as *Sayings of the Fathers* (New York: Behrman House, 1945).

Miskawayh. *Fī Tahdhīb al-Akhlaq* (Beirut: Dār Maktabat al-Ḥayyāt, 1961); tr. Constantine Zurayk as *The Refinement of Character* (Beirut: American University of Beirut, 1968); French tr. Mohammed Arkoun as *Traité d'Éthique* (Damascus: Institut Français de Damas, 1969).

Mohaghegh, Mehdi. "Rāzī's *Kitāb al-ʿIlm al-Ilāhī* and the Five Eternals," *Abr-Nahrain* 13 (1972/73) 16–23.

Naḥmanides. *Perush ha-Torah*, ed. Charles B. Chavel (Jerusalem: Mossad ha-Rav

Kook, 1995) 2 vols.; tr. Chavel as *Ramban: Commentary on the Torah* (New York: Shilo, 1971) 5 vols.

Naimark, Norman M. *Stalin's Genocides* (Princeton, NJ: PUP, 2010).

Niẓām al-Mulk. *Book of Government or Rules for Kings*, tr. Hubert Darke (London: Routledge and Kegan Paul, 1960).

Novak, David. *Athens and Jerusalem: God, Humans, and Nature* (Toronto: University of Toronto Press, 2019).

O'Callaghan, Joseph F. *A History of Muslim Spain* (Ithaca: Cornell University Press, 1983).

Onkelos. *On the Torah: Understanding the Bible Text*, ed. and tr. Israel Drazin and Stanley M. Wagner (Jerusalem: Gefen, 2011) 5 vols.

Origen. *Commentary on the Song of Songs*, tr. R. P. Lawson (New York: Newman, 1956).

Parnes, Yehudah. "Torah U-Madda and Freedom of Inquiry," *Torah U-Madda Journal* 1 (1989) 68–71.

Pines, Shlomo. *Collected Works*, ed. (Jerusalem: Magnes Press, 1979–97) Five vols.

Pines, Shlomo, and Michael Schwarz, "Yaḥyā ibn ʿAdī's Refutation of the Doctrine of Acquisition (*iktisāb*)," *Studia orientalia memoriae D. H. Baneth dedicata* (Jerusalem: Magnes Press, 1979) 49–94 = *Works* 3.110–155.

Plotinus. *The Enneads*, tr. Stephen MacKenna (New York: Pantheon, 1969, 4th ed.). Revised by B. S. Page with foreword by E. R. Dodds.

Plutarch. *On Isis and Osiris*, ed. and tr. F. C. Babbitt, LCL 5.

Proclus. *Commentary on Plato's* Timaeus, tr. Glenn R. Morrow and John M. Dillon (Princeton, NJ: PUP, 1987).

———. *The Elements of Theology*, ed. and tr. E. R. Dodds (Oxford: OUP, 1963); *Neoplatonici apud Arabes* (*al-Aflāṭūnīyah al-Muḥdathah ʿinda ʾl-ʿArab*), ed. ʿAbd al-Raḥmān Badawī (Cairo: Maktabat al-Nahḍah al-Miṣrīyah, 1955); "Hitherto Unknown Arabic Extracts from Proclus' *Stoicheiosis Theologike*," ed. Pines, in *Works* 2.283–93.

———. *Ten Problems concerning Providence*, tr. Jan Opsomer and Carlos Steel (London: Bloomsbury, 2012).

Ptolemy. *Almagest*, tr. G. J. Toomer (New York: Springer, 1984).

———. *Harmonics*, ed. and tr. J. Solomon (Leiden: Brill, 2000).

al-Rāzī, Abū Ḥātim. *Aʿlām al-Nubuwwah*, ed. Salah al-Sawy (Tehran: Imperial Iranian Academy of Philosophy, 1977).

al-Rāzī, Muḥammad b. Zakariyāʾ. *Al-Ṭibb al-Rūḥānī*, in Kraus, *Opera*; tr. A. J. Arberry as *The Spiritual Physick of Rhazes* (London: Murray, 1950).

———. *K. al-Madkhal ilā Sināʿat al-Ṭibb, wa-huwa Isaghuji*, Introduction to the Art of Medicine, ed. and tr. Maria de la Concepción Vasquez de Benito as *Libro de la introducción al arte de la medicina o "Isagoge," Acta Salmanticensia, Filosofía y letras* (Salamanca: Instituto Hispano-Arabe de Cultura, 1979).

———. *K. al-Manṣūrī* in *Trois Traités Anatomie Arabes*, ed. Pieter De Koning (Leiden: Brill, 1903).

———. *Munāẓarāt al-Rāziyayn* (Debates of the Two Rāzīs), in *The Marks of Prophecy* by Abū Ḥātim al-Rāzī, ed. Paul Kraus in *Abi Bakr Mohammadi Filii Zachariae Raghensis* (Rāzīs) *Opera Philosophica Fragmentaque quae supersunt* (Cairo: Universitatis Fouadi I Literarum Facultatis Publicationum, 1939) part I (all that was published) 295–313; tr. Goodman in "Rāzī vs. Rāzī: Philosophy in the Majlis," in *The Majlis: Interreligious Encounters in Medieval Islam*, ed. Hava Lazarus-Yafeh, Mark R. Cohen, Sasson Somekh, and Sidney Griffith (Wiesbaden: Harrassowitz, 1999) 84–107.

———. *Shukūk ʿalā Jālīnūs* (*Critical Thoughts on Galen*), ed. M. Mohaghegh (Tehran: Institute of Islamic Studies, 1993; repr., Kuala Lumpur: International Institute of Islamic Thought and Civilization); and see Jon McGinnis and David C. Reisman, *Classical Arabic Philosophy: An Anthology of Sources* (Indianapolis: Hackett, 2007).

Reale, Giovanni. *The Concept of First Philosophy and the Unity of the* Metaphysics *of Aristotle*, tr. John R. Catan (Albany: SUNY Press, 1980).

Reiser, Daniel. *Derashot mi-shnot ha-Zaʿam*, Sermons from the Years of Rage (critical edition).

Richards, I. A. *The Philosophy of Rhetoric* (London: Routledge, 1936).

Robinson, Ira. "The Evolution of Divine Worship according to Maimonides," in *The Thought of Moses Maimonides: Philosophical and Legal Studies*, ed. Ira Robinson, Lawrence Kaplan, and Julien Bauer (Lampeter, Wales: Edwin Mellen Press, 1990) 266–76.

Robinson, James T. "Some Remarks on the Source of Maimonides' Plato in *Guide of the Perplexed* I.17," *Zutot* 3 (2003) 49–57.

Rosenzweig, Franz. *The Star of Redemption*, tr. from the 2nd ed. (1930) by William Hallo (Boston: Beacon Press, 1972).

Rosner, Fred. "Moses Maimonides and Air Pollution," *New York State Journal of Medicine* 87 (1987) 574 ("Air Pollution")

Runia, David. *Philo of Alexandria and the* Timaeus *of Plato* (Leiden: Brill, 1986).

Russell, G. A. *The "Arabick" Interest of the Natural Philosophers in Seventeenth-Century England* (Leiden: Brill, 1994).

Rustow, Marina. "Ibn al-Dastūr, Samuel ben ʿAlī," *Encyclopedia of Jews in the Islamic World*, ed. Norman A. Stillman (Leiden: Brill, 2013).

Saadiah ben Joseph al-Fayyūmī (Saadiah Gaon). *The Book of Conviviality in Exile* (on the Book of Esther), ed. and tr. Michael G. Wechsler (Leiden: Brill, 2015).

———. *K. al-Mukhtār fī 'l-Amānāt wa 'l-Iʿtiqādāt* (The Book of Critically Chosen Beliefs and Convictions), ed. with Hebrew tr. Y. Kafiḥ (Jerusalem: Yeshiva University, 1970); tr. Samuel Rosenblatt as *The Book of Beliefs and Opinions* (New Haven: Yale University Press, 1948).

———. *Mishlei ʿim Targum Rasag*, ed. Y. Kafiḥ (Jerusalem: Akiva Yosef, 1976).

———. *Perush* Ayyūb, *K. al-Taʿdīl*, ed. Y. Kafiḥ (Jerusalem: Committee for the Publication of the Works of R. Saadiah Gaon, 1973); tr. L. E. Goodman as *The Book of Theodicy* (New Haven: Yale University Press, 1988).

Sabra, Ali I. "The Andalusian Revolt against Ptolemaic Astronomy: Averroes and al-Biṭrūjī," in *Transformation and Tradition in the Sciences: Essays in Honor of I. B. Cohen*, ed. E. Mendelssohn (Cambridge: CUP, 1984) 133–53.

Sarachek, Joseph. *Faith and Reason: The Conflict over the Rationalism of Maimonides* (New York: Hermon Press, 1935; repr., 1970).

Schwarz, Michael. "Some Remarks concerning Maimonides' Discussion of God's Knowledge of Particulars," in *Torah and Wisdom: Studies in Jewish Philosophy, Kabbalah, and Halacha* (Essays in Honor of Arthur Hyman), ed. Ruth Link-Salinger (New York: Shengold, 1992) 189–97.

———. "Who Were Maimonides' Mutakallimūn? Some Remarks on *Guide of the Perplexed*, Part 1, Chapter 73," *MS* 2 (1992) 159–209; 3 (1995) 143–72.

Sedley, D. N. *Creationism and Its Critics in Antiquity* (Berkeley: UC Press, 2007).

Seeman, Don, Daniel Reiser, and Ariel Evan Mayse, eds. *Hasidism, Suffering, and Renewal: The Prewar and Holocaust Legacy of Rabbi Kalonymus Kalman Shapira* (Albany: SUNY Press, 2021)

Seeskin, Kenneth. *Searching for a Distant God: The Legacy of Maimonides* (New York: OUP, 2000).

Setia, Adi. "Atomism vs. Hylomorphism in the Kalām of al-Fakhr al-Dīn al-Rāzī: A Preliminary Survey of the *al-Maṭālib al-ʿĀliyyah*," *Islam and Science* 4 (2006) 113–40.

Shapira, Kalonymus Kalman. *Esh Kodesh* (Sacred Fire), ed. Daniel Reiser in *Derashot mi-shnot ha-Zaʿam*, Sermons from the Years of Rage (Northvale: Aronson, 2021).

Shapiro, Marc B. *The Limits of Orthodox Theology: Maimonides' Thirteen Principles Reappraised* (Oxford: LL, 2005).

———. *Studies in Maimonides and His Interpreters* (Scranton: University of Scranton Press, 2008).

Siddur. Ed. J. Hertz. *The Authorised Daily Prayer Book* (New York: Bloch, 1948; rev. 1957).

Simmons, L. "The Letter of Consolation of Maimun ben Joseph," *JQR* 2 (1890) 62–101.

Simplicius. *On Epictetus'* Handbook *27–53*, tr. Tad Brennan and Charles Brittain (Ithaca: Cornell University Press, 2002).

Skalko, John Mark. "Avicenna's Argument against Infinite Regress in *The Metaphysics of the* Healing as a Step in Proving the Existence of God: Is It Successful?" Center for Thomistic Studies, Houston, 2013.

Spinoza, Barukh. *Opera*, ed. Carl Gebhardt (Heidelberg: Winters, 1925; repr., 1972) 4 vols.

Starr, S. Frederick. *Lost Enlightenment: Central Asia's Golden Age from the Arab Conquest to Tamerlane* (Princeton, NJ: PUP, 2013).

Steane, Andrew. *Science and Humanity: A Humane Philosophy of Science and Religion* (Oxford: OUP, 2018).

Stern, Josef. *The Matter and Form of Maimonides'* Guide (Cambridge: HUP, 2013).

Stitskin, Leon. "A Letter of Maimonides to Samuel Ibn Tibbon," *Tradition* 4 (1961) 91–95.

Strauss, Leo. *Persecution and the Art of Writing* (Chicago: University of Chicago Press, 1952).

———. *Philosophy and Law: Essays toward the Understanding of Maimonides and His Predecessors*, tr. Fred Baumann (Philadelphia: JPS, 1987; first published as *Philosophie und Gesetz*, Berlin: Schocken Verlag, 1935).

Stroumsa, Sarah. *Andalus and Sefarad: On Philosophy and Its History in Islamic Spain* (Princeton, NJ: PUP, 2019).

———. *Freethinkers of Medieval Islam: Ibn al-Rāwandī, Abū Bakr al-Rāzī, and Their Impact on Islamic Thought* (Leiden: Brill, 1999).

———. *Maimonides in His World: Portrait of a Mediterranean Thinker* (Princeton, NJ: PUP, 2009).

———. "Prophecy versus Civil Religion in Medieval Jewish Philosophy: The Cases of Judah Halevi and Maimonides," in *Tribute to Michael: Studies in Jewish and Muslim Thought Presented to Professor Michael Schwarz*, ed. Sara Klein-Braslavy, Binyamin Abrahamov, and Joseph Sadan (Tel Aviv: Tel Aviv University Faculty of Humanities, 2009) 79–102.

Taylor, A. E. "Some Incoherencies in Spinozism," *Mind* 46 (1937); repr. in *Studies in Spinoza*, ed. S. Paul Kashap (Berkeley: UC Press, 1973) 189–211, 289–309.

Todd, Robert B. *Alexander of Aphrodisias on Stoic Physics: A Study of the* De Mixtione *with Preliminary Essays, Text, Translation and Commentary* (Leiden: Brill, 1976).

Tosefta. Ed. Saul Lieberman (New York: Mekhon Meir Lev Rabinovits, 1955).

Twersky, Isadore. *Introduction to the Code of Maimonides (Mishneh Torah)* (New Haven: Yale University Press, 1980).

———. *Rabad of Posquières: A Twelfth Century Talmudist* (Cambridge, MA: HUP, 1962).

Urbach, Ephraim. *The Sages: Their Concepts and Beliefs* (Jerusalem: Magnes Press, 1975) 2 vols.

Urban, Martina. "Persecution and the Art of Representation: Schocken's Maimonides Anthologies of the 1930s," in *Maimonides and His Heritage*, ed. Idit Dobbs-Weinstein, Lenn Goodman, and J. A. Grady (Albany: SUNY Press, 2009) 153–79.

van der Heide, A. "Maimonides and Nahmanides on the Concept of Trial (Nissayon)," in Peláez del Rosal, 305–14.

Vlad, Marilena. "Damascius and Dionysius on Prayer and Silence," in *Platonic Theories of Prayer*, ed. John M. Dillon and Andrei Timotin (Leiden: Brill, 2015) 192–212.

Wasserstein, David. "A Family Story: Ambiguities of Jewish Identity in Medieval Islam," in *Islamic Cultures, Islamic Context: Essays in Honor of Professor Patricia Crone*, ed. Behnam Sadeghi, Asad Q. Ahmed, Adam Silverstein, and Robert Hoyland (Leiden: Brill, 2015)

Wild, John. *Plato's Modern Enemies and the Theory of Natural Law* (Chicago: University of Chicago Press, 1953).

Wolfson, Elliot. "Beneath the Wings of the Great Eagle: Maimonides and Thirteenth-Century Kabbalah," in *Moses Maimonides (1138–1204): His Religious, Scientific, and Philosophical Wirkungsgeschichte in Different Cultural Contexts*, ed. Görge K. Hasselhoff and Otfried Fraisse (Würzburg: Ergon, 2004) 209–37.

Wolfson, Harry. *Crescas' Critique of Aristotle* (Cambridge: HUP, 1929).

———. "Halevi and Maimonides on Design, Chance, and Necessity," *PAAJR* 11 (1941) 105–63; repr. in *Studies in the History of Philosophy and Religion*, ed. Isadore Twersky and George H. Williams (Cambridge, MA: HUP, 1977) 2.1–59.

———. "Maimonides and Halevi: A Study in Typical Jewish Attitudes towards Greek Philosophy in the Middle Ages," *JQR* 2 (1918) 297–337.

———. *Philo: Foundations of Religious Philosophy in Judaism, Christianity, and Islam* (Cambridge, MA: HUP, 1947) 2 vols.

———. *The Philosophy of Spinoza: Unfolding the Latent Processes of His Reasoning* (Cambridge, MA: HUP, 1961) 2 vols.

———. *The Philosophy of the Kalām* (Cambridge, MA: HUP, 1976).

———. *Studies in the History of Philosophy and Religion*, ed. Isadore Twersky and G. H. Williams (Cambridge, MA: HUP, 1973, 1977) 2 vols.

Yaḥyā b. ʿAdī. *Philosophical Treatises*, ed. Sahban Khalīfāt (Amman: Al-Jāmiyya al-Urdūniyya, 1988).

Zori, David. "Comments on the Opening and Closing Poems of the *Guide of the Perplexed*," in Michael Schwarz's Hebrew translation of the *Guide*, 767–69.